To Jim & Karen McCloskey

With Best Wishes

Your Wilmington University Buddy,

Jack Fatty field

Feb. 23, 2012

Saving
BIG BEN

Lt. Cdr. Joseph T. O'Callahan

Saving
BIG BEN

The USS *Franklin* and Father Joseph T. O'Callahan

John R. Satterfield

NAVAL INSTITUTE PRESS
Annapolis, Maryland

Naval Institute Press
291 Wood Road
Annapolis, MD 21402

Library of Congress Cataloging-in-Publication Data
Satterfield, John R.
  Saving Big Ben : the USS Franklin and Father Joseph T. O'Callahan /
John R. Satterfield.
    p. cm.
  Includes bibliographical references and index.
  ISBN 978-1-59114-808-1 (hbk. : alk. paper) 1. Franklin (Aircraft carrier)
2. O'Callahan, Joseph Timothy, 1904–1964. 3. Military chaplains—United
States—Biography. 4. Jesuits—United States—Biography. 5. World War,
1939–1945—Personal narratives, American. I. Title. II. Title: USS Franklin
and Father Joseph T. O'Callahan.
  D774.F7S38 2011
  940.54'78092--dc23
  [B]
                              2011023452

∞ This paper meets the requirements of ANSI/NISO z39.48-1992
(Permanence of Paper).

Printed in the United States of America.

19 18 17 16 15 14 13 12 11   9 8 7 6 5 4 3 2 1
First printing

For Roxanne

Laudo te, benedico te, adoro te, glorifico te,
Gratias ago tibi propter magnam gloriam tuam.

Gashed with honourable scars,
Low in Glory's lap they lie,
Though they fell, they fell like stars,
Streaming splendour through the sky.
  —James Montgomery, *The Battle of Alexandria*, 1811

I never saw them again. The sea took some . . . the
graveyards of the earth will account for the rest. . . . So be
it! Let the earth and the sea each have its own. . . . A gone
shipmate, like any other man, is gone forever; and I never
met one of them again. But at times the spring flood of
memory sets with force up the dark River of the Nine Bends.
Then on the water of the forlorn stream drifts a ship—a
shadowy ship manned by a crew of Shades. They pass and
make a sign in a shadowy hail. Haven't we, together and
upon the immortal sea, wrung out a meaning from our sinful
lives? Good-bye, brothers! You were a good crowd. As good
a crowd as ever fisted with wild cries the beating canvas of
a heavy foresail; or, tossing aloft, invisible in the night, gave
back yell for yell to a westerly gale.
  —Joseph Conrad, *The Nigger of the Narcissus*, 1897

Show me a hero and I will write you a tragedy.
  —F. Scott Fitzgerald, *The Crack-Up*, 1945

Contents

Acknowledgments

Writing is hard work, but thanking those who offer their knowledge, guidance, and help is a genuine pleasure. I have been working on this manuscript for years, so the list of people to whom I owe so much is a long one.

First, my dear wife has labored far too much and been far more understanding than I had any right to expect while I ignored my responsibilities at home and banged away on my laptop. All my other debts pale in comparison to Roxanne's contributions, all of which are based on a devotion that I certainly have never deserved.

My deepest thanks go to the men of *Franklin*, several of whom graciously shared their time in telephone interviews and made efforts to correspond with me. Tom Leo, Bob Blanchard, the late Robert Wassman, and the late Robert St. Peters all were exceptionally helpful.

The staff at the College of Holy Cross, Worcester, Massachusetts, was uniformly professional and forthcoming during my visit there. The late college archivist Father Paul Nelligan, S.J., and his colleagues, the late Father Frederick Harkins, S.J., and Father Eugene Harrington, S.J., shared useful recollections of Father O'Callahan in personal interviews.

Members of the O'Callahan family also were generous and helpful, eager to share many interesting details about Father Joe and his life. Jay O'Callahan, a master storyteller in his own right, and Maureen Madell provided useful information and photographs.

James Sawruk, who has completed extensive research on Japanese aviation in World War II, kindly translated relevant squadron records, enabling me to trace the identities of the aircrew most likely to have bombed *Franklin* on March 19. The intrepid Gina Swanberg kindly handled research in the Boston Public Library on my behalf.

The staffs of the Operational Archives and the Ships' History and Photographic Sections of the Naval History and Heritage Command, in Washington, D.C., guided me to the right materials to facilitate my early research.

Lawrence Duggan and Gary May, both professors of history at the University of Delaware in Newark, were especially helpful in enabling me to complete this volume at long last.

Finally, to the extent that I can regard myself as a military historian, I owe more than I can convey to my friend and mentor Raymond Callahan, associate dean and professor emeritus of history at the University of Delaware. Ray is an excellent role model, professionally and personally, for anyone who aspires to do history with reason, tolerance, and, most of all, class. Thank you, Ray.

Introduction

*Sicut erat in principio et nunc, et semper,
et in saecula seculorum. Amen.*[1]

When Joseph Timothy O'Callahan drew his first breath, on May 14, 1905, he entered a world of massive change. Changes in societies and cultures were so pervasive, unprecedented, and radical that in many cases decades would pass before humanity could absorb their meaning and implications for the future.

The central element in O'Callahan's public life would be World War II, and O'Callahan would become the most unlikely of World War II heroes. He was an Irish Catholic from Boston, a bespectacled Jesuit priest and scholar approaching forty years of age at his moment of achievement. He had spent most of his adult life in religious studies and teaching mathematics and physics at Boston College, Weston College, Georgetown University, and the College of the Holy Cross, all Jesuit institutions. He would become a chaplain in the U.S. Navy, the first Jesuit to serve in that role. Despite his noncombatant status, he would win his nation's most distinguished decoration for bravery, for courageous action in the face of horrendous destruction. He would, however, pay a steep, life-altering price for this achievement, a price in its own way as miserable as the pervasive death and devastation he witnessed.

Of course, it is foolish to claim that O'Callahan's experiences were the outcomes of anything more than coincidental connections, random confluences of disparate events. Still, the possibilities that time and chance presented to O'Callahan and millions of other people whose lives intertwined irrevocably in the mid-twentieth century were remarkable indeed. Their genesis resides in trends seemingly so diverse that detecting the resonance of their implications

1

upon one another can be as difficult as hearing the faint harmonic response of idle tuning forks that vibrate nearly imperceptibly when the tines of another are struck.

In North America and Western Europe, change came with remarkable velocity in the nineteenth century, as political revolution and industrial growth altered the socioeconomic landscapes of whole continents, which saw changes that accelerated almost beyond comprehension as the decades unreeled to 1900 and beyond.

The impact of these rapid transitions spilled over into the less developed world. Change rocked even Russia, the most atavistic and repressive of empires. In January 1905, saber-wielding mounted Cossacks had hacked their way through a crowd of factory workers outside St. Petersburg's Winter Palace as the people tried to deliver a petition of labor grievances to Tsar Nicholas II. Discontent quashed for generations finally overflowed, triggering the revolution of 1905. This tremor transformed Russia into a reluctant constitutional monarchy and set in train another revolution a decade later that would challenge the traditional balance of European powers.[2]

Less than two weeks after O'Callahan's birth, Russia figured again in a shocking event, when Japanese naval forces decimated the tsar's Baltic Fleet in the naval battle of Tsushima Strait, the climactic act of the Russo-Japanese War. The decisive defeat of a European empire by a nation that had capitulated without resistance to Commodore Matthew C. Perry and opened trade with the United States barely fifty years earlier astonished the West. In the course of a year, Japan had defined itself as a world power in its own right. These new challenges would engender technical competition between England and Germany, rivals over expanding colonial and continental power, and lead to the development of advanced warships to implement the global goals of these nations. After the cataclysmic conflict known as the Great War, when the combatants used these ships to deadly effect, the world would attempt, briefly and unsuccessfully, to curtail their further development and production.[3]

Global transformation was not merely political or economic. It seemed to affect nearly every facet of human activity. Less than eighteen months before O'Callahan's birth, the Wright brothers succeeded in flying the first powered aircraft, an invention that would revolutionize our concepts of travel and warfare and directly affect Father Joe and his shipmates.[4] In 1905, physicist Albert Einstein published groundbreaking papers on Brownian motion and special relativity, the latter a theory that would revolutionize our concept of the universe and ultimately contribute to the end of World War II.[5]

The first telephone line between Berlin and Paris opened that year as well. President Theodore Roosevelt initiated financing for the Panama Canal, established the U.S. Forest Service, and institutionalized conservation in America. Booker T. Washington, who preached accommodation with white America to advance black interests, published *Tuskegee & Its People,* and W. E. B. Du Bois, who disagreed with Washington, established the Niagara Movement, a precursor of the National Association for the Advancement of Colored People. The U.S. government returned Confederate battle flags captured in the Civil War to the southern states whose units had carried them. In 1905 Franklin Delano Roosevelt married his fifth cousin, Eleanor Roosevelt. French science-fiction writer Jules Verne and American Lew Wallace, author of *Ben Hur,* died. Among others sharing O'Callahan's birth year whose lives would leave lasting and significant marks in various venues were Howard Hughes, Dag Hammarskjold, Jean-Paul Sartre, Christian Dior, Henry Fonda, Ayn Rand, and Greta Garbo.[6]

Changes in Boston, O'Callahan's home, in the years just before his birth were in many ways comparable to those occurring on a broader scale. Boston had once been the center of New England Puritanism and the blue-blooded Brahmin families who had founded the city and formed the core of the East Coast establishment. By 1905, Boston had become an Irish city. History measures the immensity of this change.

The Irish had lived in Boston almost from its start, but their Catholicism guaranteed only marginal roles in the city's social order. In 1688, for instance, Boston authorities hanged Goody Anne Glover as a witch, although the Puritan minister Cotton Mather claimed she was executed for being "a scandalous old Irish woman, very poor, a Roman Catholic, and obstinate in idolatry."[7] Less than a century later, after England's victory in the Seven Years War, King George III extended religious freedom to his Catholic subjects in Canada, but Boston and New England declared Catholics "subversive of society."[8]

Irishmen would fight in large numbers in the American Revolution, and Massachusetts adopted a bill of rights protecting Catholics in its 1779 constitution. Still, Catholics in Boston had no record of a public Mass in the city until 1788. The first great wave of Irish immigration to America, one million strong, began as early as 1815. Ireland suffered a year-long famine in 1817, and by 1820 the city was home to about two thousand sons of Erin. Just five years later, the Irish population had risen to more than five thousand.

In the early 1800s Boston had begun the first of more than a dozen landfill expansions, some still continuing, that filled the coves and bays surrounding the three-hilled peninsula where colonists had first settled. Workers first reduced Mount Vernon to cover West Cove; later they dug sixty feet off of Beacon Hill to fill in Mill Pond. By 1835, when excavation of Pemberton Hill began, more than three-quarters of the project's laborers were Irish.[9] For the next fifty years or more, Boston expanded its land area largely on the backs of Irishmen, as thousands more immigrants poured into the city. Even with expansion, this influx brought intense conflict. As Oscar Handlin wrote, "Space was lacking. Boston offered few attractions in either agriculture or industry. Its commercial ranks were not broad enough to absorb the sons of its own merchant class, and the fields of retail trading and handicraft artisanry were limited."[10]

In the summer of 1837, when a Boston fire company collided with an Irish funeral while racing to a call, a riot ensued; the Irish procession invaded and captured the fire house. Firemen throughout the city joined the fray, with as many as 15,000 other residents. To stop the street fight, the mayor called out the militia, which promptly jailed some Irish mourners but no firemen. Just months later, a mob of Bostonians, numbering again in the thousands, surrounded and threatened the barracks of an Irish militia company known as the Montgomery Guards. Boston's mayor, Samuel Eliot, courageously intervened to prevent a riot when neither other militia nor police appeared.

In the 1840s the Great Hunger afflicted Ireland. British policy ultimately brought about the deaths of a million people, who starved or succumbed to disease, and a third of the population fled their homeland. From the mid-1840s until 1855, 37,000 immigrants arrived in Boston, more than 13,000 in 1847 alone. "If the influx of Irish Catholics alarmed native Bostonians during the 1820s and 1830s, the unprecedented flood of immigration from Ireland during the late 1840s and early 1850s shocked local residents into even greater expressions of fear and apprehension."[11] By 1855, 50,000 Irish constituted about a third of the city's population.[12] For nearly all these people, life was particularly squalid. An 1849 report from a city health committee investigating a recent Boston cholera epidemic offered a typical description of the conditions facing the immigrants:

> The average age of Irish life in Boston does not exceed fourteen years. In Broad Street and all the surrounding neighbourhood, including Fort Hill and the adjacent streets, the situation of the Irish is particularly wretched. During their visits last summer, your committee were witnesses of scenes too painful to be forgotten, and yet too disgusting to be related here. It is sufficient to say, that the whole district is a perfect hive of human beings, without comforts and mostly without common necessaries; in many cases, huddled together like brutes, without regard to sex, or age, or sense of decency: grown men and women sleeping together

in the same apartment, and sometimes wife and husband, brothers and sisters all in the same bed.[13]

Handlin notes that the Irish met the two conditions for remaining in Boston, despite its unfriendly reception and limited opportunities and resources— they were so desperate to escape Ireland that they didn't care about the conditions in their destination, and their abject poverty made it impossible to go elsewhere.[14]

If proper Bostonians recoiled at Irish poverty and the crime, filth, and aberrant behavior it engendered, they did little to alleviate it. One nineteenth-century visitor reported that it was "perhaps as aristocratic, vain and vulgar a city, as described by its own 'first people,' as any in the world."[15] Wealth and power could insulate the wealthy from the pervasive unpleasantness surrounding their exclusive enclaves. Nor did the well-to-do provide opportunities to immigrants interested in working their way, however modestly, into economic respectability. A contemporary local advertisement was emblematic of Brahmin attitudes: "Wanted—A good, reliable woman to take the care of a boy two years old, in a small family in Brookline. Good wages and a permanent situation given. No washing or ironing will be required, but good recommendations as to character and capacity demanded. Positively no Irish need apply. Call 224 Washington Street, corner of Summer Street."[16]

Only the most menial work was available to Irishmen, many of whom continued to toil as beasts of burden on the great landfill projects that created South Boston and Back Bay. Still, however hopeless their lives may have seemed, however hard the work and low the pay, the Irish persevered. Their numbers alone gave them increased political power, most of which they exercised in support of the Democratic Party and against Abraham Lincoln and the abolitionist movement. Opposition to the elevation and enfranchisement of African Americans was a response from people the upper classes regarded as no better, and possibly even worse, than blacks. Nevertheless, ten thousand Massachusetts Irishmen formed regiments and fought with distinction for the North in the Civil War. In the 1870s hundreds of Irish police officers walked beats throughout the city, as thousands of Irish laborers saved enough wages to use the new trolley lines and move into new suburban houses they had helped to build.

The city's annexation of Roxbury, Dorchester, Charlestown, and Brighton combined with a high birth rate to develop the critical mass that initiated a power transfer. Irishmen promptly elected their own to public office. In the 1870s and '80s Irish Catholics served on the Board of Police and were elected to Congress, the presidency of the Boston Common Council, and finally, the mayoralty. Hugh O'Brien, an immigrant himself, served from 1885 to 1889, kept municipal taxes low, and built the Boston Public Library, wider streets, and larger parks. Sports stars, including the champion heavyweight bare-knuckle boxer John L. Sullivan, Olympic triple-jumper and gold medalist James Connolly, and baseball players Jimmy Collins and Mike Kelly, emerged as well.

By 1890, Boston was the only large American city where more than half of foreign-born residents were Irish. Even with greater trappings of social legitimacy, old-school resistance to increased Irish power continued. Charles Francis Adams Jr. abandoned the family home in Quincy and moved to the Massachusetts countryside to avoid growing Irish political dominance. Massachusetts senator Henry Cabot Lodge sponsored legislation to regulate immigration, arguing that new arrivals, mainly Irish, were responsible for the rise of professional politics, local corruption, an inept, patronage-driven city administration, and mounting public debt. Boston was his prime example.[17]

In 1902 Irish-born Patrick Collins won every ward in the city's mayoral election, the first candidate to carry the entire city. Collins had learned the upholstery trade, served in the State Assembly, graduated from Harvard Law School, won election to Congress, and became a leading lawyer and Democratic Party leader. He died in 1905 and his successor was John "Honey Fitz" Fitzgerald, the first American-born Irish mayor, the first clean-shaven city leader, and the maternal grandfather of John F. Kennedy.[18] Boston had become an Irish city, and the world careened toward several rounds of global conflict.

1

Prologue

神風[1]

Before dawn on Monday, March 19, 1945, dozens of men moved with quiet urgency in the darkness around shapes indistinct but ordered about the open ground. The men labored at their tasks on these objects, parked in a row at intervals as precise as the work flowing about them. In the cool vestigial night, dew would not yet have formed on the metal surfaces of the workmen's charges. The objects were warplanes being girded for attack. They would strike against an enemy sure to bring a firestorm from the east with the first radiance of morning sun.

The men, mechanics, and armorers of the Imperial Japanese Naval Air Force at Kokubu No. 1 Airfield, near the head of Kagoshima Bay, hastened to prepare the first eight of more than a dozen aircraft for takeoff. These airplanes, a flight of D4Y3 Suisei (Comet) dive-bombers, would initiate an onslaught against the American navy to stop its assault on the Japanese homeland. The planes, carrying one or two bombs each, would seek out ships, blast them into oblivion, and, if possible, return to repeat the errand.[2]

Each plane's pilot and observer, seated in tandem under the greenhouse canopy of their Suisei, could if necessary make their aircraft and themselves implements of destruction. For the honor of the emperor and the protection of his subjects, the fliers could try to careen through protective curtains of naval gunfire, shrapnel, and shell to foment a collision between Japanese and American steel and flesh that could disable or sink an enemy vessel.

The aircrewmen undoubtedly were ready long before their planes. They were members of Kogeki (Attack) 103 Hikotai (Squadron), in Kokutai (Air Group) 701 of the Fifth Air Fleet, one of many land-based air-defense forces assembled on Kyushu, Japan's southernmost island, to defend against the coming invasion of Okinawa. Three more air fleets, the First, Third, and Tenth—long since bereft of imperial navy aircraft carriers, destroyed in earlier sea battles—gathered on Formosa, around Tokyo, and at other bases on Japan's largest island, Honshu, respectively. Among them they marshaled at least 2,100 airplanes. These were almost twice the numbers in the combined air groups of the fifteen American flattops, arrayed among protective rings of one hundred warships, in history's largest naval striking fleet, the U.S. Navy's Fast Carrier Task Force 58.[3]

Perhaps one in fifty American sailors, airmen, soldiers, and marines in the massive armada of more than a thousand combat and transport ships steaming for Okinawa had ever heard of the place before. For 103 Hikotai's pilots and observers, however, Okinawa, principal among the Ryukyu Island chain arching southwest from Kyushu to Taiwan, was as dear as the home islands. The division's veteran airmen knew that Okinawa was not merely home ground that stirred patriotic fervor. It lay barely 360 miles from Kyushu and only 840 miles from Tokyo. In American hands, Okinawa would put those places within easy range of the American bombers that already were flying from and landing on Iwo Jima in Japan's Volcano Islands. Even as U.S. Marines still fought to kill the last of that rocky fortress's defenders in their caves and bunkers, Iwo Jima now served as an American air base.[4]

Since their unexpected victory at Midway in June 1942, the Americans had attacked relentlessly in the Pacific, despite heavy losses at sea and in island invasions, and they had ultimately prevailed by weight of numbers. The Imperial Japanese Navy prided itself, with good reason, on its professional and ruthless surface and air forces. Even the most proficient and courageous warriors, however, could not forever stem an unending surge of enemies, barbaric though the Japanese thought the Americans were. And the U.S. Navy, amateurish and chaotic in imperial eyes, *was* unending.

America entered the war with eight fleet carriers. By March 19, barely forty months later, its navy had commissioned eighty-one more. The Henry J. Kaiser Company's West Coast shipyards launched an escort carrier every six days in the spring of 1944, so many that they strained the navy's convention of naming flattops for famous American battles and soon honored obscure skirmishes or year-old clashes at their christenings.

Meanwhile, Japan launched only fifteen new carriers for the Kido Butai (Carrier Striking Force). These lopsided odds were impossible for the Empire, which sank five of the first eight U.S. carriers and six light or escort carriers as well, but lost fifteen of its own, leaving only two afloat—in port—on March 19.[5]

Nothing short of a miracle, such as the typhoon known as kamikaze (Divine Wind) that had vanquished the great Kublai Khan's armada in 1281 and ended forever the threat of invasion from China, seemed likely to stem the American flood tide. Loss of territories since 1941—the Solomons, New Guinea, the Ellices and Gilberts, the Marshalls, Carolines, and Marianas, even the Philippines—to an incompetent adversary, and the attendant loss of face, was a crushing burden for Japan and its military forces. But an American flag resplendent in the wind over Iwo Jima, long part of the Japanese homeland, was an unspeakable horror. And now, the Americans were coming for Okinawa.[6]

The Imperial Japanese Navy's high command had abandoned by mid-March any consideration of a successful fleet engagement to stop the Allies (twenty-one warships, including four carriers, of the British Pacific fleet, designated Task Force 57, were present as well). As the American ships approached, however, the home islands themselves could serve as flight decks for the airplanes that would bring about the miracle sought so desperately. The time was at hand for sacrifice exponentially more profound than that of the Iwo Jima garrison, which had given more than twenty thousand lives to spill American blood in torrents seemingly beyond measure.

The obscenely high cost extracted for the U.S. victory on Iwo Jima should already have dissuaded the Americans from further assaults on the homeland. Tiny, isolated Iwo represented an infinitesimal level of violence compared to what awaited the Allies in Japan itself, and Okinawa was to presage that horror unambiguously.[7]

On Okinawa, defense forces at least three times larger than Iwo's were dug in for a deadly contest of attrition that could last months. In support of the land troops, naval air fleets and the army's air forces were committed to swarm around and into the U.S. Navy from the campaign's start to finish and beyond. Japanese industry was intensely dedicated to supplying this effort. By focusing almost entirely on aircraft production, factories were turning out two thousand new warplanes a month, and the Japanese army's inventories, not regularly involved in seaborne battle, counted three times more planes than did the navy.[8]

Nor did the Imperial Japanese Navy suffer a shortage of pilots. Young men volunteered in large numbers expressly to sacrifice themselves for the emperor by flying—with little training and virtually no skill—their airplanes into enemy targets. This impulse was nothing new. Japanese troops had launched banzai charges on Guadalcanal and throughout the early island campaigns, preferring death to the ignominy of surrender. Pilots often had rammed into ships, other aircraft, or troop formations when their planes were damaged in flight.[9]

The ethos of these Pyrrhic efforts began to change, however, in the autumn of 1944. On October 15, Japanese and American fleets and air forces clashed in the Philippine Sea in history's largest naval battle. Rear Adm. Masafumi Arima, commander of the First Air Fleet's 26th Air Flotilla, personally led a wave of nearly a hundred attack aircraft and fighters from an airstrip near Manila. The target of his raid was an American carrier task force stationed three hundred miles offshore.[10] By this time the war had decimated the Japanese naval air force. Nearly all of its most experienced pilots were dead or convalescing from wounds. Replacements, although imbued with comparable samurai spirit, flew with only rudimentary training against capable American naval aviators who gunned them down with near impunity at the "Marianas Turkey Shoot" and in later campaigns. Arima and his pilots, outmatched and outnumbered, could count on inflicting only negligible damage against the enemy in exchange for their lives. On October 15, the admiral set a new and more terrible standard.

As American Hellcat fighters ripped into Arima's attackers, the admiral sought cover in a cloudbank. When the blue-gray deck of a U.S. carrier loomed below him, he pushed over the nose of his Suisei dive-bomber, known less gloriously to the Americans as a "Judy," and swooped toward it as if to release a bomb. No release came. Instead, Arima, his gunner, and his airplane smashed into the ship.

Arima's deliberate sacrifice, a "sublime gesture" in the eyes of his pilots, quickly assumed a folkloric aura. Radio Tokyo praised Arima and recognized the potential for destruction his final flight demonstrated. Air units throughout Japan's shrinking defensive perimeter soon would replicate Arima's deadly method.[11]

Vice Adm. Takijiro Onishi, one of the navy's most seasoned aviation officers, arrived in Manila to assume command of the First Air Fleet within days of Arima's death. Among his first directives was an order implementing a special warfare corps, known as the Shimpu (another reading of the characters denoting kamikaze) Attack Unit.

Onishi assigned twenty-six planes under the command of Lt. Yukio Seki to begin *tai-atari* (body-crashing) attacks against the American warships off the coasts of the islands of Luzon, Leyte, and Samar. On October 25, Lieutenant Seki led five bomb-laden Zero fighters with a four-plane escort to strike U.S. ships in Leyte Gulf. His group sank the escort carrier *St. Lo* (CVE 63); heavily damaged *Kalinin Bay* (CVE 68), *Kitkun Bay* (CVE 71), and *White Plains* (CVE 66); and hit two larger escort carriers, *Suwanee* (CVE 27) and *Santee* (CVE 29), which nevertheless remained in operation—four carriers out of action for five aircraft, a most favorable exchange for the Japanese.[12]

Thenceforward, the Americans would contend with a shock wave of remarkably effective kamikaze attacks. The special attack corps quickly developed tactics to elude nets of enemy fighters and protective fire from ships' guns, and they rained death from the Philippines on the U.S. Navy. The kamikazes scored far better than imperial surface forces that spent themselves to little effect in the engagements of the Sibuyan Sea, Surigao Strait, Samar, and Cape Engaño on October 24–26, collectively known as the battle of Leyte Gulf.

By January 1945, when imperial naval air forces in the Philippines had sacrificed their last airplanes in that campaign, the kamikazes had sunk sixteen ships, including one light and one escort carrier, three destroyers, five transports, and six other vessels. Eighty-seven warships, including twenty-three fleet, light, and escort carriers; five battleships; nine cruisers; twenty-three destroyers; and twenty-seven other combatants and auxiliaries had suffered damage, much of it severe. More importantly, every pilot scoring successfully against American ships could virtually count on killing dozens, even hundreds, of American sailors. This equation, measured as it was in lives and equipment, was exponentially more vicious than the unfulfilled efforts of Iwo Jima's defenders, who had hoped but failed to kill ten American marines and sailors for each of their own killed.[13] No U.S. naval warship engaged within range of Japanese aircraft could now consider itself secure from attack until the war's conclusion.[14]

Later in January, kamikazes deployed from Formosa engaged the American Third Fleet in the South China Sea, smashing into the fleet carrier *Ticonderoga* (CV 14), the light carrier *Langley* (CVL 27), and the destroyer *Maddox* (DD 731). In late February, after the landings on Iwo Jima, a special attack unit of twenty attack aircraft under the command of Lt. Hiroshi Murakawa, with twelve escorts, flew from Honshu in the home islands to Hachijo Jima before launching assaults on the American invasion fleet. The escort carrier *Bismarck Sea* (CVE 95) went to the bottom after this attack, which also damaged the prewar carrier *Saratoga* (CV 3), the escort carrier *Lunga Point* (CVE 94), an auxiliary, and two landing ships.[15]

Finally, in the evening of March 11, a force of twenty-four twin-engine medium Ginga (Milky Way) bombers flew south from Kagoshima on Kyushu to attack the American fleet at its great anchorage at Ulithi Atoll. During the long flight, thirteen Gingas, known to Americans by the seemingly pejorative codename "Frances," dropped from the formation with mechanical problems, and later others fell away, their fuel tanks dry. At least two made it to Ulithi, and of these, one struck the fleet carrier *Randolph* (CV 15), managing only to damage her.[16]

Less than sixty hours after the attack at Ulithi, on March 14, Task Force 58 sortied from the atoll. The American fleet organized itself into four carrier battle groups containing fifteen flattops—*Randolph*'s damage eliminating her from the force and wrecking the battle groups' symmetry—and shaped a course for Japan to commence preinvasion assaults around Okinawa.[17]

Within a day, Japanese picket boats and scout planes spotted the enormous American flotilla at sea, heading north. Radioed messages quickly informed Vice Adm. Matome Ugaki, commander of the Fifth Air Fleet, with headquarters on Kyushu, that the Americans were on the way. Ugaki, who had ordered the Gingas' attack on Ulithi, inspected many of his units on Friday, March 16, but spent much of Saturday pheasant hunting with friends. That evening, he and his staff began planning strike operations against the approaching force.[18]

Early on Sunday, March 18, Ugaki ordered his air fleet, organized in both special and conventional attack units, to begin its assault. Twin-engine bombers and other aircraft, a total of forty from Kokubu, set off for the Americans, who by then were about seventy-five miles south of Shikoku, the small home island just north of Kyushu and separated by the Inland Sea from Honshu. The planes, striking before dawn, hit the prewar fleet carrier *Enterprise* (CV 6), which was saved from heavy damage only because the single bomb that hit her failed to explode. The newer, *Essex*-class carrier *Intrepid* (CV 11), suffering its fourth aerial attack in barely more than a year, fared less well in the near miss of a crashing bomber whose shattered remnants sprayed the ship's catwalks and flight deck. Finally, another wave of attackers found and bombed *Intrepid*'s sister ship, *Yorktown* (CV 10), damaging the carrier's signal bridge, island, and hull with bombs that also inflicted more than thirty casualties.[19]

As Ugaki's warriors charged through the air, however, American fighters swarmed by the dozen over Japanese airfields, blasting hangars and other installations but failing to find many planes on the ground. The air fleet, fully aware of its need to protect limited aircraft inventories, dispersed its warplanes in camouflaged revetments or launched them to disrupt the American attacks. Still, the interlopers were so numerous, aggressive, and constant that Ugaki suspended further raids on Sunday. Only eighteen of his attackers returned. After sundown, Japanese search planes kept track of the American armada, circling at slow speed only a few dozen miles off the coast as if to taunt the Empire's inability to stop its incursion. In the night, the orders came to 103 Hikotai and other units at Kokubu: nearly two dozen kamikazes would take off by 5:00 a.m. The Comets, too, would streak before dawn on March 19.[20]

The aircrewmen of 103 Hikotai strapped into formidable attack planes. The D4Y3 Suisei, first produced in 1944, was an advanced naval dive-bomber that had debuted in 1942 to replace the Aichi D3A Type 99 carrier bomber. The "Val," as Americans named it, had entered service in the mid-1930s. Although it performed well at Pearl Harbor and in early Pacific engagements, the Val's slow airspeed, fixed landing gear, and wheel spats marked it quickly for obsolescence. The Suisei, nearly twice as fast as the Val, was a vast improvement for dive-bombing missions. The first models utilized an in-line engine, giving the plane a sharklike nose, but the D4Y3 mounted a fourteen-cylinder, air-cooled Mitsubishi radial power plant with nearly 1,600 horsepower. The radial engines, their cylinders primed with gas as mechanics rotated the propeller blades by hand, coughed and spurted hesitantly when started and chugged loudly at full throttle, but they provided the Suiseis with abundant power, capability, and range—820 nautical miles—for the flight ahead of them. In addition to their bomb load, carried under the fuselage or on two racks under the wings and just outboard the landing gear, the planes carried two fuselage-mounted 7.7-millimeter (.30-caliber) machine guns and a single flexible-mount, rear-firing, 13-millimeter (.50-caliber), belt-fed machine gun for the observer.[21]

The Comets taxied in line from their positions on the apron to the runway. To avoid detection by American night fighters, they would fly without lights, only the blue flames of their engine exhausts visible, and maintain radio silence. A tight formation while flying in total darkness with no radio communication risked aerial collision, a waste of men and planes, so each pilot waited thirteen minutes for the airplane preceding him to clear the area. The crews—pilot and observer—would head for battle alone, in the darkness, on an eastward heading.

Naval tradition dictated that the senior officer in the group lead the formation. This honor fell to Lt. Hiroshi Kashi, a graduate of Class 69 of the Imperial Japanese Naval Academy at Etajima in 1941 and the 37th Class of Aviation Students in early 1943. Kashi flew as the observer in the first Suisei with his pilot, Ens. Hirotomo Kawabata. His backseat role did not diminish Kashi's responsibility for or authority over the mission. Freed from responsibility to control his airplane, he could direct the attackers by radio once over their targets to ensure maximum destruction. Ensign Kawabata, likely a university student and recent flight school graduate, was certain to do exactly what his flight leader directed over the airplane's intercom. At 5:45 a.m., Kawabata thrust the throttle forward to its detent and gunned his aircraft down the runway, flying, for all he knew, into eternity.[22]

The pilot of the second Comet to fly, carrying on its under-wing racks two 250-kilogram bombs, one ship armor–piercing and one general purpose, with quarter-second delayed fuses, was the force's most experienced aviator. Lt. Tominori Kawaguchi, a graduate of the 20th Hei Reserve Enlisted Trainee Class in July 1933, was, in U.S. naval parlance, a "mustang," commissioned from the ranks. In the hidebound and hierarchical Imperial Japanese Navy, this promotion was a singular achievement and signaled that Kawaguchi was an outstanding flyer. Trained as a carrier fighter pilot, Kawaguchi had twelve years of flying and likely five or more years of combat under his belt by March 19. That he had survived was a distinction, and his position in the second aircraft made for smooth and well-earned transition in command if Kashi came to grief.[23]

Sharing the cockpit with Kawaguchi was Warrant Officer Toshihira Yamashita, a graduate of the 3rd Ko Flight Reserve Enlisted Trainee Class in 1941. Yamashita, the dive-bomber's observer and machine gunner, had also done well, advancing from enlisted to warrant rank, a category according some officer privileges. His training program had been established for students with more extensive education than that required for standard flight-reserve enlisted aviation specialists.[24]

Airmen of such value could not be sacrificed lightly. Admiral Ugaki had not ordered them to end their flights with suicide attacks. He wrote in his diary:

> Some skilled [S]uisei pilots, regretting [that] the result of their attacks could not be confirmed, made a low-altitude bombing and confirmed their attacks amidship on an enemy vessel. After returning to base, they immediately reloaded bombs and started out on another attack. With skilled pilots this method is more economical and effective. However, if we applied this in general [such was the skill level of most pilots], we wouldn't be able to expect a sure hit. This is a very difficult point with which to cope. I believe, however, that we still must place more importance on the spirit of the special [kamikaze] attack.[25]

Far less capable crews—young, noncommissioned pilots, college boys, and recent Naval Academy graduates—manned the remaining Comets, rising for Kokubu in quarter-hour intervals until, by the last departure at 7:15 a.m., the sun had risen. None of them would return, but their squadron mates, already airborne for an hour or more, had by this time done grievous mischief to Task Force 58, well worth, in their own eyes, a mere sixteen lives and eight warplanes.

After takeoff, Kawaguchi eased back the Comet's throttle and set propeller pitch and fuel mixture for cruise speed, 206 miles per hour. He probably set a course due east, 090 degrees true, expecting to find American ships within 150 miles of his base. Yamashita peered behind them, searching for American fighters, his Type 2 machine gun at the ready. He would call over the intercom for evasive action if he spotted the enemy closing on them.

Kawaguchi's long experience played well during his mission's outbound leg. He stayed relatively low, scudding around and through the cloud layer forming a two-thousand-foot ceiling over the ocean. He and Yamashita probably saw flocks of American aircraft, highlighted in the surging dawn, winging well above them toward his homeland. Perhaps his training as a fighter pilot brought pangs of remorse at lost opportunities for attack, but the importance of his mission this day prevailed. The American warplanes were terrible, but if deprived of the aircraft carriers that brought and nurtured them, they would threaten the home islands no longer.

As they neared the target, Kawaguchi flew into the clouds. He knew that enemy fighters would be circling over the carriers in combat air patrols, ready to pounce on intruders as soon as shipboard radar operators called out the vectors and azimuths of approaching "bogeys." His only chance to close on the American fleet lay in the dingy morning vapor that might obscure his presence from the radarmen below who stared at scopes blinking with bright contact "blips" denoting airplanes. If he was exceptionally lucky, enough American planes would be aloft to register on radar screens and confuse their operators sufficiently to cause them to miss him.

Kawaguchi's plans could, of course, unravel at any second. He did not know where Ensign Kawabata and Lieutenant Kashi, presumably ahead of him, were, if they had made it to a target or remained undetected. The moment the first plane attacked, if it attacked, the jig would be up. Patrolling American fighters, now probably complacent in the dawn, would instantly be alert, their pilots shocked and enraged.

For Kawaguchi, however, good fortune born of long and distinguished experience almost certainly shone brightly that morning.

He would have seen it through a break in the clouds and haze—a large American aircraft carrier steaming northeast, churning frothy wake showing unmistakably that it was making speed to launch planes. Bombs exploding among warplanes with full gas tanks and weapon loads would create carnage beyond description.

Kawaguchi and Yamashita, tense and expectant, prepared to strike. The pilot banked his Comet in the clouds and aligned it for the bomb run. He dove steeply, breaking through the ceiling within a mile of the carrier's boxy prow. The flight deck loomed ahead as Kawaguchi rammed the throttle forward. The Comet accelerated as he peered into the bombsight and grasped the bomb release. Now the dark and dirty, blue-gray flight deck was a blur, not a hundred feet beneath him; the carrier's island would whiz by in a second, within feet of his left wingtip. He may have glimpsed American planes, their propellers turning, bunched just beyond him, ready for takeoff. What he almost certainly did not see, however, was the large black numeral "13" painted on the flight deck's bow.

Ichi! Ni![26]

Lighter by more than a thousand pounds, the Comet leaped up and away, Yamashita called the hits on the intercom. Both bombs had penetrated the flight deck. The gunner may have seen flashes from the carrier's antiaircraft batteries, tracers arcing toward them, but only for a second or two. As Kawaguchi pulled up into the protection of the low clouds, both he and Yamashita may have witnessed an unimaginable eruption of smoke and flame from the ship they had just attacked.

Now it was time to get away. Kawaguchi banked right, climbing to 2,500 feet, and headed due west. If he could strike so hard once, he might do so yet again. In less than an hour, the Comet could get back to Kokubu to load more bombs. Then he and Yamashita could return. Kawaguchi knew death would come, but not this day, if fortune smiled again.

Yamashita called excitedly, yelling into the intercom, as a bent-winged American fighter roared in behind the Comet. Seconds later, .50-caliber slugs from the fighter's six machine guns ripped the Japanese aircraft, and Yamashita slumped in his seat. Kawaguchi pulled up, aiming the plane's nose skyward to begin a looping escape maneuver. He could not, however, outrun the American, whose powerful warplane easily followed him, guns winking destruction. The death he had hoped to forestall probably came at the top of the Comet's loop. Kawaguchi may have seen the sky, then the sea descending in front of his windscreen like a curtain as the dive-bomber wound through its final trajectory. In another breath, the sea—dark, menacingly clean and unrelenting, containing the totality of life and death on earth—enveloped everything and flowed over and around, leaving not a trace of who he had been and what he had done.[27]

By the war's end in mid-August, kamikaze attacks by the Imperial Japanese Navy and army air forces had sunk 55 Allied ships and damaged more than 350, some so miserably that they never returned to service. More than 1,200 of the imperial navy's pilots had died wreaking about 70 percent of the total carnage.

About two weeks after the March 19 attack, Admiral Ugaki directed far more extensive strikes to defend Okinawa. His *kikusui* (Floating Chrysanthemum) units, many piloting Okha flying bombs, took 17 Allied ships with them and damaged 198 in this single, horrible campaign. Young Japanese men willingly, almost joyfully, threw themselves in the path of the Americans. One of them, twenty-one-year-old Ens. Heiichi Okabe, wrote:

> Like cherry blossoms
> In the spring,
> Let us fall
> Clean and radiant.[28]

This finely honed Japanese resolve sorely tested the relentless Americans, but their flood tide surged onward. It came at last to rest in Tokyo Bay, where on September 2, 1945, on the deck of the U.S. battleship *Missouri,* Japanese officials signed the instrument of unconditional surrender to the Allied forces that ended World War II.

It is to the story of American character in this conflict we now turn, a story framed in the structure of one ship, the lives of one crew, the actions of one man. The story just told and the story to come are much the same, for they describe the futility of struggle and the nobility of individual responsibility against forces immeasurable, albeit stories on far different stages and of far different dimensions. Within even one man, the power of action, generous, decent, and courageous though it may be, may exert itself at great and fearful cost. War displays this equation of human frailty perhaps more poignantly than does any other drama, and it is to war we will soon return after exploring decades of a life focused on piety, charity, and scholarship.

2

Introit

Introibo ad altare Dei. Ad deum qui laetificat juventutem meam.[1]

The O'Callahan family—Joseph Timothy, his parents Cornelius and Alice, and his brothers and sisters—fully reflected the Boston Irish cauldron of change and growth. Cornelius' father, Timothy O'Callahan, and his family were typical of the poorest Irish immigrants to reach America. Timothy and his wife Julia left Ireland in the 1860s but could afford passage only to England, where their two sons, John and Cornelius, were born. Timothy saved enough to move his family in the early 1870s to Boston, where Julia gave birth to two daughters, Mary and Margaret. In the 1880 U.S. census, Timothy resided with his family in a tenement at 64 Cove Street, probably one of many alleyways, long since redeveloped, in which landlords literally stacked inadequate housing for destitute residents. He listed his age as thirty-eight and his occupation as laborer, the category assigned to unskilled workers. Julia's occupation was "keeping house," not necessarily her own, although she may have been at home looking after one-year-old Margaret while her three older children worked or attended school.[2] Cambridge city directories published in the late 1880s contain references to Timothy, listing occupations as wool sorter, wool packer, and junk dealer, respectively, and at various addresses. Although it may be coincidental, a directory in 1890 lists Julia, widow of Timothy, living in Dorchester. Another 1889 entry shows Cornelius O'Callahan, possibly Timothy's son, working as a teamster, from the same business address where his father may have been employed.[3]

The 1880 census also shows an entry for Michael Casey, age thirty-eight and born in Ireland, and his family at 89 Elm Street in Cambridge. For Michael's occupation the census taker wrote, "Works marble shop." His wife, Ann, thirty-four and also born in Ireland, kept house for his six children at the time, ranging in age from ten years to eight months, and all born in Massachusetts—Ester, Christopher, Alice, James, Annie, and Mary. John would arrive in 1884, and another daughter, Rose, apparently was born later and died some time between 1889 and 1894. Michael was a marble cutter, then and now considered skilled craft work, and their residence in Cambridge reflected, if not affluence, a more solid life than most Irish immigrants enjoyed. Michael immigrated to America in 1865, five years after Ann had arrived. The Caseys seem to have had better prospects than the O'Callahans, including opportunities in Democratic Party politics. By 1900, the family had moved to 90 Concord Avenue in Somerville, a blue-collar community north of Charlestown but more rural in appearance, with tree-lined streets and squares, than the industrialized areas by the River Charles. Christopher was a lithographer. James, who initially followed his father's trade, would become principal tax assessor in Cambridge. Michael's daughters still at home worked as a bookbinder and cracker wrapper. The two oldest daughters, Ester and Alice, were no longer at home.[4]

The reason for Alice's absence was marriage. She had married Cornelius O'Callahan, Timothy's second son, in late 1899 or early 1900 and lived with her new husband in a duplex house at 51 Armory Street, on the town line between Charlestown and Cambridge. If Michael Casey's children had done well as first-generation Bostonians, Cornelius O'Callahan was on his way to spectacular success, despite his more humble origin. The 1900 census listed his occupation as produce grocer, the business he would ply for the next twenty years. Cornelius traded in produce at Boston's Faneuil Hall, buying from farmers and selling to Boston restaurants, making a handsome daily profit that provided a living far beyond anything his parents could have imagined.

Cornelius and Alice shared their good fortune with a rapidly growing family. Daughter Rose was born January 9, 1901. John was next, on June 26, 1902, followed by Cornelius Jr., known as Neil, on November 21, 1903. Joseph arrived on May 14, 1905, and sister Alice was born almost exactly two years later, on May 4, 1907. Edward came last, on March 31, 1912. The O'Callahan brood required far more room than the duplex afforded. Cornelius purchased a large, two-story frame house on 9 Leonard Avenue in Cambridge's Agassiz neighborhood, between the grounds of Cambridge and Youville Hospitals. Built in 1892, the house had room enough for four boarders, as well as Alice's younger brothers James and John and younger sister Mary. By 1910, both Cornelius' and Alice's parents had died. Family lore reports that Michael and Ann Casey died of influenza within a day of one another, but they apparently were not victims of the 1918 Spanish flu pandemic.[5]

By 1920, the O'Callahan family, with John and Mary Casey, occupied the entire Leonard Avenue house. James Casey, by then the Cambridge city assessor, had married and moved into his own home on Fresh Pond Parkway. Casey's prominence in local politics probably helped Cornelius' business prospects and added to his own status as a "commission merchant." He also was prominent in his community, serving as a member of the St. Mary's Parish Catholic Association and of the Bunker Hill Council of the Knights of Columbus.[6]

Joe O'Callahan's early childhood was a happy one. The religious intolerance that Catholic families faced in the nineteenth century was a fading memory by the time Joe was old enough to understand its significance. He could play and carouse with his brothers, sisters, and neighbor children and enjoy the privileges of affluence that his father's business success afforded. That affluence was significant for the time. A photo of Alice and Cornelius taken before 1920 shows the couple dressed in driving clothes, then the fashion. She smiles shyly, but he grins broadly, holding a cigar while both sit on a rocky outcropping in the countryside. They both appear supremely satisfied, probably out for a drive in their Pierce-Arrow automobile (then the height of luxury and a symbol of the status that Cornelius loved), sporting handsome and stylish formal outfits.

Ben Fiekers, one of Joe O'Callahan's school chums who also was to become a Jesuit, remembered their active days in class and at play. Joe attended St. Mary's of the Annunciation Parochial School in Cambridge through the primary grades, where nuns, Sisters of Notre Dame de Namur, had charge of the first six years. Lay teachers, Miss Crowley and Miss O'Connell, taught seventh and eighth grades, respectively. Reaching perhaps for school-year antecedents explaining Joe's later naval service, Father Fiekers recalled watching a silent movie in 1914 about Columbus' discovery of America, the impact of the Panama Canal's opening, and the sinkings of *Titanic* and *Lusitania*. O'Callahan, however, professed these incidents had no effect on his later interest in the navy. The Great War probably had little impact on Joe or his family, no member of which was old enough for military service. The economic boom attendant upon war production, however, undoubtedly helped Cornelius' business.

Joe O'Callahan was one of about eighty boys to complete St. Mary's in June 1918 and among the half of the class that enrolled in Boston College High School for boys. The Jesuits had founded Boston College and "BC High" in

1863 in response to Harvard's discrimination against Catholics, and both schools had developed into prestigious institutions. Five years before Joe O'Callahan arrived, BC High had moved with the college from their original South End location to Chestnut Hill, a suburb west of Boston Common.[7] For three of the four years Joe attended BC High, a Jesuit priest, Joseph A. Slattery, ran the "home room" for his class, "a tumbling bunch of good kids." The daily trip to school involved a tram ride, but sometimes O'Callahan and his school friends spent their tram fares on lunch and, ignoring school sanctions against the practice, hitchhiked from Chestnut Hill back to Cambridge.

Joe was a solid student, clearly college bound, also fully involved in extra-curricular activities, including the "tyro" basketball team for smaller players, the drama club, and the school newspaper; he was anchor man for the track team's relay quartet and set a school record in the sprint. Father Fiekers also recalled O'Callahan's proficiency with mathematics. "Joe amazed all of us in freshman," he wrote, "the way he could systematically factor algebraic expressions like $x^{64} - y^{64}$, an indication of a proclivity he would turn to good advantage in later life."[8] In the O'Callahan family, Joe's academic bent was not unique. All his brothers and sisters were clever. His sister Rose would become a nurse. John was headed for a career in law, and Neil would become a businessman in New York and later run a welding-supply company in Philadelphia. Alice would follow her brother into the church in the Maryknoll order, working as a missionary and teaching at a religious college in the Philippines. Ed was to attend Boston College (as would brothers John and Neil), do graduate work at Harvard, become a college professor, and later found the Wyndham School in Boston. "All the O'Callahans were very intelligent people," said Ed's daughter, Maureen Madell. "Although their father Cornelius was self-made, he and their mother valued education, and there was no question that all of their children would do well."[9]

Father Fiekers also remembered that his classmates all liked Joe O'Callahan, who seemed to get along with everyone. "He was not overbearing, but very decisive," his nephew, Jay O'Callahan remembered. "He was competitive, and he projected confidence and competence, without condescension. He was a natural leader." Jay O'Callahan added, however, that Joe suffered from one odd behavioral trait—claustrophobia. "He had a real fear of confinement in small, dark spaces. Claustrophobia affected him even as an adult," Maureen Madell agreed. "Father Joe hated any kind of confinement. His didn't fasten the buttons on the cuffs of his cassock because he didn't like binding around his wrists."[10]

Suddenly, however, about midway through his high school years, Joe O'Callahan's happy, privileged, and well-adjusted life crumbled. By the spring of 1920, the American economy was in trouble. Government support of war matériel production programs that had fueled manufacturing and the Great War's unprecedented exports ceased after the Armistice that ended the conflict. Exports fell by about half, and with no domestic demand to take up the slack, industries across the nation laid off workers. Unemployment reached 10 percent. The plight of farmers was especially bad, as commodity prices fell by more than 20 percent and remained low throughout the 1920s. Government help was almost nonexistent from the Wilson administration, closing out a failed second term, or later from the short-lived and corrupt tenure of Warren G. Harding. On the contrary, the Federal Reserve tightened credit in 1920 to control postwar inflation, accelerating a national recession that lasted through 1922.[11]

Cornelius O'Callahan, the commission merchant, might have weathered the downturn in commodity prices, but apparently he was deeply leveraged in the stock market and unable to sustain his losses. "He came home one night," Ed's son Jay O'Callahan said, "and told my grandmother, 'I've lost it all!'"[12] The pressure of possible financial ruin must have been intense for Cornelius. In 1920, diagnosis of chronic hypertension would have been unusual and effective treatment nonexistent. The first study documenting hypertension as a serious public-health issue would not appear until 1925.[13] Cornelius was almost certainly at risk because of the disease, however, and the Christmas season probably sharpened its effects on his system. On Sunday, December 26, Cornelius collapsed, victim of a massive "shock," the common term at the time for a stroke. He died at home on Monday evening, surrounded by his family, "of the effects of a shock. He was ill only a few hours, having been apparently in the best of health up to 1 o'clock Sunday afternoon."[14] In those precarious hours, while Joe O'Callahan watched his father pass from the here and now, he decided on his own future. With his entire family around him, over his father's body, Joe O'Callahan announced that he would become a Jesuit priest.[15]

3

Iudicium

Iudica me Deus, et discerne causam meam de gente non sancta.[1]

Joe O'Callahan's commitment to the Jesuits may have seemed sudden, even rash, made in the heat of a tragic moment, but it also derived from broad experience and inclination. The Jesuits had guided Joe's entire secondary-school experience, and he had responded well to their instruction. Although neither he nor his brothers had served as altar boys or sung in the choir at St. Mary's Church, the Jesuit order's reputation for scholarship and teaching clearly appealed to him.[2] With his father's death, economics also would have been a major consideration. Cornelius' business was a sole proprietorship, and there was no one to fill the void his death created. Joe's older brother John was just eighteen, but he volunteered to leave college, take over the business, and try to organize his father's finances—a tall order even for an experienced businessman. The best he could hope to do was help to liquidate his father's enterprise. Fortunately, John Casey, Alice's younger brother, still lived at 9 Leonard Avenue. He worked as an accountant for the telephone company, and his salary, coupled with savings and income the O'Callahan children could earn, kept the family going.[3] Still, with six children planning professional careers, expenses for college would have a major impact on the O'Callahans. Joe's early decision to take holy orders would alleviate some of this financial burden.

Father Fiekers said extracurricular activities had apparently affected Joe's grades in his senior year at Boston College High, creating some worry about his final acceptance to St. Andrew-on-Hudson, then a Jesuit seminary north of Poughkeepsie, New York, in the spring of 1922, but his concerns turned out to be groundless. O'Callahan passed a series of examinations that several of his teachers at BC High and the order's provincial, the senior Jesuit in the region, probably administered.

The Society of Jesus is one of the largest of the nearly 140 religious orders for men and women in the Catholic Church. The society's founder, Iñigo López de Loyola, originally wanted to name his organization the Company of Jesus, reflecting a martial tone, but the pope preferred the less military name.

Loyola, a Spanish courtier and soldier, had found religion after recuperating from a serious wound. In his thirties, he studied for the priesthood in Paris and founded his order with six associates in 1534 to adhere to vows of poverty, chastity, and obedience (and special obedience to the pope), to "enter upon hospital and missionary work in Jerusalem, or to go without questioning wherever the pope might direct." Pope Paul III ordained the men and approved their order during their visit to Rome in 1537, and within twenty years the society was large enough to establish a constitution for a strictly regimented organization emphasizing "absolute self-abnegation and obedience to Pope and superiors." The society's motto, *"Ad Majorem Dei Gloriam"* (For the Greater Glory of God), reflected a notion that Jesuits could claim broad license to further their cause, a view many others disputed. The order's fervency and Loyola's military background earned them the nickname "Footsoldiers of the Pope."

Early on, Jesuits established schools, colleges, and seminaries that offered not only religious discipline and instruction but also set the foundation for some of the West's most rigorous and advanced scholarly study. They also concentrated on missionary work around the globe. Jesuits preached to gain converts in Japan, India, China, Tibet, and in North, South, and Latin America. Their successes, many of which others attributed to excessive determination, gave them significant power within the church, but their doctrinal conservatism led to their undoing after more modern Enlightenment doctrines took hold throughout Europe and in the church. Several nations expelled the Jesuits, and Pope Clement XIV formally suppressed the order in 1773, a ruling that remained in force for more than forty years. The Jesuits hung on, however, in Orthodox Russia, where papal authority was not respected. After the order's restoration in 1814, the Jesuits found a haven in the United States, establishing or taking over nearly thirty colleges throughout the country, of which Boston College became one of the most prominent. For a budding scholar and teacher, life as a Jesuit could offer considerable advantages. The life also was challenging. The Jesuits remained among the most conservative and doctrinaire orders, insisting on the highest level of dedication in all aspects of ministry and personal demeanor. Unlike diocesan priests, who are not members of religious orders, Jesuits are subject first and foremost to the discipline and authority of the order's superiors. Credentialing, too, was intense; in the 1920s, ordination required about thirteen years of training and practice.[4]

Although several of his classmates, including Ben Fiekers, attended Boston College and later entered the priesthood, Joe O'Callahan went directly into Jesuit novitiate study at St. Andrew-on-Hudson, arriving on July 30, 1922. St. Andrew had opened in 1903 on an eighty-acre campus by the Hudson River in Dutchess County, just a couple of miles from Franklin D. Roosevelt's family home, "Springwood." The school offered instruction to Jesuit novices, both lay brothers and aspirants to the priesthood, and for sixty years it trained priests and scholastics from the entire East Coast.[5]

Even among Catholics in the early twentieth century, Jesuits were something apart, focused, unlike most parish priests, on "theological niceties," according to some not in the order who displayed a bit of jealousy: "If a young Jesuit, brought in to hear the extra hordes [i.e., of penitents] at confession before a feast day, got up at his allotted Mass the next morning and actually *said* something, the pastor would warn his congregation next Sunday that it is sinful to want one's ears tickled with novelty, or to come to Mass in pride as if it were a classroom where one argues or debates."[6]

Joe's probationary training at St. Andrew emphasized "the spirit and discipline of the order," not philosophical debates. He spent his first ten days on campus contemplating the life to which he had committed himself. Next came a retreat and more meditation on personal motives. After admission as a novice, O'Callahan could wear the order's habit. For nearly two years he concentrated on verifying his vocation, on introspection, and on commitment to his religion. He pursued daily Jesuit practices, with periods of meditation, study, manual labor, and prayer.

On July 31, 1924, O'Callahan took his first simple vows, received his vow crucifix, and became a "junior," or formed scholastic in the order. Aspirants could spend anywhere from two to fifteen years completing studies in philosophy, theology, classics, or other specific disciplines, such as mathematics, depending on personal skill. Joe's talent in math and his education at BC High undoubtedly helped him to finish the juniorate in two years. He completed the "regency" (a period of work in the Jesuit "provinces") under Father John Tobin, a physics professor at Boston College, and his contributions as a student helped to build the department's reputation in the late 1920s. O'Callahan was interested in radio circuits, and he helped to edit notes from a series of Rev. Henry M. Brock's lectures on physics for publication in the *Jesuit Science Bulletin,* the publication of the eastern division of the American Association of Jesuit Scientists. He received his bachelor of arts degree and reported to Weston, the Jesuit theological seminary in Weston, Massachusetts, a Boston suburb. Weston was a new school, opened in 1922, reflecting the growing prestige and size of the order, and had about two hundred students. Weston contained the Philosophical School, where Joe studied logic, epistemology, and cosmology: the systematic philosophy based on the teachings of Aristotle and St. Thomas Aquinas and the Scholastics. He graduated with a master of arts degree in 1929, after which he taught physics at Boston College until 1931. Teaching, scholarship, and academic training would occupy Joe throughout the worst years of the Great Depression, insulating him from the depths of the national economic downturn. His family also fared well enough, despite occasional money shortages and the era's difficulties. O'Callahan returned to Weston's Jesuit Seminary in 1931 to complete his formal theological studies.

On June 20, 1934, nearly twelve years after Joe had joined the order, the bishop of Jamaica, in the British West Indies, Thomas A. Bennett, S.J., ordained Joseph Timothy O'Callahan a priest and professed member of the Society of Jesus. He received the bachelor of sacred theology degree from Weston in the spring of 1935 and moved to St. Robert's Seminary in Pomfret Center, Connecticut, about thirty miles south of Worcester, Massachusetts, to complete his "tertianship," the third year of novitiate or probation, and then pursued advanced studies for another year at Georgetown University in Washington, D.C., where he earned the STL degree, the licentiate in sacred theology. He also published a mathematics paper, entitled "Jesuits Die in Threes," in the *Jesuit Science Bulletin*. The paper was a summary of his graduate thesis at Georgetown, finished under the supervision of the seismologist and math and astronomy professor Rev. Frederick Sohon. O'Callahan later presented his argument to a Jesuit colloquium in Chicago marking the four hundredth anniversary of the society's founding. The paper evaluated the statistical grouping of historical events and presented a mathematical basis for the claim that events happen in cycles of three. O'Callahan was satisfied that his research, while demonstrating no absolute proof of this dubious proposition, showed that the notion is not just an old wives' tale.

His formal education complete, Father Joe returned to Weston College in 1937 to teach cosmology, presenting all his lectures and classroom discussions on the philosophy of science in Latin, as was then the norm for study in Catholic seminaries. In the summer of 1938, the Jesuits transferred the priest to the College of the Holy Cross in Worcester, to replace a Jesuit math professor who had died suddenly. For better or worse, and with one great exception, Holy Cross, on Mount Saint James Hill overlooking Worcester, would be Father O'Callahan's home for the rest of his life.[7]

4

In Hoc Signo Vinces

*Emitte lucem tuam, et Veritatem tuam, ipse me deduxerunt,
et aduxerunt in montem sanctum tuum, et in tabernacula tua.*[1]

In the early nineteenth century the bishop of Boston, Benedict J. Fenwick, S.J., founded the College of the Holy Cross, New England's first Catholic college, as Saint James Seminary, in Worcester, Massachusetts, after Boston's Protestants blocked his efforts to establish a similar Jesuit school for young men in that city. An associate purchased land for the campus on the hillside of Mount Saint James, one of Worcester's seven promontories, in 1836. Seven years later the Jesuits laid the cornerstone for the campus' first building, and the first class graduated in 1849. Bishop Fenwick's brother, George, also a Jesuit and nicknamed "Dad," taught algebra, classics, and philosophy at Holy Cross and whiled away idle time playing checkers with students. Fenwick Hall, the college's main building, burned in 1852, but the Jesuits rebuilt it as a spired red-brick structure the following year; it remained the campus' only building until 1895. The Massachusetts legislature, known as the General Court, refused to approve a charter for Holy Cross, so the president of Georgetown University, the nation's first Catholic college (founded in the 1780s), signed all the graduates' diplomas until the legislature finally granted accreditation in 1865. Holy Cross remained largely isolated and stringently focused on Jesuit instruction throughout its first fifty years. After the turn of the century, the school adopted a more modern approach, developing more rigorous academics and a strong reputation in regional collegiate athletics. The administration also established a Naval Reserve Officers' Training Corps (NROTC) program in 1926.

When Father Joe arrived in 1938, about 1,200 students attended the college. Father Francis J. Dolan, S.J., who was president at the time, died unexpectedly the following year after minor surgery. Rev. Joseph R. N. Maxwell, S.J., succeeded Dolan and would be in charge at Holy Cross until 1945. Major buildings on Mount Saint James, overlooking the football stadium and baseball field, were Fenwick and adjacent O'Kane Halls, which by the late 1930s housed administrative offices and rooms for faculty (nearly all of whom were Jesuits), and classrooms and a small theater, respectively. The Dinand Library, Kimball Hall (which housed the campus dining room), and Saint Joseph's Chapel rounded out the campus, with the Loyola (renamed Carlin in 1941) and Wheeler dormitories, the latter finished in 1939.[2]

From his first days on campus, O'Callahan was popular with students, faculty members, and other college staff. "He was very gifted in math, very friendly and loved people," said Rev. Frederick Harkins, one of his colleagues at Holy Cross. "He was a great example for everyone at the college, not interested in pursuing a career for personal enrichment, a true religious interested in the work of the Church and the work of the order. He was a real soldier of the order."[3]

Father Joe's complete and unwavering faith may seem a curiosity in the secular, materialistic twenty-first century, but his belief was nonetheless very real. The tenets of his order and the church were as matter-of-fact for him as the rising of the sun in the morning, the flow of tides, or the drawing of breath. In the Memorial Acclamation of the Mass, the sacrifice of the Mass that he served countless times in his priesthood, he intoned, *"Mysterium fidei."*[4] For O'Callahan, however, the "mystery" of faith was no mystery at all. It was a central fact that informed his entire world. His correspondence reveals not a shred of internal doubt about the rightness of his teachings or his practice as a priest. He devoted himself not only to the ministry of his Catholic students, parishioners, and laity, but also to instruction and conversion of Protestants. He was an externally focused man, not much given to preoccupation with self, likely to minimize or dismiss the physical aspects of his life in favor of rational or intellectual elements. Nearly everyone who met O'Callahan commented on his open, confident personality, clearly arising from his sense of certainty about the world and his place in it.

In addition to work with physics and math students, O'Callahan continued his affiliation with the American Association of Jesuit Scientists, providing frequent notes for the *Bulletin* on activities at Holy Cross. In the classroom and around the campus, Father Joe was an enthusiastic and involved professor, interested in the activities and opinions of both students and other faculty members. O'Callahan also served as the prefect of the senior dormitory, providing advice and counsel to his charges on a wide variety of issues. His room always was open, the locus of many discussions with his friends about teaching, academic ethics, and related topics. He was very interested in current events and loved academic arguments, although he rarely discussed politics with his colleagues.

"We had a lot of fun, and he'd stir things up," Rev. Eugene Harrington, another Holy Cross professor, recalled—adding, with a smile, "He was full of the devil in that sense." Father Harkins agreed: "Mathematical problems delighted him, and he loved mysteries and puzzles. He was very quick." O'Callahan's interests did not, however, extend into literature, except for Dante, or music. Nor, aside from ecclesiastical Latin and Greek and a smattering of Italian, did he have any fluency in foreign languages. "We visited Paris once," said Father Harkins, "and the only French word he knew was '*ici.*'"[5]

Father Joe's academic capabilities and credentials were impressive enough to warrant his appointment as director of Holy Cross' Department of Physics and Mathematics in 1940. He also established the first departmental library at the college, a new math and physics collection. In addition to his scholarly pursuits, O'Callahan pursued ministry, serving as acting chaplain at Boston City Hospital and assistant curate of St. Patrick's Church in nearby Wareham. At the age of thirty-five, he had mastered a calling as an academic priest and successfully assumed a leadership role at one of the most distinguished Catholic colleges in the United States.[6]

Worcester, Massachusetts, and Holy Cross seemed comfortably removed from the concerns of the rest of the country and the world, the right setting for a promising scholar. At the end of the decade, however, the world was ready to intrude with an extraordinary rush even into the cloistered campus on Mount Saint James. With the outbreak of World War II in September 1939, Europe descended into turmoil. Japan had invaded Manchuria in 1931 and begun a more general incursion in China in 1937. On September 8, 1939, immediately after Germany invaded Poland, President Roosevelt declared a national emergency and called for the United States to increase "the national defense within the limits of peacetime authorizations." On the same day, an executive order permitted the nearly instantaneous expansion of the armed forces. Mobilization had begun. The U.S. Navy, Marine Corps, and Coast Guard, with fewer than 160,000 members at the time, would add an average of nearly seven thousand enlistees a month from October 1938 until June 1940, expanding thereafter until more than four million men and women had joined the sea services by August 1945. Nevertheless, every aspect of O'Callahan's future still centered on the Society of Jesus and the College of the Holy Cross.

It is doubly surprising, then, that Rev. James H. Dolan, then head of the New England Province of the Society of Jesus, received a handwritten letter, dated June 23, 1940, from Father Joe O'Callahan.

Dear Fr. Provincial:

P.C. [The Peace of Christ]

There are two topics about which I wished to see you when I telephoned. It may well be however that both of them can be handled by letter. I'll begin with the more important.

After thinking over the question for several weeks and making it the point of election in my retreat that I just made at Pomfret, talked with Fr. McCormick [Rev. Robert E. McCormick, J.C.D. (Doctor of Canon Law), head of the U.S. Military Ordinariate, a special diocese that serves the religious needs of the armed forces] there about the wisdom of becoming a chaplain in the navy. We discussed the matter in some detail, had he agreed with me both in the fact that with an expanding navy chaplains are needed even apart from the eventuality of war, & he agreed also that I have to a sufficient extent the qualities needed for doing good work in this rather hard assignment. And so he advised my volunteering through you. Hence if you see fit to put me in the navy, I'm ready to go.

O'Callahan added a paragraph requesting permission to visit Georgetown University to consult Father Sohon and complete research for a paper on "educational measurements" O'Callahan was preparing, with great reluctance, for a symposium. "If you put me in the navy immediately I'll have a perfect excuse [to cancel the presentation]!"[7]

O'Callahan's request was unprecedented. As the letter shows, the Jesuit order placed unusually stringent disciplinary requirements on its members, even to the point of needing to request permission to travel to another college. Because Jesuits owed complete obedience to the order and its superiors, in fact, they had little or no discretion to take independent action. Instead, much as military subordinates obey their superior officers, they obeyed orders from the society's leaders, who determined the tenure and location of assignments. No Jesuit had ever served as a U.S. armed forces chaplain. The Chaplain Corps in all services were small, with relatively few Catholic priests, none of whom had been from orders. Jesuit rules of obedience generally meant superiors, not priests, would bring up assignments, so O'Callahan's approach was unique, although not contrary to the life of the order. If Reverend Dolan approved his request, Father Joe would become the first Jesuit chaplain in the U.S. Navy's history. Approval, while not necessarily disruptive to the Jesuit order, would set something of a precedent, since other promising young Jesuits undoubtedly would—and did—follow O'Callahan's example as the war effort expanded.

Father Dolan replied two days later, writing, "I would have no objection to your proposal about applying for a chaplaincy in the Navy. Since this proposal results from your retreat election and meets with the approval of good Father McCormick, I am confident that it has God's blessing upon it. In the light of your new status assignment I commend the matter to further reflection and prayer."[8]

O'Callahan's rapid rejoinder to Dolan's approval was so enthusiastic that it could have been misinterpreted as disingenuous:

> For consultation I chose Fr. Quigley [a Holy Cross faculty colleague] who of course knows me well—better than anyone else here at Holy Cross; and who besides would be inclined to favor my continuing with Fr. Sohon. On my part while I recognize that the Navy work has a surface glamor [sic] wholly lacking in the study assignment, yet it seems to me that my awareness of this aspect ensures that I have duly discounted it. In any case I did not want to follow my own judgement [sic] and by no means tried to argue Fr. Quigley into agreement with any decision I might have reached alone. Rather we quietly discussed the pros & cons and came to the conclusion that the Navy chaplaincy is the proper choice. . . . I think, then, Father, . . . I should apply for chaplaincy in the Navy and that the application should be made at once.[9]

O'Callahan added that he wanted to carry out his busy summer schedule, including preaching and counseling obligations in the region—requiring him to leave Holy Cross and take temporary residence in Boston—in part because he wanted to be near the navy yard there to facilitate his chaplaincy application.

Father Joe's decision clearly surprised most of his colleagues at Holy Cross. "I don't know why he went in the Navy," said Father Harkins, "but his calling enabled him to reconcile war with the goodness of God." Father Harkins continued, "In Catholic philosophy and theology, as St. Thomas Aquinas noted, evil is not a positive reality, but rather the privation of something good. God can allow things to happen because He's the Almighty and knows how to draw good from evil. God allowed, but did not cause, the fall of Adam and Eve because He created man with freedom. God promised to redeem us and repair the damage our freedom created." For Father Joe, naval service could be interpreted as a test of faith. "We believe that faith is a gift. We pray for help from God to withstand our doubts," Harkins concluded. "Joe O'Callahan was very confident in the strength of his faith and his vocation as a Jesuit."

"O'Callahan certainly understood that the world was facing crisis, and I think he wanted to play a larger role in resolving those enormous problems. He didn't want the world to pass him by," Father Paul Nelligan added. "He knew war was coming, and I think he wanted to be involved in it."[10] Father Joe's decision reflected a mix of rational, religious, and other—very human— motives. He certainly believed in the rightness of his choice, and "logical arguments were of little avail with the adamant Father O'Callahan."[11]

The New England Province supported the commissioning process, sending endorsements of his application to the church's Military Ordinariate in New York. On August 7 the Department of the Navy commissioned Father Joe as a lieutenant (junior grade) in the Naval Reserve.

O'Callahan completed induction, including a physical exam, at the Boston Navy Yard. He was about five feet, ten inches tall, slender, and apparently in reasonably good health for a recruit approaching middle age. But there were issues. Father Joe had inherited his father's hypertension, an ailment of which the Jesuits were well aware. As Rev. Richard Dowling would note much later, "Many of his friends [at Holy Cross and in the order] sincerely remonstrated with him. His hyper-tense nervous nature did not augur well for the stringency of combat. More, his obvious talents in physics and mathematics could be used better for the war effort by teaching at Holy Cross, soon to be one of the top Naval ROTC units in the United States."[12] Furthermore, his eyesight may not actually have passed muster; he wore glasses and apparently memorized the eye chart ahead of time, pretending to see the rows of letters clearly enough without spectacles to meet the vision standards. Somehow the Navy overlooked these infirmities, as well as O'Callahan's claustrophobia, and he pinned the single silver bar of a lieutenant (jg) and a chaplain's cross on the wings of his uniform shirt collar.[13] (Many staff officers, such as chaplains and judge advocates—that is, attorneys—are permitted to enter the service at more senior commissioned grades, more commensurate with their professional standing, than the usual entry grade of ensign.)

Other approvals were not immediate, however. O'Callahan's assignment as a chaplain and the appointments of two other priests in the Army Reserve were still pending in mid-October. In the interim, O'Callahan probably learned naval protocol and turned himself into a reasonable facsimile of a naval officer.

Finally, just before Thanksgiving, Chaplain O'Callahan got his assignment. He would become the Catholic chaplain at Naval Air Station, Pensacola, Florida.[14]

5

Pensacola

The Annapolis of the Air

Lieutenant (jg) O'Callahan officially reported on board the naval air station on November 25, 1940, but he had arrived a few days earlier and had immediately begun corresponding with Father Dolan about a request for a car. "The station itself spreads over vast acres, & crack ups may occur at any of several landing fields & there is no official car to bring the chaplain to the scene. . . . Due to the increased personnel, the officers newly arriving must find accomodation [*sic*] in the city (for which a government rental allowance is of course granted) & the city is a $1.00 taxi ride from the station."[1] Father Dolan approved acquisition of a secondhand car, though Father O'Callahan was to make "every effort to keep this expenditure as low as possible."[2]

O'Callahan certainly needed transportation. Pensacola was indeed a large base. Located on the Gulf of Mexico at the tip of the Florida panhandle, by the Alabama border, the base originally had been a navy yard, established in 1826. A hurricane and tidal wave wiped out the yard in 1906, and a subsequent yellow fever epidemic led to its closure. The navy's burgeoning interest in aviation, however, gave the site new life as a training facility for seaplanes, almost exclusively the navy's early focus in the air. By 1917, as training accelerated during World War I, the site became a naval air station, but it trained only about a hundred pilots annually in the early 1920s. With the start of the naval aviation cadet training program in 1935, however, Pensacola began to grow rapidly. The station's airfield expanded to five paved runways in 1938, and the navy purchased land for an outlying landing field about twelve miles from the station in 1940, the year Father Joe reported for duty. As training require-ments increased during World War II, other auxiliary fields grew around the station, and eventually the navy would turn out more than 1,100 naval aviators a month there. The entire facility, including outlying fields, would encompass nearly ten thousand acres. Pensacola eventually trained more than 28,000 avi-ators, slightly fewer than half of the total produced for the war at dozens of air facilities around the country.[3]

When Lieutenant (jg) O'Callahan checked in, joining two Protestant chap-lains already on station, prospective naval aviators were learning to fly a wide array of aircraft, many of which would remain in service throughout most of the war. All of these planes seem remarkably frail and vulnerable today, but in the 1930s they reflected the state of a technology with a thirty-year history. The air station's seaplane ramps accommodated Consolidated PBY Catalina flying boats and Vought OS2U Kingfishers, Curtiss SOC Seagulls and Naval Air Factory N3N float planes—the last of which, a biplane, sported such colorful nicknames as "Yellow Peril" and "Rhapsody in Glue." Pilots plan-ning to specialize in carrier aircraft trained in North American SNJ Texans, Vultee SNV Vindicators (known pejoratively as "Vibrators"), Yellow Perils, and another biplane, the Stearman N2S Kaydet.[4]

O'Callahan set up temporary living quarters at the St. Michael's Catholic Church rectory in Pensacola. Within days, he bought a 1936 coupe for a few hundred dollars and called on the station's commanding officer and depart-ment heads. He scheduled his first Mass for Sunday, December 1, and worked with the medical department, which had the only records of the religious affili-ations of assigned personnel, to prepare a roster of Catholic sailors. He noted also, "There is a large Army Camp [Fort Barrancas] adjoining and I have been asked to look out for the Catholic boys there, so my flock will be very large."[5] Father Joe also visited Mobile, Alabama, home of Pensacola's diocese and Bishop Thomas J. Toolen, who expressed concern that the navy was hindering O'Callahan's work and reflecting anti-Catholic bias by not providing the chap-lain quarters on the base. O'Callahan, however, did not share the bishop's view, assuring him of the navy's cooperation. "Bishop Toolen is very good to me, but I really believe he is too prone to see slights & insults where none are intended, and to insist on special rights & privileges." In fact, O'Callahan's main worry was the relatively small percentage of sailors attending Mass and confession. "Please God by Christmas I'll have most of them in line. It's a happy season in which to begin work. And there is plenty of it to be done." With help from the station commander, Capt. Albert C. Read, he soon had base quarters and worked long days to help his congregation.[6]

Within a month, he filed a report on his busy daily routine, which he completed with full cooperation from "everyone from high command to Petty Officer" and from the two Protestant chaplains, who "have welcomed me heartily and we work together perfectly." Father Joe's weekly tasks included celebrating Mass for about eight hundred enlisted men, aviation cadets, and officers on station, hearing confessions, welcoming newly assigned training-class members, and providing a variety of social services, including counseling, allotting Navy Relief funds, and visiting patients in the base hospital. One such case involved a man charged with desertion who was being held in the hospital brig:

> Alone all day in a cell he was in a way worse off than if he were not [*sic*] in the hospital. I made it a point to visit him every day, and each day he was mentally worse. The corrective was obviously reading material, but a rigid rule for men in the brig for charges . . . forbad [*sic*] all reading matter. The matter was brought to the attention of the executive officer, who thought [*sic*] personally sympathetic couldn't see his way to making an exception to the rule. Then a happy solution occured [*sic*] to me—I saw a loop hole. Navy regulations for brig men must be enforced, but, Navy regulations for [the] Chaplain Corps had also to be enforced. The one forbade the reading of books the other insisted on the need of religion [*sic*] help—and that certain included the reading of the bible! Laughingly we both agreed that was the perfect solution—and the lad is now a Bible scholar, he averages about 6 hours of Bible reading each day. It was significant though that the only Bible available was a St. James edition. Where can I get a copie [*sic*] of the Catholic edition especially the new American Translation?[7]

In another case, O'Callahan rode in the passenger seat of an open cockpit biplane and sprinkled holy water as part of a memorial flight for a Chilean officer killed in a crash at sea while in training.[8]

By March 1941, Father Joe's diplomatic and friendly approach, which he bolstered by attending many social events in Pensacola and at the air station, led to the navy's authorization for conversion of a vacant building into a Catholic chapel, which was open for business in May. Mass attendance exceeded four hundred sailors. O'Callahan also spent many hours on station morale, counseling on a variety of issues he itemized in monthly reports, and writing and publishing the station's newsletter, *The Gosport*,[9] the name of the primitive communication system connecting pilots to instructors in training aircraft, most of which had no radios. From the end of June to mid-July, however, Father Joe wound up in the station hospital himself—"too much heat, too much work and a severe attack of shingles."[10] Despite his ailment, the priest continued to offer Mass, but he promised to cut back on his activities.

O'Callahan did not keep the promise, though the summer was unusually hot, too hot for a New Englander. "I do know that [in] four months (with no relief in sight) there has not been a cool day or a cool night. Heat rash is a hair shirt just as uncomfortable as those worn by the old monks, just like five hundred mosquito bites simultaneously itching."[11]

Father Joe tended to rigorous daily chaplain duties, including therapy for mental patients in the base hospital, marriage counseling, religious instruction for sailors (Catholic and Protestant), planning marriages, and helping those interested in conversion to Catholicism. He also continued to edit the station magazine, planned a Christmas party for a thousand children on the base, and worked on finding low-cost housing for enlisted men as the ranks at Pensacola swelled beyond the base's barracks capacity, especially after the attack on Pearl Harbor and full mobilization.

In general, however, O'Callahan did not notice significant change after December 7. "There is no direct change in my work here since the outbreak of war, and no reference whatsoever to the war. It is however somewhat intensified, the work I mean, both religious & morale."[12] By year's end, a second Catholic chaplain, Father Wheaton, arrived to help, although this did not stem the flow of visits to Father Joe's office. "I seem to have the happy or unhappy faculty of attracting to my office an unending series of heart-breaking and head cracking cases, from Catholics and non-Catholic alike. I believe that I am helpful to the parties, and I know that at the close of the case whether it be two days or two weeks, whatever their religion, they have learned to pray and are nearer to God."[13]

The 2,400 members of the station's officers club also elected Father Joe as a director, recognition that pleased him. He attributed the choice to positive influence with other officers, "not a popularity that comes from being a 'good fellow' (with my sending a big check to you every month I have no money to spend being a good fellow!); I think rather that I have succeeded in trying to help people and in my efforts to put across a religious message in a way that will not antagonize. (The Jesuit training is mostly responsible for that, and Jesuits should be the best chaplains.)"[14] O'Callahan also made it clear that he expected to take on a different assignment. "I don't want to spend the war at Pensacola, and have little doubt that before many months, I might well be at sea." He added an ominous postscript, "You recall my little sister, the Maryknoll nun in Manilla [sic]. We didn't hear whether she is alive or dead at the time the Japs took the city, and now we won't know anything. Say a prayer for her."[15]

Father Joe's enthusiasm for service at sea probably increased because of his sister's situation, but he had long been interested in ships. "From the day I entered the Navy," he wrote later, "I sought sea duty and I wanted to be aboard a carrier."[16] Not everyone, however, encouraged his interest, even though his increasingly positive reputation had spread beyond the naval air station.

Father Maurice Sheehy, chaplain at the naval air station in Jacksonville, Florida, wrote a memo to "the Pensacola Padre" on O'Callahan's promotion to lieutenant in January 1942, noting that he had recommended, albeit without success, additional advancement for Father Joe: "Sorry you didn't get another stripe which you richly deserve. You would be greatly flattered if you only knew how the Protestant chaplains . . . speak of your work."

"And get the idea of sea duty out of your head," Sheehy added. "You'll never be anywhere where you can do more good than you are doing now."[17]

Around the same time, O'Callahan's mother requested financial help from her son, prompting a question about classifying her as his dependent, eligible to receive an allowance from his pay, most of which he sent to the provincial's office. He also wanted to designate his mother as beneficiary of his military life insurance, since regulations prohibited naming the society or a similar organization, but he felt he needed permission from Father Dolan. He made a similar request before spending eighty dollars for a motorbike the navy proposed to authorize for him and other departmental officers to get around the base, another reflection of his insistence on keeping his vow of obedience to the order.

For a year and a half O'Callahan had done exceptionally well at Pensacola, adapting well to his new service responsibilities and to the service itself. He had proved to be a pragmatic, practical, and effective chaplain who regarded his Catholicism and Jesuit training as assets and advantages in dealing with the predominately Protestant community he served. He was a pleasant, capable, competent, and committed pastor whose demeanor prompted respect from nearly everyone with whom he dealt, in both official and unofficial situations. Father Joe summarized his service at the air station:

> In my eighteenth months there [Pensacola] I had learned naval procedure and acquired an amateur familiarity with naval aviation. I had made hosts of friends: administrative heads who were now captains and executives of carriers; aviation instructors who now in war were the squadron leaders of planes flying from flattops into combat; many hundreds of cadets who had earned their wings at Pensacola and were now piloting those combat planes from carriers; other hundreds of mechanics and

metal smiths and radiomen, the bluejackets and chiefs who kept those planes in good flying conditions.[18]

Father Joe continued to fill his days with instructions for a large number of sailors interested in conversion to Catholicism, and premarital counseling for aviation cadets ready to take advantage of relaxed military regulations, in many cases after quick romances. O'Callahan did what he could to dissuade trainees from hasty weddings but still had plenty of marriage ceremonies to conduct. He also worked to establish facilities for Mass and other religious services at the outlying airfields to accommodate Catholics unable to get to the main base.[19]

By mid-April, however, O'Callahan had no further need to plan for new chapels around Pensacola, or to buy a motorbike. Orders from the Chief of the Bureau of Navigation, titled "Change of Duty" and dated April 10, 1942, read:

> When directed by the Commandant, Naval Air Station, upon the reporting of your relief, you will regard yourself detached from duty at the Naval Air Station, Pensacola, Fla., and from such other duty as may have been assigned to you; will proceed to Norfolk, Va., and report to the Service Force, Atlantic Subordinate Command, Naval Operating Base, for such transportation as he may designate to the port in which the U.S.S. *Ranger* may be, and upon arrival report to the commanding officer of that vessel as the relief of Lieutenant Commander Edward J. Robbins (ChC), U.S.N.[20]

Father Joe was heading for an aircraft carrier, going to sea, and going in harm's way.

6

Ranger

Chaplain of "The Ghost Ship"

anger was the navy's fourth aircraft carrier and the ninth naval ship (laid down or commissioned) to bear the name. Those vessels shared a distinguished history and tradition. The first *Ranger,* an 18-gun sloop built in 1777 and displacing 308 tons, was one of the 33 ships in the Continental Navy. Under the command of Capt. John Paul Jones and with a ship's company of 140 men, *Ranger* sailed on her maiden voyage to France. Flying the ensign of the new American nation on Valentine's Day, 1778, she received a formal gun salute from a French flotilla, the first official international recognition of the American government and its flag. In April, *Ranger* became the first American vessel to defeat a British Royal Navy (RN) ship in British waters, taking HMS *Drake,* twenty guns, near the Irish port of Carrickfergus. However, the British captured *Ranger* in 1780, renaming her HMS *Halifax.*

Other *Ranger*s, all small vessels, served in the War of 1812, during the latter nineteenth century, and in World War I. After the war, two planned cruisers carried the name for short times, but both were scrapped before completion.

The ninth *Ranger,* designated CV 4 as the navy's fourth fleet aircraft carrier, was the first flattop the navy planned and built from the keel up. The first of her three predecessors, *Langley* (CV 1), was a collier converted in 1920 to serve primarily as an experimental and training vessel; the others, *Lexington* (CV 2) and *Saratoga* (CV 3), were more sophisticated carriers built on cruiser hulls and commissioned in late 1927.

Newport News Shipbuilding & Drydock Company laid down CV 4 on September 26, 1931, at its shipyard near Virginia's Hampton Roads, and launched the ship on February 25, 1933. Mrs. Herbert Hoover, the first lady, sponsored *Ranger* at the commissioning at the Norfolk Navy Yard on June 4, 1934. Capt. Arthur L. Bristol, USN, took command.[1]

Ranger proved to be an inadequate design, its shortcomings reflecting the navy's uncertainty about the appropriate size for carriers within the fleet-tonnage restrictions of the 1922 Washington Treaty. After a refitting in September 1941, she displaced less than 20,000 tons fully loaded; she had a 709-foot flight deck and carried 79 aircraft, including fighters, dive-bombers, and scout aircraft. A crew of 2,148 in the ship's company and air group manned the carrier. For defense, *Ranger* carried eight 5-inch, .25-caliber, dual-purpose guns and forty .50-caliber machine guns. Her turbine engines could generate a top speed of nearly thirty knots. Both *Lexington* and *Saratoga* were much larger, displacing more than 43,000 tons fully loaded, with 866-foot flight decks accommodating 76 aircraft each—fighters, dive-bombers and scouts, and torpedo planes—and complements of 2,751 officers and men in the ship's companies and air groups. Their top speed was thirty-five knots. Defensive armament included eight 8-inch, .55-caliber guns and twelve 5-inch, .25-caliber, dual-purpose guns.

Ranger's smaller size dictated that she carry less defensive armor and armament, making her more vulnerable than either the *Lexington*-class ships that preceded her or the *Yorktown*- and *Essex*-class carriers that followed. During World War II, this vulnerability kept *Ranger* in the Atlantic, where German U-boats posed the major threat. Deployment to the Pacific would have exposed her to Japanese carrier attacks that would have ensured her destruction.

For nine months after her commissioning, *Ranger* completed shakedown and training cruises off the eastern U.S. and South American coasts, but she spent the next four years in the prewar Pacific, based in San Diego and conducting exercises and fleet problems from Seattle to Peru. In January 1939 she returned to the Atlantic for winter exercises near Cuba's Guantanamo Bay, then docked in Norfolk in April. In autumn 1939 *Ranger* began neutrality patrol operations along the eastern seaboard, sailing routes from Bermuda to Argentia, Newfoundland.

The outbreak of war on December 7, 1941, found the carrier returning to Norfolk from an ocean patrol. In late March 1942, after about three more months of South Atlantic duty, the flattop returned to Norfolk Navy Yard for repair and refit. While she lay in port, Rear Adm. Ernest D. McWhorter assumed command of Atlantic Fleet carriers, breaking his flag in *Ranger* in early April.

During April and May, the carrier ferried two groups of P-40 fighters destined for the Tenth Air Force in Karachi, India, from the Quonset Point Naval Air Station on Narragansett Bay, Rhode Island, to Accra, off the Gold Coast of Africa. On the way home, *Ranger* made a port call at Trinidad and passed Martha's Vineyard on May 28, returning to Quonset Point the next day.

Father Joe detached from Pensacola on April 29, 1942, but could not report on board *Ranger,* which had departed on its second aircraft-ferry voyage on April 22. He certainly must have enjoyed the chance to see his family, friends, and colleagues in Boston and Worcester while waiting for the carrier's return to Narragansett Bay, where he joined the ship.[2] On May 30 Capt. Calvin T. Durgin relieved Capt. William K. Harrill as *Ranger*'s commanding officer, probably on the same day O'Callahan reported on board. On June 1 the carrier had put out from Narragansett Bay and was under way the following day to "Base Roger," Argentia, Newfoundland, where she arrived on June 5.

Argentia was a new naval facility, built near Placentia Bay during the first half of 1941 to accommodate the ships and patrol aircraft that provided escorts to merchant vessels convoying war matériel from the United States to Great Britain on the dangerous northern route. German U-boats played havoc with supply convoys early in the war, sinking ships more rapidly than shipyards could build them. To protect the vulnerable lifeline to Britain, the Allies built a strategic network of bases stretching from Canada to Greenland, Iceland, Ireland, and Scotland, enabling corvettes and patrol bombers to keep an almost uninterrupted web of bombs and depth charges primed for attacks against submarines, and greatly improving the odds that freighters would complete their voyages safely. In August 1941 President Roosevelt and Prime Minister Winston Churchill met at Placentia Bay and negotiated the Atlantic Charter, a plan for global governance after the war ended. Just a couple of months before *Ranger* arrived, a Lockheed Hudson patrol bomber attacked and destroyed *U-656* southwest of Newfoundland, the first time U.S. forces sank a German submarine.[3]

After conducting flight training and operations in the area for two weeks, *Ranger* departed for "Base George," Narragansett Bay, on June 20, joining the light cruiser *Juneau* (counting the five Sullivan brothers among her crew) before making port two days later. July 1 found *Ranger* under way again, ferrying more army aircraft, with a stop at "Base Dog," Port-of-Spain, Trinidad, on July 6 before launching the aircraft at Accra on July 19 and returning to "Base Hypo," the Norfolk Naval Operating Base at Hampton Roads, eleven days later. Just before entering port, Father Joe wrote to Father Provincial Dolan, reflecting on his first month of sea duty:

> Twenty years a Jesuit. I'm getting to be an old man! I never thought I would be spending [my anniversary of service] far away from a Jesuit home. But I'll say Mass in my little chapel aboard and there will be a goodly number of men attending. It is very edifying to have a group of Men [sic] every morning, the number increasing weekly. Also increasing is the number under instruction—as I told you I run daily Catholic lessons.

> I'm very happy & not at all bored. On the other hand it isn't too exciting. An atmosphere is deliberately built whereby the men assume there is a quiet permanence and so are by no means jittery. The chaplain is supposed to build up such an atmosphere & I believe successfully. My usual bad scrawl is made worse by a rolling sea.[4]

If O'Callahan was worried about a lack of excitement while at sea, the concern soon would pass. Planning for Operation Torch, the invasion of North Africa, began the week before Christmas 1941 during the Arcadia war conference in Washington, D.C. By the time *Ranger* returned from ferrying P-40s to Accra, the plans for Torch were ready, and the operation could begin. American forces would attack Morocco's Atlantic coast while British ships and troops would assault Oran and Algiers in Algeria, both French colonies under the control of the German-surrogate Vichy government.

The carrier took on Air Group 4's fighter and scouting squadrons, VF-41, VS-41, and VF-9 replacing the bombing squadron VB-42, since *Ranger's* mission would be air cover for the landing force. Throughout August and September the carrier remained in Norfolk, conducting brief cruises into Chesapeake Bay and to Quonset Point for gunnery and flight training. In October the flattop headed for Bermuda, rendezvousing with four *Sangamon*-class escort carriers, converted from tankers. These ships would constitute the carrier task group supporting Task Force 34, the naval armada that would disembark the U.S. Army's Western Task Force, Maj. Gen. George S. Patton commanding, which would hit three points in French Morocco—Port Lyautey to the north, Casablanca in the center, and Safi to the south. More than 100,000 soldiers and sailors were to participate in the attack.

By October 25, *Ranger* and the four escort carriers were headed toward Casablanca, part of a flotilla that would contain three battleships, seven cruisers, thirty-six destroyers, thirty-one transports, eighteen auxiliaries, and four submarines—104 ships in total. At 4:15 a.m. on Sunday, November 8, the order "Play ball" initiated the invasion.

By 6:15, as the sun rose, the carrier's flight-deck crew had launched eighteen F-4F Wildcat fighters from VP-9 to attack Rabat and Rabat-Sale airport, where they destroyed twenty-one French aircraft on the ground and then patrolled to establish air superiority over the landing force. In short order, seventeen SBD ("Slow But Deadly," as nicknamed by their crews) Dauntless dive-bombers from VS-41 and another eighteen Wildcats from VF-41 also launched to attack and destroy hostile submarines, ships, and shore batteries while covering troop landings, as well as Port Lyautey airfield.

Throughout the morning, as *Ranger*'s aircraft landed and took off in successive sorties, Vichy French naval forces attempted to leave port in Casablanca and take on the American invaders, and defenders on the beaches organized increasingly determined resistance. Aircraft dropped depth charges and ships fired at submarine contacts, although they reported no hits. Several *Ranger* aircraft bombed and strafed French ships as well as ground positions, and others engaged in dogfights with obsolescent red-and-yellow-striped French Curtiss Hawk and Dewoitine D.520 fighters, claiming sixteen shoot-downs—a strong performance against veteran French pilots for the well-trained American aviators in their first combat. Even Curtiss observation float biplanes, launched from battleships and cruisers and carrying depth charges with impact fuses, bombed a French tank formation. As the hours passed, however, American aircraft losses mounted, with several reports of aircraft in the water. Fortunately, many of the pilots in these aircraft survived, and American or French vessels picked them up.

All of this action would have been completely remote for many of the men on board *Ranger,* most of them working below decks, had it not been for Lieutenant O'Callahan. In his after-action report on Operation Torch, Captain Durgin explained, "For the benefit of men below decks handling bombs and ammunition, manning engine room stations, standing by damage control posts and providing coffee, sandwiches and frequent hot meals for the ship's company, the chaplain, Lt. J. T. O'Callahan, USNR, broadcast a running commentary of the USS *Ranger*'s attack on French Morocco over the ship's loud speaker system. This battle commentary was welcomed with especial interest and understanding."[5]

Just before 2:30 in the afternoon, the war came a lot closer for several *Ranger* crewmen, including the chaplain. With each American sortie, Vichy antiaircraft fire bored in with increasingly deadly accuracy. Captain Durgin reported forty-three of *Ranger*'s planes returned to the flight deck with damage, one aircraft with twenty-seven hits. One of these was an SBD Dauntless dive-bomber from Scouting 41 that had attacked French gun installations at Point El Hank. A .50-mm antiaircraft shell had hit the aircraft, penetrating the rear cockpit and hitting the gunner, Aviation Radioman Third Class (ARM3) Aubra Talmadge "Pat" Patterson, in the leg. Patterson bled to death in moments. By the time the plane landed on *Ranger,* blood swathed the cockpit. Plane handlers covered the cockpit canopy but did not remove Patterson, leaving that grisly task to hospital corpsmen—and Father O'Callahan. The priest helped to lift Patterson's body out of the Dauntless's cockpit, helped clean up the gore, and buried the airman at sea the following afternoon, all without betraying a second's hesitation or reluctance. If any fear or other emotions gripped Father Joe in those moments, his first exposure to combat, he suppressed them, just as he minimized or ignored other internal responses that could have affected his ability to carry on. Years later, however, Father Harkins recalled the real impact on O'Callahan. "We talked about his war experiences every now and then. He said that when he went to his bunk on the ship, he'd grip the rail around it so tightly his knuckles turned white. He was terrified of submarines and torpedoes and being blown up any minute."[6]

The following morning, air operations continued, including the launches of three army L-4 Piper Cubs, used as observation aircraft. Capt. Ford Alcorn, the senior army air forces pilot of the unit, took off into a thirty-five-knot headwind that provided plenty of lift to get the little plane off of *Ranger*'s deck. Because Captain Durgin refused to break radio silence to let other ships know the Piper Cubs were taking off, Alcorn and the other pilots had to evade fire from American ships that did not recognize the unfamiliar craft. Over the French shore, antiaircraft fire wounded the captain and brought down his L-4, making him the first U.S. army aviator to be shot down and captured in North Africa.[7]

A naval aviator, Lt. (jg) Charles Shields of VF-41, shot down at least two Vichy fighters, emptied his guns on a strafing run over a French airfield, and bailed out when four Vichy Hawks blasted his Wildcat. As Shields floated under his parachute toward the ground, the French planes looped menacingly around him, firing at him occasionally. Incensed, the aviator drew his pistol and shot back as the aircraft buzzed him. Shields made it to the ground unhurt, one of four navy pilots on *Ranger* taken prisoner in the battle.[8]

Captain Durgin credited two late-afternoon attacks on November 10 with speeding the Vichy government's cease-fire the following day. Nine dive-bombers carrying 1,000-pound bombs struck the French battleship *Jean Bart* in the port of Casablanca, where it had been berthed throughout the battle. The French had brought the ship's guns to bear against the American invasion fleet on November 8, but she suffered considerable damage from bombings and could only operate one turret on November 10. The Tuesday mission ended any threat from the vessel. Nine more aircraft similarly armed hit antiaircraft batteries at El Hank and within the Casablanca harbor itself, putting all out of commission.

Before hostilities against Vichy forces ceased on November 11—coincidentally the anniversary of the Great War's Armistice Day—*Ranger*'s air group and other Task Force 34 elements claimed the destruction of or severe damage to one light cruiser, one destroyer leader, four destroyers, and a submarine at sea. Subsequent attacks damaged the battleship *Jean Bart* and up to seven submarines, all in port. CV 4 fighters tallied seventy-one enemy airplanes destroyed or damaged on the ground and more than twenty in aerial dogfights. Airman also strafed about twenty tanks and more than eighty trucks.

Operation Torch also exacted a steep price in Allied lives and treasure. Total Allied casualties were 479 dead and 720 wounded. (French forces lost about three times that number.) Task Force 34 lost ten airmen and twenty-three aircraft. *Ranger* counted six dead. From VF-9, Lt. (jg) S. M. Amesbury, Lt. Edward Micka, and Ens. T. M. Wilhoite sacrificed their lives. VS-41 lost Ens. Charles E. Duffy and his gunner, Aviation Radioman George E. Biggs, and ARM3 Patterson. The Vichy French captured four *Ranger* pilots, all from VF-41 (and all destined for quick release). The carrier lost sixteen fighters and dive-bombers in combat or other operations, nearly 25 percent of its available aircraft. A couple of planes crash-landed on the ship's deck or were damaged "beyond economical repair," in Captain Durgin's words. One of these, an SBD with one 500-pound and two 100-pound bombs in its racks, had hit a tree during a strafing run, smashing its keelson and empennage. Several other planes ditched at sea after running out of gas.

Ranger's crewmen did well in Operation Torch, their first combat. The deck crew handled nearly 500 launches on more than 60 missions that dropped 48 tons of ordnance and fired nearly 21,000 rounds of machine-gun ammunition. Captain Durgin summed up the performance: "The large number of flights, with the damage of only two planes on landing and no accidents to plane handling crews nor any breakdowns in arresting gear showed that the flight deck personnel had been well trained and the flight arresting devices well designed and well maintained."

"The general sentiment of the ship's crew was 'this is just like battle practice and it doesn't seem like the real thing,'" Durgin continued. "All hands turned to with a will and the years of careful training made actual battle procedure run as smoothly as the previous battle practices."[9]

Fighting on the ground and in the air stopped on November 11, but *Ranger* still faced danger. On the morning of Thursday, November 12, submarines attacked the carrier, firing at least five torpedoes that bracketed the ship. Two crossed the bow, one narrowly missing, while three passed the stern, in one case almost under the fantail. For more than two hours *Ranger* maneuvered to avoid strikes as its planes, guns, and escort destroyers pounded submarine sightings with bombs, shells, and depth charges. At one point a submarine appeared to surface between two of the many Spanish fishing trawlers in the area, raising concerns about possible coordination between subs and the commercial fleet. Nevertheless, *Ranger* did not turn her guns on any trawlers but ordered them to clear out of the area as fast as possible, giving the commands through a bullhorn in Spanish and Portuguese. Captain Durgin reported that *Ranger* had maintained vigorous antisubmarine patrols and watches throughout its voyage and that this discipline paid off. He noted that after the November 12 action, the carrier "encountered no further serious trouble."[10] Perhaps Father O'Callahan relaxed his grip on his bunk rail.

At 12:35 p.m., the *Ranger*'s battle diary noted, "Formed cruising disposition, 1-T modified, with *Cleveland, Brooklyn, Suwannee, Fitch, Forrest, Ellyson, Ludlow* and *Swanson; Ranger* guide—base course 275°, speed 14 knots, and departed Torch area." The carrier was heading home.

On November 21, the flotilla put up for a day at "Base Mike," in Bermuda's Port Royal Bay, then made way for "Base Hypo," in Hampton Roads, and then Norfolk, where *Ranger* anchored on November 25. After a month in a navy yard dry dock for overhaul so the ship could handle larger, heavier aircraft, including the Grumman TBF Avenger torpedo bomber, the carrier loaded more army P-40s for transport to Morocco. Under way on January 8, 1943, *Ranger* reached her destination eleven days later. Tragedy marred the return voyage, however, reflecting the dangers of even routine operations at sea.

On January 23 Lt. (jg) George O'Mary attempted to fly an antisubmarine patrol despite a case of nausea. The TBF veered to port on takeoff and hit the water. O'Mary and his two crewmen scrambled out of the aircraft. The pilot hesitated for a moment and remained standing in the aircraft's cockpit as the others dove into the sea and swam away. As O'Mary waved to his shipmates on *Ranger* and fumbled with his parachute harness, depth charges in the Avenger's bomb bay, set to discharge at twenty-five feet below the ocean's surface, suddenly exploded, obliterating everything in a huge geyser of water and foam.

Returning to Norfolk on January 30, *Ranger* repeated the ferry operation, loading more P-40s for another voyage to Casablanca. She departed the naval base on February 13, delivered the Warhawks to Casablanca on February 23, made home port on March 6, and then anchored once again at Quonset Point, Rhode Island, on March 10. While conducting training in the area, new commanders came on board. Rear Adm. Alvah D. Bernhard succeeded Admiral McWhorter and took over Task Force 22, and Capt. Gordon Rowe relieved Captain Durgin. Day-and-night flight training from Maine to Nova Scotia sharpened the air group, but the pilots were not flawless. *Ranger* docked at the South Boston Navy Yard in early April to repair a gun emplacement damaged in a crash landing. Father Joe welcomed the opportunity to visit his family, but the sojourn was a short one. The carrier embarked for Argentia, Newfoundland, on April 2, operating there into the summer.

On July 1 the navy promoted Chaplain O'Callahan to lieutenant commander, reflecting both his outstanding service and the urgency of wartime requirements.

Another yard period in Boston came at the end of July, as did a voyage providing air cover for the SS *Queen Mary,* carrying Prime Minister Churchill to the Quebec Conference with President Roosevelt.

After months of North Atlantic operations, *Ranger* was ready for more offensive action. In mid-August she joined the Royal Navy's Home Fleet, based at Scapa Flow, a quiet bay in the middle of Scotland's Orkney Islands at the northern tip of the British Isles. From the Orkneys in early October 1943, the carrier would take U.S. naval aviation's first action against German forces, off the coast of Norway in Operation Leader, a combined effort under the command of Adm. Sir Bruce Fraser, RN, Commander in Chief, British Home Fleet.

Operation Leader's objective was the Norwegian port and airfield at Bodö, its target German naval and merchant ships. The combined task force reached launch position off Vestfjord, Norway, before dawn on October 4, catching the Germans completely by surprise. *Ranger* launched twenty SBDs and eight Wildcat fighters as escorts. Several dive-bombers attacked the eight-thousand-ton freighter *LaPlata,* while others hit a German convoy, damaging a tanker estimated at ten thousand tons and a smaller troop transport. *Ranger*'s aircraft also sank two small German merchant ships in the Bodö roadstead. A second attack, with ten Avenger torpedo bombers and six F-4Fs, sank a German freighter and a small coastal ship and damaged another transport filled with troops. The carrier's combat air patrol also shot down two of four German patrol airplanes that found the carrier group, chasing the others away.

The carrier lost one TBF and two SBDs, all to antiaircraft gunfire around Bodö. Lt. (jg) John Palmer, the TBF pilot, successfully parachuted from his stricken craft, but his crewmen, Aviation Radio Technician First Class Joseph

Zalon and Aviation Machinist's Mate First Class Reginald Miller, did not. Lt. (jg) Sumner Davis and his gunner, Aviation Radioman Second Class D. W. McCarley, ditched their SBD near a small island and inflated a rubber raft. Norwegian fishermen picked them up, and the Germans soon took them into custody. Lt. (jg) Clyde A. Tucker's Dauntless hit the water and exploded, killing him and his gunner, ARM2 Stephen Bakran. Tucker's wife Louise of just over a year was pregnant with his son, Clyde Jr.[11]

Ranger arrived safely at Scapa Flow on October 6. Captain Rowe said later of Operation Leader, "It was a very fine attack, and many German troops were killed. My pilots drove home their attacks in the face of strong anti-aircraft fire. We struck quickly and departed before the Germans knew what had hit them."[12]

The Germans told a much different story, and *Ranger* soon would figure prominently in the news throughout America and Europe. German radio broadcasts and newspapers announced proudly that on April 25, 1943, Kriegsmarine kapitänleutnant Otto Von Bülow, captain of the submarine *U-404,* "in addition to torpedoing four steamers, caught and sank the American aircraft carrier *Ranger.*" Von Bülow's feat warranted Adolf Hitler's personal presentation of Oak Leaves to the officer's Knight's Cross.

Concerned about the effects of this story on the families of *Ranger*'s crew, the navy quickly issued a denial, but the German press issued no corrections. Lieutenant (jg) Palmer, by this time in Stalag Luft 3, a German prisoner-of-war camp for captured American and British airmen, said later, "I was the only Navy guy in this camp, and the other prisoners thought I was a German plant because they had seen the German news account of the sinking of the *Ranger.* Of course, I told them that I was off the *Ranger,* and they didn't believe me. They believed the newspaper."

The carrier continued patrols with the British 2nd Battle Squadron and then entered dry dock in Rosyth, Scotland, for repairs on October 24. In November she ranged throughout the North Atlantic, anchoring in Hvalfjord, Iceland, on October 26 before shaping course for Boston, where she arrived on December 4, remaining through the year's end. The ship transited to Quonset Point on January 2, 1944, to assume its primary role for the remainder of the war, carrier-qualification training for new naval aviators. In early February an Associated Press story on *Ranger*'s exploits in Operation Leader ran throughout the country, calling the carrier "a ghost ship on Nazi record." The new, ironic nickname stuck. The war correspondent Quentin Reynolds, then working for CBS Radio, visited the carrier and interviewed Captain Rowe and several crew members about Operation Leader and the report of *Ranger*'s demise.

The report, broadcast on February 15, quoted the captain:

We on the Ranger have put in a strenuous year. The North Atlantic and the Arctic Oceans have been ours as part of a Task Force of the Atlantic and the British Home Fleet. As Mr. Reynolds has told you, we've been a pretty lively ghost. The story that we were sunk was a coward's trick— spreading anxiety and fear among the innocent. *We* knew we were all right, but there were a lot of our relatives and our friends who didn't know it. That's why at Bodö we were so eager to make the enemy pay heavily for his lie.

Well, we hit 'em hard and got out with few losses. We spread panic and chaos in the Norwegian shipping lanes. Only one thing we regret. We kept looking for the *Tirpitz*, but either she wouldn't or couldn't come out. We may have a chance later to dig her out, but meanwhile, the *Ranger*, still very much afloat, is doing her job. And I'm grateful for the chance to say a word on behalf of the officers and men of the *Ranger* and the *Ranger* Air Group.

The submarine commander, Von Bülow, who survived the war, later corrected the record, claiming an unsuccessful attack on the British escort carrier HMS *Biter*.

Ranger's training routine, from her base in Narragansett Bay near the Quonset Point Naval Air Station, continued through the spring. On April 3 the carrier took a break from her war preparations and sailed to Staten Island, New York, to load seventy-six P-38 Lightning fighter planes and army, navy, and French naval personnel for another delivery to Casablanca, with a return to the United States in mid-May. Father O'Callahan, however, was not on board. He detached from *Ranger* on that day with orders to report to Naval Air Station, Alameda, California, for duty ashore as base chaplain. After nearly two years of service at sea, the priest could look forward to a cushy stateside assignment. Father Joe reported to Alameda in late May after taking a well-earned rest at home in Cambridge.[13]

O'Callahan had seen his share of a new and frightening world, as distant from his Jesuit experience as another planet is from Earth. He had struggled with his own physical frailties, fought against the fear that touches all men, and served as a source of comfort, stability, solace, and leadership for boys and young men even more frightened and uncertain than he. The academic priest had become a sailor, tested in battle, acclimated to the hard life all sailors live on an unforgiving sea. He had come to know and like the men he served as pastor, men who relied on his counsel and learned from his faith. He had lived and worked at close quarters with officers and men he regarded as parishioners and friends. He had watched them toil, risk their lives, and, too often, die. O'Callahan would remember his time on *Ranger* with particularly strong fondness and pride. He wrote:

The USS *Ranger* was my first ship. . . .

Sea duty to any naval man is naturally preferable to shore duty, and, to one who has been connected with naval aviation, aircraft carriers are superior to any other ship. They are the queens of the fleet, Fighting Ladies, always in the thick of the fray.

But no ship, not even the queens of the fleet, would expect loyalty to such an extreme as to demand that any member of her crew forget that "First ship is first love." The *Ranger* had been my first ship. She always will be my first love. . . .

When reporting aboard the *Ranger* I found myself on a hangar deck so big and symmetrical I could not tell where was forward and where aft. I trust that the *Ranger* crew found me a ready pupil. I found them willing and expert instructors, particularly Scotty, the electrician, Vermersch, the carpenter, and young Peterson [*sic*—O'Callahan is referring to Alvah T. Patterson], the gunner who bled to death in his bomber as she returned from a strike at Casablanca. . . .

Seldom did the *Ranger* make headlines, and her praises are not sung in Navy folklore, [but] I think the best work of my Navy career was performed aboard her.[14]

7

Interlude

A Tale of Two Sisters

The war in the Atlantic was an enormous undertaking involving count-less ships, aircraft, and men, but the *navy's* war was in the Pacific. Even before fighting began, the Pacific Fleet was America's major naval fight-ing force, with secondary Atlantic and Asian squadrons. Adm. Ernest J. King, Commander in Chief, U.S. Fleet, resurrected the Atlantic Fleet in early 1941. King agreed with President Roosevelt, Prime Minister Churchill, and the Combined Chiefs of Staff that the Allies' primary concern must be the defeat of Nazi Germany in Europe. His allocations and scheduling of resources, how-ever, clearly demonstrated the navy's preference for Pacific operations.

Naval campaigns in the Pacific outnumbered Atlantic operations by nearly five times, forty-three to nine. Of the seven American aircraft carriers in active service before Pearl Harbor, only *Ranger,* the least capable, served in the Atlantic. More telling, every one of the thirteen *Essex*-class fleet carriers and nine *Independence*-class light carriers that were fully operational during the war joined the Pacific Fleet after shakedown. Fewer than a dozen of the seventy-eight "jeep," or escort, carriers (designated CVEs, which their crews suggested stood for "Combustible, Vulnerable, and Expendable"), most con-verted from merchant vessels or oilers, or built to merchant-design hulls, served in the Atlantic to protect convoys and hunt German U-boats.

America built about 80,000 vessels of all types, an astonishing total, in World War II, and most of them were Pacific bound. Just before the D-day invasion, for example, U.S. naval landing craft in England and the Mediter-ranean numbered about 2,500; the Pacific area accounted for nearly four thousand. More than 1,200 warships participated in the D-day invasion, the entire fleet totaling about four thousand vessels, from battleships to landing craft. Fewer than two hundred naval vessels were American; nearly 80 percent were British.[1]

Inevitably, the Pacific siphoned in ever more ships and support activities. As the Allies tightened the noose around Japan's home islands, American naval bases sprang up on or around Pacific islands almost as soon as army and marine invaders wrested them from Japanese control. The navy's center of gravity moved inexorably west and drew with it the vast network of resources and support services—including a Catholic chaplain—that kept the sea service going.

Father O'Callahan's new assignment at Alameda was in splendid contrast to his *Ranger* sea duty. A commercial airfield located on Alameda Island, by the eastern shore of San Francisco Bay near Oakland, had opened for operation in the late 1920s. The army had expanded the facility and opened an air base, named Benton Field, in 1930. Five years later, Pan American Airways had inaugurated Clipper flying-boat routes to Hawaii and the Orient.

The navy had taken over Benton Field in 1940, building enough storage and repair hangars to accommodate two carrier air groups and five seaplane and two utility squadrons. San Francisco was the navy's main West Coast surface and supply center in World War II, the "Aviation Gateway to the Pacific," and Alameda became one of its primary air stations, with more than 2,300 acres and 5 asphalt runways. Army air force lieutenant colonel Jimmy Doolittle's crews loaded their sixteen B-25 Mitchell bombers on the carrier USS *Hornet* at Alameda in 1942 and sailed on the long voyage culminating in the Tokyo raid. Throughout 1943, the navy opened outlying training fields in Crescent City, Concord, San Luis Obispo, Paso Robles, Half Moon Bay, and Cotati, and Clear Lake and Tulare Lake for seaplanes, much as it had set up satellite bases around Pensacola. More than one thousand aircraft of all types, most in repair and overhaul, filled the area's runways, and more than ten thousand sailors, all in need of material and spiritual nurturance, trained or worked at these facilities.

A month after Father Joe's arrival in May, Alameda opened another auxiliary station in Fallon, Nevada, to provide aerial gunnery training.[2] This facility and the other outlying fields would keep O'Callahan racing at full speed, as he reported to the Father Provincial: "I am very busy, but I had anticipated that I would be. It's a very big station here, and there are in addition nine outlying stations within a radius of a few hundred miles. Fortunately I travel by plane. I've succeeded in getting authorization for Catholic chapels for nine stations as well as a second chapel for the main station. Fast talking! But I won't count them until they are hatched."[3]

The chaplain's duties in the Alameda area were similar to his work at Pensacola. He counseled parishioners, celebrated Mass, visited the hospital, dealt with the surrounding communities, and administered the sacraments. The navy was moving west, however. O'Callahan spent about six months at the air station before receiving new orders for Naval Air Station 128 on Ford Island, Pearl Harbor, Hawaii. He left Alameda in early December and reported at Pearl on December 23, 1944.[4]

Ford Island sits in the middle of Oahu's Pearl Harbor, then and now the navy's main Pacific base. The naval base occupied the harbor's lochs, which extended like fingers from the central basin encircling Ford Island. Adm. Chester Nimitz, Commander in Chief, Pacific Ocean Areas, maintained his headquarters at Pearl, and the base housed dry docks and repair and overhaul facilities, as well as berthing for warships. The mooring quays for "Battleship Row" surrounded Ford Island. Here, on the morning of December 7, 1941, had been tied up *Nevada, Arizona* (with the repair ship *Vestal* outboard), *Tennessee* (with *West Virginia* outboard), *Maryland* and *Oklahoma* side by side, the oiler *Neosho,* and *California;* these ships had borne the brunt of the Japanese air attack. On the island itself, Japanese bombers and strafing fighters also had devastated the naval air station, with its large runway and hangars for utility and patrol aircraft. By Father O'Callahan's arrival the navy had long since repaired the air station's damage, but the hulk of *Arizona* still lay by its moorings off the island's southeastern edge, and *Utah,* an obsolete battleship converted for gunnery training, lay wrecked on the island's northwestern shore.[5]

Father Joe admitted that the Ford Island assignment as senior chaplain was "a cushion." The air station had relatively few residents, and the hub of naval activity had shifted to the western Pacific, to bases at New Caledonia, Ulithi, and other islands and atolls. Regarding his duty in Pearl as interim, he requested a naval staff slot in the Philippines. His reason was clear and personal:

> My sister, Alice[,] . . . had been imprisoned there since early in the war when the Japs had captured Manila. For three years neither my mother nor myself had heard a word of her. We did not know whether she was alive or dead.

> The battle of Manila was at its height. Daily the headlines shouted of wholesale murder: "Japs in defeat go berserk." Even if "La" had survived the early phases of the war, such news gave us little hope that she still lived. Were I assigned in the Philippines, I could make inquiries and perhaps settle my mother's uncertainty which was in its way more taxing than even the worst, but definite, news would have been.[6]

O'Callahan's sister Alice had taken first vows in 1930, as Sister Rose Marie, after entering the order in 1927 at age twenty. Before she decided to enter into religious life, she had worked briefly as a governess for Joseph P. Kennedy, helping to raise his younger children, including Robert, then about two years old. As a nun she had become a missionary, working in Malabon, a fishing village on Manila Bay in the Philippines. In 1938 she took a new assignment in Baguio in northern Luzon, where she taught and worked with a primitive tribe, the Igorots, indigenous peoples of the Cordillera central mountains, known for building remarkable terraces to cultivate rice. Two years later, she had reported to St. Paul's Hospital in the Intramuros section of Manila. She remained at the hospital when the Japanese took the city on February 1, and they interned her.[7]

That Father Joe's younger sister was a prisoner of the Japanese, if she still lived, made the priest's decision to participate in Pacific combat not only a supremely personal issue but also a leaden irony. On the one hand, the resolute enemy O'Callahan was sworn to help defeat held and may already have killed an innocent and defenseless loved one. At the same time, his family included a new member of Japanese heritage, his sister-in-law Ann.

Earlier in the war, during Father Joe's service on *Ranger*, his older brother John had visited Montreal in Canada with some friends. They stopped by the city's cathedral, and there John saw an exceptionally beautiful young woman.[8] She was Ann Catherine Yoshida, whose life story reflected the complex texture and depth of recent American history. Although she had grown up in Toronto and Montreal, Ann had been born in America—in Atlantic City, New Jersey, to be exact. Her father, Manzo Yoshida, had come to the United States from Japan around the turn of the century to attend college and study business. After graduation, Manzo had decided not to go home. He had worked in New York City in the art business and attended several art auctions in Wildwood, a well-to-do resort town on the New Jersey shore. At one of these events, Yoshida had met an attractive Irish girl named Mary Kearney. They married in June 1906, and their first child, christened Anna but known as Ann, was born in 1907. Manzo moved his family to Canada, where he set up an import business, the Tokio Trading Company, in Toronto; the firm expanded to Montreal, where the family eventually moved. Two more children, Richard and Rosemary, followed in 1911 and 1914, respectively. Mary raised her children as Catholics, although Manzo did not convert to Catholicism until the end of his life—so he could be buried next to his wife, who had died many years before his passing in the late 1950s.

Manzo's business did well. His grandson Richard recalled stories about Ann, well known in Montreal as a great beauty and socialite, and of her mother driving around the city in a fancy car and visiting the United States on frequent shopping trips.[9] Manzo and his son Richard were prominent amateur tennis players, well known in the community. All of Manzo's children worked intermittently in the family business as they grew up.

Then came the war, which brought major and unwelcome changes to the Yoshida household. Canada replicated U.S. policy toward its citizens of Japanese heritage. Soon after Pearl Harbor, acting on misguided fears of Japanese-Canadian collaboration with Japan, the national government confiscated the boats of Japanese fishermen in British Columbia. In March 1942 the Canadian government confiscated the property of more than 20,000 Japanese on the West Coast and forced them to move at least one hundred miles from the Pacific into inland towns created for them. Men were forced to work on road crews or as farm laborers, and the government imprisoned those who resisted. Japanese-Canadians had to wait until 1949 for restoration of their citizenship rights.[10]

In Montreal, the Japanese-Canadian population was much smaller and security concerns less immediate, though enormous difficulties still confronted the Yoshidas, the same property confiscation other Japanese citizens endured. But Manzo's affluence and standing in the city undoubtedly helped him avoid disaster. According to his grandson, Yoshida successfully negotiated with government officials, who allowed him to keep his home on Stewart Avenue in the Outremont section and serve as honorary Japanese consul in Montreal for propaganda purposes after the arrest of the official consul. Before the forced closing of his store on Notre Dame Street, in the city's old business district, Manzo and his children posed for a newspaper photo, probably a reflection of his unusual situation in Montreal. Deprived of his regular income, Manzo eventually turned to farming. He had acquired land in Laval, a nearby rural area, where he grew vegetables for Chinese restaurants in the city. After the war, as Montreal expanded, suburban sprawl greatly increased Laval's real-estate prices, and Manzo profited handsomely from his investment.[11]

When John O'Callahan met Ann, she was in her mid-thirties, about five years younger than he, and uncommonly attractive. He was smitten, and apparently so was she. In 1943, after a whirlwind courtship, they married and moved to the O'Callahan family home on Leonard Avenue in Cambridge. If Ann expected an easy time in the United States, she was mistaken. Despite American citizenship, her parentage, and her beauty, Cambridge residents recognized Ann's Japanese heritage. She frequently was the target of derision from people on the street. One man even spat on her.

The O'Callahan family, however, embraced Ann with enthusiasm. They welcomed John's bride into the house, remodeled so that the newlyweds could occupy the first floor. The family recognized the irony of their situation, and even Father Joe's young nieces and nephews understood how unusual it was to have a Japanese aunt while the nation fought against Japan and they waited for word on another aunt in a Japanese prison camp.[12] Father Joe shared his family's affection for Ann. He probably met her for the first time while on leave from *Ranger* and accepted his new in-law without hesitation before he reported to the Pacific. O'Callahan's references to the Japanese against whom he fought reflected the hostility common among combatants in the Pacific War, but Ann apparently never figured in these criticisms. The inconsistency may never have crossed Father Joe's mind. Human nature seems to allow us to ascribe unflattering characteristics unhesitatingly to entire nations, races, and ethnic groups, but to be unwilling to apply the same attributes to people we know well who happen to belong to the same groups.

John and Ann had no children, but they remained devoted to one another and the extended O'Callahan family for many years, especially enjoying visits from John's nieces, nephews, and grandnieces and grandnephews. He practiced law in a Boston firm until bad health forced an early retirement, and she worked in the administrative office of Cambridge Hospital. The Leonard Avenue house remained a happy gathering place for generations of O'Callahans.[13]

Despite the burdens their unusual situation imposed on the O'Callahans, the family lived and worked day by day, coping with their concerns for Father Joe, Sister Rose Marie, and new sister-in-law Ann. In Hawaii, Father Joe focused on the task at hand. While he waited for orders, O'Callahan stayed busy in the "vast 'playing at house'" that is the shore-bound navy: "I listened to gripes, shuttled between the men and their officers on many small and some important missions of reconciliation. I arranged movies, coffee breaks, and I fulfilled all the apparently picayune roles given to that mother–psychologist–efficiency expert, the unmilitary morale officer. At the same time I said Mass, heard confessions, and tried in an inadequate way to stretch the scope of my intentions and ministrations to the size of the need of a world at war. But mostly, I waited."[14]

On March 2 the wait ended. Capt. John Moore, Admiral Nimitz's fleet chaplain, sent O'Callahan word that orders were on the way. They duly arrived: "To Joseph T. O'Callahan, 087280, Lieutenant Commander, USNR: Hereby detached from Chaplain duties, Naval Air Station, Pearl Harbor. Proceed immediately and without delay, reporting for duty to Commanding Officer, USS *Franklin* (CV-13)."[15]

Before the day was out, the priest said goodbye to the air station CO, packed, and made his way to Ford Island's Fox Two dock. He climbed the forward gangway to the big ship's quarterdeck as a line of sailors loaded provisions, reporting on board "between two bags of potatoes."[16]

The next morning, March 3, 1945, *Franklin* slipped her moorings and slowly put out of Pearl Harbor, shaping a westerly course. She would become part of Task Force 58, under the command of Vice Adm. Marc A. "Pete" Mitscher, with seventeen other fleet carriers, eight battleships, and two cruisers, the primary striking arm of Adm. Raymond A. Spruance's Fifth Fleet. That vast assemblage totaled nearly 1,400 vessels of all types. Within it was Task Force 51, the fleet's amphibious component, under Adm. Richmond Kelly Turner, with 18 escort carriers, 12 cruisers, 10 battleships, 136 destroyers, 134 transports, and more than 600 landing ships. Also subordinate to Admiral Spruance was the British Pacific Fleet, Vice Adm. Sir Bernard Rawlings, RN, commanding, which became Task Force 57, with one battleship, four carriers, four cruisers, and twelve destroyers. The carriers' air groups totaled about two thousand aircraft. In addition, more than 180,000 soldiers and marines constituting the invasion force were embarked on the transports.

This extraordinary armada, the most powerful in history, headed for Okinawa, the largest of the Ryuku Islands, a chain stretching southwest from Kyushu, the southernmost of Japan's four main islands, toward Taiwan.

Codenamed Operation Iceberg, the Okinawa campaign was intended to set the stage for Operation Downfall, the invasion of Japan itself. Iceberg would involve far more troops, ships, and matériel than the D-day assault in Normandy. The fast carriers arrayed themselves so their air groups could attack not only Japanese forces on Okinawa but also neutralize Japanese aviation within range of the Ryukus, on the home islands.

The U.S. Navy had amassed a force beyond comprehension, and as it steamed northwest Father O'Callahan and *Franklin*'s crew mixed the shared apprehension normally preceding combat with a measure of confidence that the war's end was approaching and that Japan's defeat was inevitable. What they could not know was that despite its size and power, their fleet would lose more ships (36 destroyed and 368 damaged) and more men (nearly 5,000 dead and 5,000 wounded) in a single battle than would be lost in any other engagement in the U.S. Navy's history. Moreover, they could not know that *Franklin*, and Father Joe, would bear immediate witness to much of this horror.

8

Franklin

"Big Ben"

When Father O'Callahan lined up to climb *Franklin*'s forward gangway at Pearl Harbor's Fox Two pier, he gazed up at the pinnacle of modern naval power in 1945.

United States Ship *Franklin*'s hull number, CV 13, signified she was the thirteenth fleet aircraft carrier in the U.S. Navy; she was also the fifth hull of the formidable *Essex* class. The navy had designed these ships without the constraints of the Washington Naval Treaty that had previously limited the size and displacement of warships.[1]

In every respect, the *Essex* carriers far outstripped the three ships in the *Yorktown* class—the other two being *Hornet* and *Enterprise*—the most advanced prewar carriers. Although similar in appearance to the earlier vessels, with extended islands and rectangular flight decks, *Essex*es were sixty feet longer, had about ten feet more beam, displaced (at 27,100 tons) at least one-third more than the earlier ships, and drew more than twenty-eight feet. Their flight decks were longer (at 872 feet) and wider (more than 147 feet), with two catapults. They also featured deck-edge elevators, which made flight operations easier. The earlier carriers had used centerline elevators, which stopped launches and recoveries when lowered to their hangar decks, leaving the ships more vulnerable to attack and unable to conduct continuous operations. These improvements enabled an *Essex*-class ship to carry an average air group of ninety larger and more powerful aircraft, including thirty-eight Grumman F6F Hellcat fighters, four F6Fs configured for night flights and three more for photoreconnaissance, twenty-seven Curtiss SB2C Helldiver scout bombers, and eighteen Grumman TBF Avenger torpedo bombers.[2]

Below decks, *Essex* carriers also were state of the art, using more efficient power-plant layouts, with steam turbines generating 150,000 horsepower and developing top speeds of up to thirty-three knots. Defensive weaponry included twelve 5-inch, .38-caliber dual-purpose guns in four twin and four single mounts, as well as dozens of quad-, twin-, and single-mount 40-mm and 20-mm machine guns, and superior armor and compartmentalization. Of the seven prewar carriers in the Pacific (including the reclassified aircraft transport *Langley*), only two—*Saratoga* and *Enterprise*—would survive. Japanese aerial attacks and later kamikazes, which sank other American ships in droves, severely damaged several *Essex* carriers, but not a single member of the class turned turtle in the war.[3]

The *Essex* design was hugely successful, the largest and most capable aircraft carrier built until well after the war. The navy built ten ships classified as *Essex* class; thirteen more, with modified bows to accommodate antiaircraft gun batteries, were later classified as *Ticonderoga*-class carriers, of which four served in World War II. One more extensively modified carrier, *Oriskany,* was the last of the basic design, joining the fleet in 1950. The navy canceled eight more hulls, in construction or on order, in 1945. Several *Essex* carriers continued in service through the Korean War and beyond. After extensive modifications including flight-deck expansions, some soldiered on as amphibious assault ships until the early 1970s. *Lexington* (CV 16, later AVT 16) provided until 1991 the flight deck on which thousands of "nugget" naval aviators landed for the first time, testimony to a remarkably robust design.[4]

Naval ship-naming conventions through most of the war gave the names of fish to submarines, those of famous Americans to destroyers, American cities to cruisers, states to battleships, and to carriers well-known American ships or battles, in some cases the names of the prewar carriers lost in early Pacific engagements. The *Essex* class included, aside from the name ship, *Yorktown, Intrepid, Hornet, Franklin, Lexington, Bunker Hill, Wasp, Bennington,* and *Bon Homme Richard.*

Most of her crew believed *Franklin*'s name honored founding father Benjamin Franklin and nicknamed her "Big Ben." Others argued, in line with the naming convention, that the name recalled the bloody Civil War battle in Franklin, Tennessee, on November 30, 1864, ending in a decisive Union victory and the destruction of John Bell Hood's Confederate Army of Tennessee.

In fact, however, as O'Callahan himself understood, the carrier carried forward the names of her four naval predecessors.[5]

The first *Franklin* had been a sixty-ton fishing vessel out of Marblehead, Massachusetts, on loan to the rebellious colonies. Then-colonel George Washington ordered her fitted out with six guns in 1775 as one of Commodore John Manly's schooner fleet that harassed British commercial shipping in the New England littoral. After a year of war service, she returned to commercial fishing.

The second ship of the name was a 155-ton brig of 8 guns, built at Philadelphia in 1795. She fell victim to pirates on the Barbary Coast, captured off Tripoli and sold to the bey of Tunis in 1802. The ship came back into American hands in 1805, served briefly as a storeship and transport in the Mediterranean, then returned for transport duty around New Orleans before the navy sold her.

The third *Franklin* was a ship of the line of 74 guns and 2,257 tons, built in 1815 as the first vessel laid down in the Philadelphia Navy Yard. She served as flagship in both the Mediterranean and Pacific Squadrons until 1824. Laid up for nearly twenty years, she served as a receiving ship, or floating office building, in Boston until 1852, when shipwrights in Portsmouth, New Hampshire, broke her up.

The fourth ship bearing the name was a screw frigate with one 11-inch gun, thirty-four 9-inch cannons, and four 100-pounder naval rifles. Laid down in Portsmouth, using parts salvaged from her predecessor, and launched in 1864, *Franklin* entered commissioned service in 1867 and served as Adm. David Farragut's flagship while he commanded the navy's European Squadron. She served in this capacity (with a couple of interruptions) through 1876. After decommissioning, she was the receiving ship in Norfolk until just before the Great War.[6]

It was this heritage, not highly distinguished but originating indirectly with Ben Franklin, that the new carrier's name embodied.

Newport News Shipbuilding Company in Virginia laid the keel for CV 13 in December 1942, with Lt. Cdr. Mildred A. McAfee, USNR, director of the WAVES, serving as her sponsor. The new ship was launched ten months later and entered commissioned service at the Norfolk Naval Shipyard on January 31, 1944, Capt. James M. Shoemaker, commanding.[7]

The ship's specifications matched those of the class. She would carry, in the ship's company and air group, a total of nearly 3,450 officers and men. Her armament also was standard, including a dozen 5-inch dual-purpose guns and forty-eight 40-mm and fifty-seven 20-mm antiaircraft guns.

The new carrier completed a shakedown cruise to Trinidad, British West Indies, and quickly headed for the Pacific for training. By June she had joined Task Group 58.2, an element in the Fifth Fleet's fast carrier striking force, off Eniwetok in the Marshall Islands. From this rendezvous point, *Franklin's* aircraft attacked the Bonin Islands, in preparation for the invasion of the Marianas. On Independence Day, 1944, the carrier's aircraft attacked Iwo Jima in the Volcano Islands and Chichi and Ha Ha Jima in the nearby Bonins, striking shore batteries and cargo ships moored off shore. More air strikes followed on Guam and Rota before the amphibious assaults on those islands began on July 21, and attacks continued against the Palau group until the end of the month. CV 13 was quickly earning her spurs in the Pacific War, and her brief operational record reflected the frenetic tempo of combat operations.[8]

Throughout these campaigns, the navy increased its fleet power until it could support MacArthur's South West Pacific theater of operations around New Guinea and the Solomon Islands as well as its own massive offensive in the Central Pacific. This latter drive was the effort *Franklin* had joined in June 1944, and it would involve literally hundreds of warships for the next fourteen months.[9]

Another week of air operations ensued, after which the ship and crew spent most of August replenishing at Eniwetok. The carrier quickly resumed its hectic pace, attacking Yap and covering the invasion at Peleliu on September 15. CV 13 conducted patrols in the Palaus for about a month, served as flagship of Task Group 38.3, and then joined other carrier groups for the invasion of the Philippines at Leyte Gulf. Here for the first time, at twilight on October 13, Japanese bombers and fighters threatened *Franklin,* which dodged two torpedoes. Another aircraft, its pilot probably incapacitated, flew directly into the ship. It struck the flight deck just aft of the island, careened across the deck, and crashed into the sea off Big Ben's starboard beam but caused little real damage.[10]

Japanese defensive actions quickened, however, and soon exacted a stiffer price from the ship. *Franklin* was steaming off the eastern coast of Luzon with her carrier group, her aircraft bombing enemy installations, when three "bogies," Japanese planes, slipped through the combat air patrol's defensive net and attacked. One bomb struck the carrier on the outboard corner of her deck-edge elevator. The blast killed three crewmen and wounded twenty-two, but the chaos never interrupted daily operations. Four days later, the air group took a bit of revenge, sinking or damaging several enemy ships and a floating dry dock in Manila Bay and destroying eleven aircraft.[11]

When landings commenced in Leyte Gulf on October 20, *Franklin's* aircraft searched the straits and approaches to the gulf in what was to be the greatest sea battle in history. On October 24 her planes were among those that discovered and attacked the Japanese "First Raiding Force," steaming toward Leyte in the Sibuyan Sea under the command of Vice Adm. Takeo Kurita. The aircraft assaults were overwhelming, sinking the superbattleship *Musashi* and destroyer *Wakaba* and damaging battleships *Fuso* and *Yamashiro*.

The following day, however, *Franklin* was part of a less distinguished episode in the battle. A Japanese feint lured Third Fleet commander Adm. William F. Halsey, his three carrier task groups, and six battleships northward beyond Cape Engaño and away from the amphibious force and its covering fleet at Leyte Gulf, leaving the landing's defense to destroyers and escort carriers in the U.S. Seventh Fleet, their aircraft armed only for land attack. This paltry force of eighteen jeep carriers, each carrying about thirty aircraft with virtually no antiship bombs, and a handful of destroyers and destroyer escorts armed with torpedoes and 5-inch gun batteries, would array itself against the remnants of Vice Admiral Kurita's battleships, with 16- and 18-inch naval rifles, emerging after an initial retreat from San Bernardino Strait, in one of the few naval engagements in the entire war in which adversaries could see one another. This running fight ended improbably with the Japanese fleet's withdrawal in the face of American aerial and sea attacks delivered at the cost to the Seventh Fleet of two escort carriers, *St. Lo* and *Gambier Bay*, destroyers *Hoel* and *Johnston*, and destroyer escort *Samuel B. Roberts*.[12]

Halsey's carriers turned around and heaped more destruction on the Japanese raiders, allowing only one ship to return to the homeland in battleworthy condition.

On October 30, about one thousand miles off Samar, the campaign in the Philippines appeared all but over for the Third Fleet and *Franklin*. Suddenly, three Japanese bombers appeared. One missed the ship altogether, crashing into the sea just off her starboard side. Another dropped a bomb that narrowly missed the ship and then dove into the flight deck of the nearby light carrier *Belleau Wood*. The other plane wrought havoc on Big Ben, crashing through the flight deck, boring into the hangar deck, and spraying destruction, killing fifty-six crewmen and wounding another sixty. This time, *Franklin* would not continue operations. She and *Belleau Wood* steamed for Ulithi and temporary overhauls. *Franklin* then headed stateside, arriving at the Puget Sound Navy Yard in Bremerton, Washington, on November 28, 1944, for major battle-damage repair.[13]

When Father Joe joined the carrier at Pearl, she had completed several weeks of fitting out and training for her new air group. She left Bremerton under the command of Capt. Leslie Edward Gehres, forty-six, who had succeeded

Captain Shoemaker in November 1944. Gehres, born in 1898 in Newark, New York, about thirty miles from Rochester, had enlisted in the New York Naval Militia in 1914. Mobilized in the Naval Reserve in 1917 with America's entry into the Great War, he received an ensign's commission before he was out of his teens. Gehres was a physical standout at six feet, four inches in height, with a football lineman's build and an aggressive demeanor. After completing a reserve course at the Naval Academy, he accepted a regular naval commission and served more than eight years as a surface officer. In early 1927, at age twenty-eight, he reported to Pensacola for flight training and earned his wings later that year. In the early days of naval aviation, it was not unusual for experienced officers to complete flight training to meet the need for pilots. Admiral Halsey, known in World War II as a naval aviation leader, probably set the record for seniority. In order to be eligible to command aircraft carriers, he earned his own naval-aviator designation as a fifty-two-year-old captain in 1934, even though he readily admitted that without his glasses, strictly forbidden for student pilots, he could hardly see the gauges on the airplane's instrument panel![14]

Gehres had plenty of opportunities to learn aviation after graduating from flight school. He flew biplane fighters from the flight decks of *Langley, Lexington,* and *Saratoga.* He commanded a training squadron at Pensacola. In 1936 he led an exhibition team that won the aerobatics trophy during the All-American Air Maneuvers in Miami. He also served on *Yorktown* and became *Ranger*'s air officer in 1938. Later, after a tour as the executive officer at the Ford Island Naval Air Station in Pearl Harbor, Gehres assumed command of Patrol Wing 4, later redesignated Fleet Air Wing 4, just weeks before the Japanese attack on December 7. By this time a captain, Gehres led his command to war far from the center of action: Patrol Wing 4's duty stations were in Kodiak, Alaska, and at Dutch Harbor in the eastern Aleutian Islands, off the Alaskan coast.

Although the Aleutians, windswept and rocky outcrops in the frigid Bering Sea, had little direct strategic value, the Japanese navy launched an attack against the American base at Dutch Harbor in June 1942 as a feint to keep the U.S. Navy away from the imperial fleet's real target, Midway Island. Gehres and his patrol aircraft supported the navy's small Task Force 8, five cruisers and fourteen destroyers under the command of Rear Adm. Robert Theobald, in its attempt to counter the Japanese assault. The Japanese failed to fool the Americans, and with the concurrent U.S. victory to the south at Midway, the first major Japanese loss at sea in 350 years, imperial navy forces contented themselves with taking two of the westernmost Aleutians, Attu and Kiska, well away from any American installations. Nevertheless, Japanese invaders were on American territory, and American forces spent more than a year driving them out. Throughout this campaign, Gehres, now the navy's first aviation commodore, in charge of the expanded Fleet Air Wing 4, covered the entire Aleutian campaign. He directed air operations in support of both naval and army attacks that finally rooted out the Japanese in August 1943, ending the struggle for the island chain.

Gehres earned two Legions of Merit for his leadership in the long battle and was ready for promotion to permanent flag rank. He turned down a rear admiral's stars, however, preferring a combat command on a carrier. *Franklin* would more than satisfy his desire to be near the fight.

The carrier's executive officer (Exec), or second in command, was Cdr. Joseph Franklin Taylor of Danville, Illinois, a 1927 Naval Academy graduate designated an aviator in 1929. Joe Taylor was among the navy's saltiest flyers, with experience in patrol and fighter squadrons. He had flown from *Langley* and *Lexington* and commanded VT-5 ("Torpedo Five") on *Yorktown* in 1941 and early 1942, leading raids against the Gilbert and Marshall Islands, Salamaua, Lae, and Tulagi. He also was a veteran of Coral Sea and Midway, for which he had received two Navy Crosses for exceptional heroism. He had been with *Franklin* from the start, helping to fit out the carrier and serving as her air group commander (CAG) before "fleeting up" as Exec.

The CO and Exec had full charge of the carrier, but *Franklin* also served as the flagship for the Commander, Carrier Division 58.2, which included *Hancock* (CV 19) and light carriers *Bataan* (CVL 29) and *San Jacinto* (CVL 30). At her truck CV 13 displayed a blue pennant with two stars signifying that Rear Adm. Ralph E. Davison and the division staff were on board. Rear Adm. Gerald F. Bogan, slated to relieve Davison in a change of command scheduled after the first strike operation in Operation Iceberg, and his staff also were on the carrier. In addition, Capt. Arnold J. Isbell, credited with sinking at least ten German U-boats in 1943 while in charge of the escort carrier *Card* in the Atlantic, was taking passage in *Franklin* on his way to assume command of *Yorktown.* Another unusual passenger was Alvin S. McCoy, war correspondent for the *Kansas City Star,* working as a pool reporter for the Combined American Press syndicate.

Reporting directly to Gehres and Taylor were the carrier's department heads, all experienced naval officers. The ship's navigator, Cdr. Stephen Jurika, born in the Philippines in 1910, was a Naval Academy graduate, class of 1933. He had served as a naval attaché in Tokyo. Early in the war, he had been the intelligence officer on *Hornet,* briefing Lt. Col. Jimmy Doolittle's Tokyo raiders before they flew their B-25 bombers off that carrier's flight deck to attack Japan in 1942. Some time later, Jurika would learn that Japanese forces had beheaded his mother when they took Manila.

Other department heads were Lt. Cdr. William R. McKinney, Naval Academy class of 1940, gunnery officer; Lt. Cdr. Thomas Jethro Greene, Naval Academy class of 1930, engineering officer; Lt. Cdr. Robert B. Downes, damage control officer and first lieutenant; Lt. Cdr. W. R. Kreamer, communications officer; Lt. Cdr. D. V. Wengrovius, supply officer; and Cdr. F. Kirk Smith, senior medical officer. Father O'Callahan's Protestant counterpart was Chaplain Charles Grimes Weldon Gatlin, known as Grimes or "Gats," a Methodist minister from Texas on his first shipboard assignment. Lieutenant Gatlin had graduated from Navy Chaplain Corps Class 12-43 in August 1943. O'Callahan, by virtue of rank and experience, was the department head.

Franklin's air officer was Cdr. Henry Henderson Hale, from Gary, Indiana; he had come on board with Gehres. The air department was responsible for shipboard operations in support of the air group, including the catapults and arresting gear, aircraft handling on the flight and hangar decks, weather, ordnance, fuel, and maintenance.

The commander of Carrier Air Group 5, assigned to *Franklin* when the carrier returned to duty from Bremerton, was Cdr. Edwin B. Parker, Naval Academy class of 1935. The squadrons assigned to the carrier included dive-bombers, torpedo planes, and fighters, with something of a twist. VB-5 ("Bombing Five," Lt. Cdr. John G. Sheridan commanding), flew Curtiss SB2C Helldivers. Torpedo Five, under Lt. Cdr. Allen C. Edwards, operated Grumman TBF Avengers. These squadrons operated about fifteen aircraft each.

The "twist" was that VF-5, "Fighting Five," under the command of Lt. Cdr. MacGregor Kilpatrick, manned Vought F4U Corsairs instead of the Grumman F6F Hellcats usually on fleet carriers. The powerful, gull-winged Corsairs were bigger and faster than Hellcats. However, their small cockpits set well back on their fuselages made carrier landings far more difficult and dangerous than those in Hellcats, because they limited visibility during the approach. Corsair pilots quickly learned to enter the landing pattern at a steep bank over a carrier deck so they could see the deck more clearly. Although the navy appreciated the Corsairs' dogfighting advantages against Japanese aircraft, it quickly dispensed with F4Us in naval fighter squadrons and assigned the aircraft to marine fighter units, all of which had been land-based thus far in World War II. Marines made excellent use of F4Us and racked up good combat records in the plane, which Japanese adversaries nicknamed "Whistling Death."

Improvements in the aircraft also made it even more formidable and facilitated carrier landings. Leatherneck aviators began training to serve on escort carriers, but Japanese tactics intervened. The kamikaze threat mounted as the fleet neared Japan, and the navy called for an increase in fighter strength to counter suicide attacks. Assigning marine squadrons to flight decks was a quicker, more expedient solution than establishing and training additional naval units, so pilots and Corsairs from the Corps joined fleet carrier air groups. When Japanese attackers were absent and continuous combat air patrols were not required, the big Corsairs could carry 11.75-inch Tiny Tim rockets, new weapons well suited to close air support against entrenched targets during island invasions.

In the first half of 1945, ten marine fighter squadrons served on carriers. Two of these served on *Franklin.* VMF-214, the famed "Black Sheep Squadron" once commanded by Maj. Gregory "Pappy" Boyington (who was by then languishing in a Japanese prisoner of war camp), flew under Maj. Stanley R. Bailey, the last Boyington alumnus in the unit. VMF-452, Maj. Charles P. Weiland commanding, was barely a year old and on its first combat tour.[15] Marines constituted about half the fighter pilots on the carrier, and about three-quarters of the more than one hundred planes on *Franklin* were Corsairs.

These ship and air-group commanders, with a few dozen chief petty officers (senior enlisted men who had grown up in the navy) and warrant officers (all former chief petty officers who specialized in various technical areas vital to the ship), formed the core of Big Ben's leadership. They made *Franklin* a fully functional carrier, entirely reflecting the level of professionalism needed to fight a ruthless war against a deadly enemy. The senior officers who commanded and headed departments on the warship—men such as Gehres, Taylor, Jurika, Hale, Parker, and others—had spent their adult lives focused on naval careers. They had prepared for these moments, accepted the risks, and mastered the methods that had brought the navy they helped to develop and shape to its unprecedented power and prestige.

As remarkable as the professionals, perhaps even more so, were the thousands of young sailors manning *Franklin* and other vessels. For the great majority of junior officers and enlisted men, the last option they would have considered before December 7, 1941, had been naval service. Most of the young officers were "ninety-day wonders," and most of the enlisted men knew only the rudiments of their assigned jobs.

Nearly all of them were boys just out of school, in their late teens and early twenties. Before enlisting, those who worked had been shop clerks, apprentices, factory workers, truck drivers. In barely three years some of them had become seasoned war-fighting technicians, part of the great destructive machine created to decimate Japan's naval capabilities. All of them—aircraft mechanics, radiomen, cooks, medics, yeomen, boiler tenders, men of every conceivable craft and specialty—contributed with considerable competence and remarkable commitment to the overriding purpose the American navy had adopted in late 1941.

Father Joe, though he was a midgrade officer, had much more in common with the citizen sailors who had interrupted their lives to fight the war than with the line officers of his seniority. While the career men could look forward to other assignments, advancement, and promotion, O'Callahan expected, as did most of the men on Big Ben, to return to home, family, and job when the war ended. Furthermore, the end seemed in sight at last. Germany's surrender was all but inevitable (it would come on May 8). The Allies were closing in on Japan, and while they expected major resistance in the planned invasion of the home islands, the Empire seemed no longer to present a significant offensive threat at sea.

An unusually high proportion of crewmen in *Franklin*'s ship's company were from New York, Philadelphia, and Boston (and New England generally); young and untested for the most part, they had less experience than many of their counterparts on other ships whose combat duty had not been interrupted by lengthy repairs. Many also were Catholics. They had joined the carrier in Bremerton as her overhaul neared completion, and their first time at sea had been the voyage from Puget Sound to Hawaii. Nevertheless, nearly everyone on board the carrier and every other naval warship shared high confidence in his own ability and that of his shipmates. All were prepared to risk their lives to end the war and get back to their homes and families in the States.[16]

For ship, chaplain, and crew, that risk would be higher than anyone could imagine, and they would face it sooner than anyone could know.

9

Murderers' Row

Qui tollis peccata mundi, suscipe deprecationem nostram.[1]

*F*ranklin anchored in twenty-one fathoms in the northern anchorage at Ulithi in the Caroline Islands on March 13. The harbor, nicknamed "Murderers' Row," contained the naval might of the United States. More than a dozen carriers and many other ships rested in the great lagoon. By 1945, the harbor's nickname accurately characterized the lethality of the fleet it contained. The U.S. Navy juggernaut had soundly trounced Japan's waning maritime power for eighteen months. The carriers and other warships resting quietly in the atoll's glassy waters represented technology bent to offensive power and apparent invincibility that had been almost inconceivable less than a decade earlier. Within days, many of these ships would face a test beyond imagination, one that would challenge any notion of invincibility the young sailors manning these vessels might have harbored. *Franklin*'s ordeal would be the most spectacular and terrifying of all.

The stop at Ulithi was a short one. On March 14 elements of Task Force 58 steamed northward to rendezvous the next day off the coast of Kyushu. The Okinawa campaign was under way, and the task force's attack aircraft would assault nearly fifty airfields on Kyushu, all of them within easy range of Okinawa and able, if not neutralized, to launch planes that could hammer the American invasion fleet when Operation Iceberg began on April 1. Task force aircraft also would fly against Japanese naval bases in the coastal cities of Kobe and Kure, on the home island of Honshu, ready to destroy any remnants of Japan's navy able to sortie against the Americans.

Task Force 58 stretched for more than fifty miles across the Pacific as it closed on its objective. The task force's four task groups steamed in similar formations, with carrier divisions at the center surrounded with screens of battleships, cruisers, and an outer ring of destroyers.

Saturday, March 17, was Saint Patrick's Day. Combat operations were slated to begin on Sunday, and there would be no time for religious services. O'Callahan offered Mass on Saturday afternoon on *Franklin*'s forecastle; about 1,200 young sailors, around one-third of the crew, jammed into the area. Father Joe described the service:

> Twelve hundred American boys crowded in the fo'c'sle area, boys ranging from seventeen years up. Boys from every section of the country, from small towns and big cities, from Minot, North Dakota, from San Francisco, California. Some were college men, graduates of professional schools, doctors and lawyers. Some were quite unlettered. Officers and enlisted men, pilots and mechanics, seamen and radio technicians—the whole assemblage of rates and ranks, lowest to highest, was there on the fo'c'sle. Steward's mate stood next to doctor, apprentice seaman beside experienced aviator. A cross section of the ship was there, more than a third of the ship's complement of men.[2]

Doctor Bill Fox, one of *Franklin*'s medical officers, who had been an altar boy in his youth, assisted the priest throughout the service and helped to recite the prayers in Latin. O'Callahan's sermon focused, as it should have, on the forthcoming action: "As we all know, boys, tomorrow morning, the fighting starts. We've known that for ten days. And before combat each one of you should go to confession and receive Holy Communion. . . . Each day the line outside the chaplain's office grew longer as more and more took advantage of the opportunity of confessing. Today the line stretched half the length of the ship. Yet there are still several hundred who have not yet received absolution. Fortunately, there is available the privilege of General Absolution."

O'Callahan described the requirements for the ritual and called for the assemblage to recite the Act of Contrition: "Twelve hundred subdued voices joined in unison, reciting phrase by phrase the solemn and familiar prayer. . . . The special public address system carried clearly to twelve hundred men the priest's words pronouncing General Absolution: *'Ego auctoritate Ipsius vos absolve a peccatis vestris in nomine Patris et Filii et Spiritus Sancti.'* The eyes of twelve hundred men seemed to mirror the peace which comes with Sanctifying Grace." Father Joe continued his homily: "We [do] not want to avoid battle; we [are] looking for it. Hence, the proper prayer should be to ask for God's help for this: that while in the fray we might do as good a job as possible for God and country. That, my shipmates and my brethren, is the intention for which this Mass today is being offered. God bless you all."[3]

As a cold, end-of-winter wind whipped the canvas screens lashed behind mess tables serving as an altar, the Mass concluded with communion, and twelve hundred men, their sins forgiven, returned with purified hearts and souls to the pressing duties of preparing for attack. Perhaps also the absolution helped Seaman First Class Frank F. Davis, a sailor who had gone missing on March 17. Davis either jumped or fell overboard and vanished.

This religious service was emblematic of something more than piety and preparation for battle. For nearly four years, young Americans who otherwise would never have met or associated with one another had lived in close quarters, often in squalid conditions and great danger. As Father Joe—who knew nothing about life in the army, army air forces, or Marine Corps, all of which offered fewer amenities than the navy—wrote, "an enlisted man aboard a warship has less privacy than any other known human being."[4] In this forced intimacy, Americans discovered, often to their surprise, similarities far more numerous and important than differences among their comrades from other regions of the country, with varied ethnic and religious heritages. In every extreme from deadly combat to the crushing boredom of daily routine, only the most obtuse and prejudiced GIs could fail to notice that others they had once dismissed with stereotyped insults and pejorative language were for the most part just like them. Americans in uniform lived through dozens of episodes of courage and fear, elation and pain, hope and anguish, generosity and selfishness, humor and sadness, in full view of one another, and they saw themselves in each other—imbued with the humanity and vulnerability of ordinary men.

The war was a great test of political and economic institutions and practices, but it also was a test of societies and cultural habits, and it engendered enormous changes across the board. In addition to creating new roles for democracy and free enterprise, the conflict set the stage for new tolerance and trust in American society, helping to establish a nation for which religion and ethnic background became far less important than they had been just a few years earlier. After World War II, Italian Catholics from San Francisco, English Episcopalians from Philadelphia, Norwegian Lutherans from Minneapolis, Pima Native Americans from Sacaton (Arizona), Scots-Irish Baptists from Murphy (North Carolina), Creole Santerians from New Orleans, Russian Jews from Brooklyn, and French agnostics from St. Louis would be less the children or grandchildren of immigrants than they were American veterans, boys who shared common experiences and insights that had made them into men intent on building families and improving their communities and, by extension, their nation.

The only characteristic not part of this great social dynamic was race. Because the U.S. armed forces remained segregated, white Americans did not associate as closely with black Americans, and they did not have an opportunity to learn that skin color meant no more than religion or ethnicity. That lesson was not lost, however, on many black Americans, who fully understood that their contribution to the war was forming the legal and ethical foundation of the quest for civil rights that would quickly gain momentum after 1945. Many of the men and women, black and white, who engineered the challenges to segregation that dominated the 1950s and 1960s were to be veterans of World War II, who fully understood that anyone willing to fight and die for a nation should expect to enjoy full access to its rights and privileges, and to the benefits of unfettered citizenship and social justice.

Few if any sailors leaving Father Joe's Mass that day would have thought about the social implications of the war, but they would take lessons learned, however implicit, home with them and help to build a renewed country with new opportunities for all their shipmates in the decades unfolding before them.

That night, Japanese scout planes dogged the American formation, dropping parachute flares that reflected off the clouds and illuminated the sky with gossamer beams of light. Destroyers and other surface ships protecting the carriers fired frequently at targets that their combat information centers designated from the bright blips that appeared on radar screens with each sweep of the antennas on their masts. Blasts from other ships' guns rumbled and flashed like thunder and lightning on the horizon around *Franklin,* and tracer rounds from Oerlikon and Bofors antiaircraft batteries made red streaks as they rose on their trajectories toward an unseen enemy.

Father O'Callahan moved through the darkened ship, the white cross painted on his helmet signifying his role and triggering recognition among the crewmen he passed. On the carrier's bridge he met Captain Gehres and exchanged comments about the air group's readiness for battle and the threat of torpedo and kamikaze attacks. The chaplain's next stops were the squadron ready rooms, where he prayed with those who wished to and offered absolution. He delivered a Saint Christopher medal to Cdr. "Eb" Parker. Parker, a Protestant, liked to wear the medal as a good-luck charm, even though Father Joe remonstrated that Our Lady of Loretto was the patroness of aviation.[5]

On March 18 the armada was just one hundred miles off the Japanese coast and ready to launch its first attacks, even as Japanese snoopers continued to prowl. *Franklin* was in the middle of the action. Before dawn, in the cold wind, twenty aircraft roared down the carrier's flight deck and into the darkness as the ship churned through the rough winter sea. The planes headed for targets at Kagoshima and Izumi, and others soon followed. Corsairs landed, reloaded, and took off again all day long. Kagoshima was an important target for the Americans. Japanese airmen had practiced the Pearl Harbor attack there, because of its similarity to the Pacific Fleet port.

O'Callahan recalled the day:

> All morning we pounded their airfields and shot down their interceptors, until we could conduct the afternoon's search practically unchallenged. In the late afternoon a flight of returning planes reported a discovery of what were certainly ships under camouflage in a hidden bywater . . . but darkness was closing in, and the strike at them would have to wait for morning.

> That strike would be primarily the *Franklin's* responsibility. We were the only ship carrying a newly developed weapon for use against naval vessels, the powerful "Tiny Tim" rockets. These rockets were expected to be able to penetrate the toughest steel; one of them could disembowel a ship. The planes from the *Franklin* would carry them by the score tomorrow.[6]

During the distant combat, Father Joe repeated the role he had played on *Ranger,* reporting as an "amateur newscaster" from the bridge over the ship's public-address system on action as it unfolded, relaying information to the ship's company, hundreds of whom worked below decks, as pilots radioed to the carrier during their missions.

The tally for Air Group 5's fighters after the first day of combat was eighteen enemy aircraft shot down, with many more destroyed or damaged on the ground, as well as extensive damage to airport facilities and several small boats. The group's sorties constituted a measurable part of the operation that destroyed 387 enemy aircraft, nearly all on the ground, and damaged 17 imperial navy warships, including the battleship *Yamato* and 4 carriers, before the task force's withdrawal on March 19.

The cost of this mayhem was four Corsairs. Flak brought down three, and the fourth loss was accidental. One VMF-452 pilot, marine lieutenant Thomas D. Pace, and a "Fighting Five" aviator, Ens. Paul Casebeer, apparently died in their aircraft. A lifeguard submarine picked up a third man, but an attempt to rescue the fourth, marine lieutenant J. Pierpont Stodd III of VMF-214, failed when Japanese sampans captured the pilot less than a mile offshore and within sight of the sub racing to save him. By sunset, all CV 13 aircraft, except the four, were back on deck.

The American attacks excited Japanese retaliation. The task group's carrier air patrols splashed several bogies near the American ships. Corsairs and Hellcats dodged in and out of heavy overcast looking for Japanese planes as ships' combat information centers repeatedly vectored them by radio to radar contacts on the perimeter of the task force. On the ship itself, deck-gun crews spotted several floating contact mines, a sign of the task force's proximity to the Japanese coast and shipping channels, and blasted them out of the water.

As darkness enclosed the carrier, Japanese air assaults continued, although only one cruiser, in Task Group 58.2, opened fire on a radar contact. Gunners fired with caution, since some of these contacts were friendly. Specially equipped carrier night fighters patrolled the skies, using their own aircraft radar to sweep, albeit without success, for enemy intruders as flares continued their weird, brilliant dances into the sea.

Despite the exhausting day, the night was not restful for *Franklin*'s crew, many members of which remained at torpedo-defense stations, alert to possible submarine attacks. Although he had no watch duties, O'Callahan was not able to sleep. "Time and time again the dim bunk rooms rattled awake to the sound of loud alarms, then a voice over the speakers: 'This is not a general alarm. Repeat: This is not a call to battle stations. Let all gun crews man their stations immediately.' All except the unfortunate gunners might go back to sleep, if they could, knowing that somewhere above them in the blackness enemy planes were circling, eager to revenge the cruel losses we had inflicted on them."

The priest returned to the bridge, then headed to the combat information center, where men, staring incessantly at blips on screens, were bathed in red light from battle lamps and the spectral luminescence of radar scopes and in swirls of cigarette smoke.

At 3:30 a.m. the loudspeaker barked again, "All hands to general quarters! Man all battle stations!" A bugle took up the call. No alarm sounded, however. The ship was not under attack. Instead, the call announced the start of the next round of operations, preparation for the morning's first aircraft launch.

Men throughout the ship turned to. Many of those who slept probably stayed in their clothes. Once up, they laced their heavy, high-topped work shoes, called "boondockers," pulled on reefer jackets or peacoats, Mae West life jackets, and helmets, and moved rapidly through the gloom to their duty stations. Indeed, the night was not restful. Nor would the new day promise any relief.[7]

10

March 19, 1945

Crucible

Before dawn on March 19, "Lucky Plus One" day in task force code, CV 13 turned into the wind. Barely five minutes later, Corsairs began launches for a fighter sweep against enemy targets on the island of Honshu. The fighters were off the flight deck before 6:00 a.m., and *Franklin* turned west-southwest. Radar screens were clear; no enemy contacts appeared. Admiral Davison ordered Task Group 58.2 gun batteries to set Condition III, ready for action but with some personnel off watch, and Condition Yoke for the task group's ships, the standard level of readiness and watertight integrity while at sea. Captain Gehres supplemented the order with modified Condition Zebra, calling for all passageways and compartments to be sealed. The modified condition allowed about one-sixth of the crew to stand down, and one hatch from the hangar deck to the crew's mess on the second deck remained open.

A second wave of aircraft would take off about 7:00 a.m., following the forty-five already airborne and over their targets, as the carrier task group closed within about fifty-five nautical miles of Kyushu. At top cruising speed, *Franklin* would have arrived in Japan in about two hours. Father Joe went through the squadron ready rooms again, stopped at his compartment to drop off battle gear, and then headed for a quick breakfast.

On the fantail, on the hangar-deck level, Chaplain Gatlin and Exec Taylor prepared to conduct a burial at sea. Ned Bennett, an aviation machinist's mate second class assigned to the ship's company, had swallowed strained torpedo propellant fluid, mistakenly believing he could get drunk on the fluid's wood-alcohol base. Instead, Bennett spent the night in agony as the brew poisoned him, eating away at his digestive tract. Doctor Fox and his pharmacist's mates could do nothing for the boy, and the sick bay resonated with his screams until, mercifully, the young sailor died. Now it was time to consign his body, wrapped in a weighted canvas mattress cover, to the deep.

During the grim ceremony, activity on the hangar deck and throughout the ship never skipped a beat. Thirty-one Corsairs, Avengers, and Helldivers were on the flight deck, propellers turning and preparing to take off. The launch began on schedule, and eight or nine planes were in the air, circling overhead and waiting to join with the rest and head for Japan.

Twenty-two aircraft, mostly Corsairs, remained on the hangar deck. Armorers had loaded several of these planes with rockets and bombs and had primed machine guns with ammunition belts. Fuel handlers pumped aviation gas into wing and belly tanks. Sailors by the dozen worked or gathered in the gallery deck, a large and largely unarmored area amidships between the hangar deck and the flight deck. Its spaces contained administrative offices for senior officers and flag staff, squadron ready rooms, the combat information center (CIC), intelligence library, and several repair shops.

Commander Jurika was on the navigation bridge, just forward of the pilothouse. Joining the captain, he informed him that *Franklin* was just fifty-two miles due south of Point Ashizuri Saki, Shikoku island's southernmost tip. He later recalled, "The sea was calm, with a 12 knot wind from about 060 [degrees] true. Sky was overcast, with occasional breaks, and lower scattered clouds at an estimated 1500 to 2000 feet. Horizontal visibility was excellent."[1] Carrier *Hancock* alerted *Franklin* over the "Talk between Ships" (short-range voice radio) that lookouts had spotted a Japanese plane in the area, heading for CV 13. CIC's radar picked up a bogey, loitering almost directly ahead of the carrier, about ten miles away, but otherwise the scopes were clear. Nevertheless, *Franklin*'s defensive armament came to life, as powered 5-inch and 40-mm gun turrets turned on their motors.

Several minutes earlier, the ship had piped chow call. Hundreds of men not performing urgent tasks lined up on the hangar deck around airplanes waiting for their turn to head down a ladder to the galley, one deck below.

Father O'Callahan was eating, too, sitting in the wardroom mess near the forward section of the second deck, one level below the hangar deck, with Lt. Red Morgan, in charge of hangar deck operations, chief engineer Tommy Greene, and a few other officers, chiding Steward First Class Tom Frasure about the tepid food that passed for breakfast. "That ain't fried bread, sirs," Frasure shot back, "that's French toast!"[2]

At 7:08 a.m., as Captain Gehres, Jurika, and a few others stood on the open bridge by the pilothouse, "without radar warning, an enemy plane dove out of the base of the clouds from less than 2,000 feet altitude, about a thousand yards directly ahead of *Franklin,* made a low-level bombing run, dropping two 250-kilo semi-armor-piercing bombs with about .25 second delay fuses."[3] In the corner of his eye, Jurika caught the shadow of the aircraft as it swept by and the flash of the bombs hurtling toward the flight deck.

Wham! Wham!

The two concussions from the blasts knocked down hundreds of men on the ship, in some cases with immense force, hurling them against bulkheads or into overheads. Father Joe and his mess mates hit the deck in the wardroom as splinters of glass from overhead light fixtures rained down. Deck guns opened fire for a moment at the retreating Japanese plane, but it already was long gone.

Almost instantly, *Franklin* seemed transported from the western Pacific into the gates of hell. "The conflagration . . . was the most severe [suffered] by any U.S. warship during the course of World War II." Fires of indescribable intensity enveloped the carrier, as gasoline and ordnance detonated immediately after the bombs penetrated the flight deck and exploded in the hangar area.

The first bomb, a semi-armor-piercing weapon filled with 133 pounds of explosive, drilled a hole through the Douglas fir planks of the flight deck just to port of the centerline by the forward 5-inch gun turret, bounced on the armored hangar deck, and detonated athwart the bridge. The blast tore open a six-foot-by-twelve-foot hole in the hangar deck, shattered offices on the second deck below, and propelled fragments into CIC, Air Plot, and other spaces, containing more than two hundred people, in the gallery deck above. The conflagration also lifted the forward aircraft elevator—all thirty-two tons of it—from its piston lifts in the center of the flight deck, blowing it about a foot above the deck before it crashed askew back into its shaft.

The second bomb, a general-purpose high explosive, holed the flight deck by the aft centerline elevator before blowing up virtually simultaneously with the first bomb right over aircraft full of gas and ordnance—and the men working and standing around them—on the hangar deck. The explosion was also directly under the planes, also fully laden, with engines turning—pilots in their cockpits and deck handlers surrounding them—on the flight deck. Aircraft fuel tanks contained 36,000 gallons of high-octane aviation gasoline, and weapon racks carried thirty tons of bombs and Tiny Tim rockets, nearly all of which began igniting.

In seconds, the entire volume of the hangar deck resembled the core of a blast furnace. No human being or anything that humans had fabricated could withstand the unleashed, almost immeasurable, power. Only two lucky men out of more than five hundred in the vast space survived, because by chance they could shield themselves from the fire long enough to run to a passageway. The explosions killed dozens instantly, but those the fragments did not shatter fared no better. If they had a moment to inhale, their lungs filled with the flames that immersed and immolated them. Most of these men had no chance even to take a step as the cauldron engulfed their bodies, turning nerve endings to cinders and boiling blood and moisture in their bodies in a trice. Death was gruesome, but suffering was not prolonged. Few would have been able to utter more than an abrupt yell before they were gone. Moments later, many bodies vanished altogether, vaporized and expunged.

The fire grew in intensity as it consumed and ignited parked planes. Aircraft and metal structures could withstand the inferno longer than a human body, but not much longer. Contained gasoline and weapons of all sorts in the airframes lit off, pushing flames outward and upward through elevator shafts and other openings, literally around the ship, enveloping nearly everything with smoke as tongues of flame lashed dozens of feet in the air.

On the bridge, Captain Gehres saw the forward elevator leap from the flight deck and tumble like a piece of cardboard. The quartermaster of the watch, John O'Donovan, saw it, too, and realized that "we were in bad shape" as he tried to write in his log book with a trembling hand.[4] Gehres later described the explosive chain reactions that were ripping *Franklin* apart:

> The first of a five-hour-long series of heavy explosions occurred on the flight deck, where there were five bombers, fourteen torpedo planes, and twelve fighters, all turning up and loaded with a maximum load of general-purpose bombs and "Tiny Tim" rockets. The explosions of this heavy ordnance progressively from forward to aft, some of it dropping into the hangar deck to explode, spread fire and destruction throughout the ship from the island down to the fourth deck. Fires from the hangar and gallery decks worked upward through the island and eventually all topside five-inch, forty-millimeter, twenty-millimeter, ready rocket, and aircraft ammunition lockers and the ammunition in all the gun mounts aft of the bridge exploded.[5]

The pilots waiting to take off on the flight deck had seconds to act. Many of the aircraft bounced into one another like jumbled toys, their propellers chopping into nearby fuselages or men. A Helldiver on its takeoff roll flipped upside down; its pilot fell out of his seat when he released his restraining harness. Other aviators tried to shut down engines, open cockpit canopies, and leap to the deck, running for their lives as the ordnance in their bomb racks began to cook off. One pilot watched a live rocket launch itself from a wing rail and shoot about five feet over his head.

Concussions blew other sailors off the ship and into the water, including many working on the flight deck or at open gun emplacements just below the deck's perimeter on the gallery deck and on the fantail. Seaman Second Class Abe Barbash of the Bronx, one of *Franklin's* best known poker players, was among those on the fantail. Barbash, who could not swim, put his own life jacket on another young sailor with two broken arms before helping to lower the boy gently into the waiting sea. He then turned back toward the hangar deck to find another Mae West for himself and stepped directly into an exploding bomb. A shipmate recalled, "Not even his dog tags were ever found."

Several men jumped to save themselves from the flames and stifling heat. Smaller ships, notably destroyer *Hickox,* would find and rescue many of the eighty or more men treading water around *Franklin,* but others, shivering in the cold winter temperatures as the ocean chill robbed them of their body heat, lost consciousness and drowned. Among these were several sailors and marines who gave their life preservers to others who could not swim, then found themselves unable to hang on.

Men in the gallery decks died in droves, peppered with shrapnel from the bomb explosions or heaved violently into unforgiving steel structures. Forty-one sailors were working in CIC, and the shock killed all but one of them outright, launching them into the steel overhead as the deck on which they stood heaved upward. Lt. W. A. Simon alone survived because he happened to be wearing his steel helmet, preventing a crushed skull. Many other crewmen were trapped on ladders when the thin metal sheathing that encased their frames crushed around them.

In VMF-214's Ready Room 51, the deck on which a dozen marine pilots stood during their preflight briefing, the thin steel sheet that was the only barrier between them and the hangar deck, buckled, peeled open like a sardine can, and propelled them all into the overhead. Only one Black Sheep, Lt. Carroll K. "Budd" Faught, survived because he was leaning against a bulkhead that did not collapse. Nevertheless, the pilot heard cracks as the impact broke both his legs and one arm. As he lay on the distorted deck, Faught could glimpse the hangar deck below, roiling and churning like molten metal. Faught later crawled to a catwalk and plunged into the sea. A ship picked him up, but he would lose one of his legs to amputation. In Fighting Five's adjacent ready room, not a single pilot lounging in the space, waiting for another mission briefing, survived.

The single positive aspect of all this destruction was its relative containment to the hangar and flight decks. Unlike the flight deck, the hangar deck was armored with sufficient shielding to withstand a thousand-pound bomb blast. Miraculously, only one Japanese bomb knocked a (relatively small) hole in the shield. Subsequent explosions penetrated several compartments on lower decks, but the armor plate protected the engineering spaces and the nearly eight hundred crewmen deep in the hull, probably saving the ship from disintegration.

Exec Taylor was standing on the flight deck aft of the superstructure, near the launch point for aircraft. Nearly one thousand others were working flight operations or in surrounding gun mounts. The blast knocked the commander into the lifelines on the deck's starboard side. Smoke immediately swirled around him, and he retreated to the starboard deck edge, lowering himself by a rope to a 40-mm gun sponson that jutted beyond the flight deck. He found the catwalk on the deck edge, crawled through a port in the island, and "found myself almost where I had started from." He crawled forward on his hands and knees, helped some men attempting to rig a fire hose along the way, then returned to the sponsons and climbed a chain ladder to the bridge, where Captain Gehres greeted him: "Joe, I'll have to say the same thing the Admiral said when you were last bombed, your face is dirty as Hell."

Admiral Davison and several of his staff members also made their way to the navigation bridge and suggested that Captain Gehres prepare to abandon ship.

Franklin continued to churn through the sea, making more than twenty knots, with all boilers functioning. Gehres, noting the smoke emanating from the carrier's starboard side, had quickly ordered the ship to slow to two-thirds speed and to turn to starboard to bring the wind over the port bow. This course change only made the situation worse, wrapping nearly everything in an acrid cocoon. Navigator Jurika noted that the light carrier *Bataan* crossed *Franklin*'s bow just a few hundred yards ahead, a dangerously close margin.

The heavy black smoke overcame the CO, who bent to his knees, racked with coughing. For a brief moment, Gehres, much like everyone else, seemed shocked and disoriented. The captain quickly recovered and took action, however, ordering the helm to turn the ship into the wind. This move pushed much of the smoke aft and cleared the bridge and the forward flight deck.

Direct communication from the bridge to the pilothouse was one of the few means left to the ship's commander. Other systems, including the ship's intercom, failed. Somehow, a single sound-powered phone circuit from the bridge to the five crewmen in the after steering compartment, buried in the lower decks, remained open. From Steering Aft, another sound-powered line ran unencumbered to the main engine control room. This fragile network would enable the ship to operate through many harrowing hours. *Franklin* also had no means to scan the sky. Masts had toppled, bringing the ship's radar antennas down with them. Even signal flags, an antique method still in use on modern ships, were useless, because fire had consumed the halyards used to raise them.

A curtain of flame covered *Franklin's* aft flight deck, and dense, black smoke arched back and upward for hundreds of feet. Photographer's mates on other ships in the armada shot still pictures and movie film of the cataclysm.[6] Witnesses must have stared at the carrier in disbelief. Even today, the silent 16-mm color film of the event is stunning and leaves the viewer with a sense of wonder that anyone could have survived the carnage.

As the smoke shifted, secondary explosions became more apparent. A wounded radar specialist who had escaped Air Plot watched in amazement as an R2800 Pratt & Whitney Double Wasp radial engine, a formidable Corsair power plant weighing more than 2,300 pounds, hurtled so far into the sky that "it seemed like it reached the horizon." Commander Taylor remembered, "The highlight of this Roman holiday was when the Tiny Tims decided to add their bit. Some screamed by to starboard, some to port, and some straight up the flight deck. The weird aspect of this weapon whooshing by so close is one of the most awful spectacles a human has ever been privileged to see. Some went straight and some tumbled end over end."

"The explosions were . . . soul-shaking," added Commander Jurika. "The ship shuddered, rocked under the impacts and would emerge from a period of vibration only to be racked by another heavy blast. Fifty caliber ammunition in the planes on deck set up a staccato chattering and the air was well punctuated by streaks of tracer. Twenty and forty millimeter ammunition next joined the cacophony of sound as the gallery mounts caught fire."[7]

Throughout *Franklin,* men struggled in the welling, poisonous smoke that churned into the bowels of the ship. Dozens stumbled in passageways, opening watertight doors as they searched for escape routes. Many found no way out. Fire or wreckage frequently blocked their progress. The oppressive heat accelerated the flow of breathable air from many spaces, and none replaced it. One such space was the sick bay, where Dr. Bill Fox, who had helped Father O'Callahan offer Mass two days before, worked with seven pharmacist's mates to save several patients, many of whom could not be moved. There they all remained, and there sailors in a rescue party found them all days later, suffocated.

Back in the wardroom mess on the second deck, dozens of sailors seeking sanctuary from the terror above them joined Father Joe and the other officers. O'Callahan remembered with a sense of irony and foreboding that March 19 was the feast of Saint Joseph, the patron of a happy death.

Officers began searching for a way out of the mess deck and found an open passageway leading to the forecastle. The priest's stateroom was by the forecastle, and from the forecastle men could exit through a scuttle, a small escape hatch within a larger hatch sealed watertight in the chaos. While waiting on the forecastle, O'Callahan retrieved his reef coat, life belt, and helmet with the white cross painted on the front. The junior aviators' bunk room, a large compartment nearby, had become a makeshift sick bay, filled with several grievously wounded or burned victims. Father Joe joined Chaplain Gatlin there to pray and help several boys utter Acts of Contrition. In a few minutes, O'Callahan decided to head for the flight deck and the island. He made his way along the starboard catwalk, passing sailors riveted in not only fear but awe. "The noise of explosion followed explosion, each blast worse than the preceding because of the cumulative horror of what had gone before; the billowing smoke, a shroud mantling a dead ship; the flames, snake-tongued, writhing high into the sky or lashing fore and aft, port and starboard, scourging those who thought themselves safely distant from the center of destruction—all this was truly awe-inspiring." At one point, Father Joe could peer into the cauldron below him. "The hangar deck was one massive blaze, not leaping flames, just one solid mass of fire. Here and there, like coals of special brilliance, were airplane engines glowing white hot, glaring so intensely that their image hurt the eye and branded the memory forever."[8]

Smoke forced the priest to retrace his steps. He returned to his room, grabbed a flashlight and long protective gloves, and smeared anti-flash-burn paste on his face. From the forecastle, he climbed to the flight deck. Through intermittent smoke, he noticed Captain Gehres and Commander Jurika on bridge. Bodies lay everywhere on the span of forward flight deck not in flames. O'Callahan found Dr. Sam Sherman, the air group surgeon, treating men with burns and horrible wounds. Father Joe would later recall that he and Dr. Sherman, who was Jewish, had become fast friends in the two weeks since the priest reported on board. The priest helped as he could with prayers and, in too many cases, last rites. Doctor and padre rested together for a moment, and Sherman treated a small shrapnel wound on O'Callahan's calf, cut when a fragment hurtled between his legs. Shards of metal and other material seemed to fly everywhere with each explosion, and each man merely scratched or not hit at all could count himself a walking miracle.

The constant explosions spelled apparent doom for the carrier. No one on board could help but contemplate the limitless catastrophe if flames reached the magazines in the lower decks. After about twenty minutes of continued torrent, with no clear evidence that damage control parties were making headway, Admiral Davison and his chief of staff, Capt. Jim Russell, counseled Captain Gehres again to abandon *Franklin*. Gehres later reported, "No action was taken on this, but the Admiral was requested to provide surface and air support, and we would save the ship."[9]

This response, admirable as it was, meant that CV 13's status as the Task Group 58.2 flagship was untenable. Admirals Davison and Bogan and their staffs prepared to transfer their flags to other vessels. The bridge used signal lamps and a bullhorn to notify destroyer *Miller*, already on *Franklin*'s starboard quarter, to provide assistance. Carrier and destroyer slowed to eight knots so the ships could rig highlines and transfer the staffs by breeches buoy, a process both dangerous—especially so given the circumstances—and tedious. Transfer of the surviving staff members would take more than an hour. Making matters worse, *Miller* signaled just before the operation began that a Japanese plane was diving on the formation from astern. Fortunately, American pilots flying carrier air patrol quickly dispensed with the intruder, well away from *Franklin*, which was hardly in shape to beat to general quarters and defend herself. *Franklin* aircraft already aloft would later land safely on other carriers.

Despite Admiral Davison's pessimistic assessment, damage control parties were at work all over the ship. Although huge fires still raged, much gasoline had burned up, much of the aircraft ordnance had detonated, and the violent explosions now occurred less frequently. Small groups of men on the forward flight deck worked fire hoses, spraying streams of water against the flames leaping upward. Exec Taylor, who left the bridge to inspect the extent of damage, encouraged others on the prow to help with untended hoses. The water knocked down some of the fire, pushing it slowly aft.

Taylor took a few minutes to look at the hangar deck, now "a nightmare of death and destruction. Bodies were everywhere, in the passageways, on the ladders where they had dropped, one hanging from a catwalk on the overhead by one arm." The explosion killed the two sailors in the conflagration station overlooking the hangar deck—a specially protected booth from which systems installed to fight major hangar-deck fires like this one were supposed to be controlled—and destroyed the space. Nevertheless, the concussion probably tripped the deck's fire-sprinkler system, and as the fire lost intensity, the water no longer evaporated instantly as it sprayed over the deck.[10]

Father O'Callahan returned for a while to the junior officers' bunk room on the forecastle. Several sailors were wearing officers' coats to shield them against the cold. Well-meaning officers had distributed the clothing to help cover several men in shirtsleeves or even underwear. An unfortunate by-product of this generosity was confusion over ranks and an impression that some officers were milling about, doing little or nothing to save the ship.

Chaplain Gatlin had stayed in the space, ministering to the wounded. Just before Father Joe had arrived, "Gats" had helped a man up a ladder to the bunk room. Only a thin bulkhead separated them from the forward elevator pit. Suddenly, a load of 20-mm and 40-mm ammunition went off, sending a hailstorm of lead around the two men. Gatlin, who was holding the boy on his feet, kept moving slowly as slugs punched holes around him. Somehow, both made it through unscathed.[11]

Hundreds of other crewmen remained trapped below decks. In the enlisted men's after mess hall on the third deck, about three hundred men had been eating breakfast. Explosions blocked every passageway, and the fire two decks above them robbed the space of oxygen and baked the sailors in unbearable heat. Two officers, Dr. Jim Fuelling and Lt. (jg) Don Gary, were among those trapped. Gary, forty-four, an assistant engineering officer, was a "mustang"— that is, a former enlisted man who had worked his way through the ranks. A twenty-seven-year navy man, Gary knew every gear locker, fan room, and vent space in *Franklin*'s hull. While Dr. Fuelling tried to keep the men calm, Gary began searching for a way out of danger.

Even deeper in the ship, below the waterline, the five men in Steering Aft remained at their battle station, buttoned up and roasting in the heat. Their one connection to the outside world was the sound-powered phone linking them to the bridge and the main engine control room. Quartermaster Third Class Holbrook R. Davis, Engineman Third Class Bill Hamel, Machinist's Mate First Class Jim "Smoky" Gudbrandsen, Machinist Mate Third Class Larry Costa, and Seaman First Class Norm Mayer probably could have escaped when the conflagration began, but not one of them considered abandoning the others or leaving his post.

Chief Engineer Tommy Greene had bolted from the forward wardroom mess instantly after the first explosion and raced to his office. Finding the space wrecked, he descended another ladder to oversee the ship's turbine engines and boilers. The men in these spaces were used to heat, an unavoidable aspect of their work, but not to temperatures that rose well beyond human endurance.

Boilers in Fireroom 2 died quickly, their uptakes destroyed in the blast. By 8:30 a.m., Fireroom 1 was down as well. Smoke filled compartments, forcing sailors to use breathing apparatuses with limited air supplies. Steam lines gave way, and pressure diminished. Greene relayed a message to the bridge through Steering Aft requesting permission to abandon the spaces. The after firerooms, numbers 3 and 4, continued operating for another hour or so, then they too failed. The men in these spaces could not work their way topside and ultimately jumped overboard from lower-deck catwalks or openings in the hull. By 10:00 a.m., *Franklin* would lie dead in the water, drifting in the current toward Japan.

One emergency diesel engine continued to run, providing just enough power for the no. 11 fire pump. Fire-main pressure dropped precipitously, and the carrier's hoses began to play out. As water already pumped flooded into lower compartments, the carrier soon developed a list to starboard that gradually increased, eventually canting the ship about thirteen degrees—navigator Jurika never admitted a steeper pitch, even though the inclinometer indicated otherwise—and making movement on the flight deck even more difficult.

Miller took the last member of the flag staffs on board about 9:00 a.m. and cleared *Franklin*'s side. When the destroyer hauled away, the *Cleveland*-class light cruiser *Santa Fe*, commissioned in late 1942 and in nearly constant action in the Pacific thereafter, stood ready to offer assistance. The young ship had an older commanding officer than did *Franklin*, Capt. Harold C. Fitz, of Somerville, Massachusetts, Naval Academy class of 1920. Fitz, an all-around athlete at Annapolis, was an experienced seaman and knew the risks he and his ship faced. As his vessel approached *Franklin*, he and his shipmates recalled the fate of cruiser *Birmingham*, which had pulled alongside the light carrier *Princeton* to help that crippled ship during the battle of Leyte Gulf. As *Birmingham* laid to, *Princeton* had exploded, killing and wounding more than six hundred of the cruiser's crewmen working topside.

Fitz and *Santa Fe* did not hesitate. With *Miller* well away, the cruiser closed on the carrier's starboard side and reduced speed. Fitz noted the stricken ship's list, the immense flames covering the aft flight deck, flaming gasoline spilling from the vessel's starboard quarter into the sea, and continuing explosions. His first question semaphored to Captain Gehres, still on *Franklin*'s bridge, addressed his concern about a sudden catastrophic explosion: "Are your magazines flooded?" Gehres answered, "Affirmative." He had so ordered, but in fact he was unsure whether his crew had completed the task. In fact, they had not succeeded. The carrier's large ordnance stores were dry. Although crewmen risked their lives to go below and open valves controlling the magazine's flood mains, the ruptured pipes contained no water. CV 13's greatest good fortune was that these spaces would not ignite.

The cruiser quickly highlined two high-pressure fire hoses to the flight deck, then rigged provision whips, lines with pulleys, to begin moving the carrier's many wounded crewmen to safety. Just before 10:00 a.m., with these vital operations under way, a ready-service magazine in an aft twin, 5-inch, .38-caliber gun turret lit off, the largest explosion of the morning. The blast pulverized huge areas of the aft flight deck and spewed debris over both carrier and cruiser, chopping up *Santa Fe*'s fire hoses. Incredibly, the rain of ruin caused no injuries among the crew on the cruiser or the firefighters on *Franklin*'s flight deck.

On *Franklin,* Commander Jurika later wrote, "The ship felt as though it were a rat being shaken by an angry cat. Whole aircraft engines with propellors [*sic*] attached, debris of all description, including pieces of human bodies were flung high into the air and descended on the general area like hail on a roof."[12]

With all lines cut in the blast and *Franklin* losing headway, *Santa Fe* had no choice but to back away. Grievously injured men on the flight deck, some with limbs blown off, watched as their only immediate hope for survival departed. In the meantime, the cruiser and destroyers *Hickox* and *Miller* rescued dozens of carrier crewmen who had abandoned ship and now floated helplessly in the cold water.

Father Joe, meanwhile, had worked his way back to the flight deck. He joined damage control parties working the few operable fire hoses on *Franklin* as they made slow progress in pushing the flames back. He could not believe that apparently no one on the bow had been killed or injured when the turret exploded.

Vice Adm. Marc Mitscher, the Task Force 58 commander, witnessed *Franklin*'s distress from his flagship, the carrier *Bunker Hill.* He ordered his signal bridge to transmit permission to CV 13 to abandon ship, on the presumption Captain Gehres was waiting for fiat to get his men to safety. Gehres ordered his own signalman to flash a curt reply: "Abandon? Hell, we're still afloat!" The young signalman blinkered the message exactly as the CO uttered it, adding one more inspiring turn of phrase to the navy's legacy of defiant quotations.

On board *Santa Fe,* Captain Fitz undoubtedly shared Admiral Mitscher's skepticism about *Franklin*'s future. Before he broke away, his crew had managed to transfer only a few injured carrier sailors. CV 13 was adrift, its list more pronounced than before, with fires still raging aft and smoke billowing. Another explosion could conceivably capsize or break apart the big ship and take down its entire complement. Fitz considered his options, then carried out what Captain Gehres called "the most daring piece of seamanship I ever saw." Fitz ordered the cruiser first to pull away and then turn toward *Franklin* with all engines ahead full. *Santa Fe* barreled toward the carrier's starboard side at twenty-five knots on a collision course. As Fitz shouted commands, engineers backed the ship's powerful turbines and the cruiser's helmsman threw the rudder hard right, veering the ship—all 570 feet and 10,000 tons of her—at precisely the right moment to shear into *Franklin's* gallery deck, scraping along gun sponsons, catwalks, safety nets, and lifelines. The crash knocked aside the useless radar antenna dangling by the carrier's island, but the massive obstacles *Santa Fe* hit helped to slow the cruiser's momentum and locked it in place, undamaged, side by side with *Franklin.* Commander Jurika and dozens of *Franklin* crewmen marveled at Fitz's remarkable maneuver, which the navigator compared to "a well-handled gig boat making a liberty float at Long Beach."

On *Santa Fe,* newly minted ensign Robert S. Hayes, Naval Academy class of 1945, saw an Annapolis classmate, Ens. Richard E. Jortberg, standing just a few feet away on the carrier. "Dick," he asked nonchalantly, "What do you hear from your wife?"

Within minutes, hundreds of men, many of them *Franklin's* badly injured crewmen, literally stepped or were carried from the carrier to the cruiser. Among those departing were surviving members of the carrier air group. Dr. Sherman, one of three physicians still alive on the ship, stayed to tend remaining crewmen, disobeying Cdr. Henry Hale, the carrier's aviation officer, who threatened to shoot or court-martial him if they survived the ordeal. Military authority did not overly impress Sherman, who wore both navy and Marine Corps uniforms as he pleased, because of the mixed air group. After the war, Sherman recalled, "[Hale] talked about the court-martial a lot but everybody in higher rank on the ship thought it was [a] really bad idea and made him sound like a damned fool. He stopped making the threats."[13] Meanwhile, Hale ordered every other "airdale" in the group and ship's company to the cruiser.

Fighting Five CO MacGregor Kilpatrick protested. Few men on board could claim to be luckier than Kilpatrick. Moments before the bombs struck *Franklin,* he had found himself riding by mistake a supply hoist elevator from the flight deck to the hangar deck. Those who watched him disappear assumed that he was one more victim in the charnel house below them. Some time later, however, he reappeared, stepping from an island compartment back to the flight deck, where he joined firefighters. Protests notwithstanding, Kilpatrick left the ship under Captain Gehres' direct order, "You are an aviator, not a firefighter! Take your pilots and get moving!"

Cornelius and Alice O'Callahan, Father Joe's parents, circa 1918
Photograph courtesy of Maureen Madell

Father Joseph T. O'Callahan, S.J., the newly ordained priest
Photograph courtesy of the College of the Holy Cross

The O'Callahan family in 1934, the year of Joe's ordination. Sitting are, left to right, Neil, Alice, Joe, Rose, and John. Standing are, left to right, Alice's brother John, Rose's husband Edward O'Brien, and Edward.

Photograph courtesy of Maureen Madell

Campus of the College of the Holy Cross, circa 1940. Fenwick Hall, with its spires, is the large building in the left center of this aerial view.

Photograph courtesy of the College of the Holy Cross

USS *Ranger* (CV 4), her flight deck full of prewar biplanes. During flight operations, her stacks rotated downward and outward, away from the flight deck.

U.S. Navy photograph

A Grumman F4F-4 Wildcat fighter taking off from USS *Ranger* (CV 4) to attack targets ashore during the invasion of Morocco, circa 8 November 1942. Army observation planes are flying overhead.

U.S. Navy photograph

USS *Franklin* (CV 13) in the Elizabeth River, off Norfolk, Virginia, February 21, 1944
U.S. Navy photograph

Franklin operating near the Marianas, August 1, 1944, in camouflage Measure 32, Design 6a on her starboard side, photographed from USS *Hornet* (CV 12)
U.S. Navy photograph

"Murderer's Row." From foreground, U.S. Navy *Essex*-class carriers *Wasp*, *Yorktown*, *Hornet*, *Hancock*, *Ticonderoga*, and *Lexington* moored at the Ulithi anchorage in the Caroline Islands, December 1944.
U.S. Navy photograph

Franklin in extremis moments after the attack on March 19. The combined effects of Japanese bombs, aviation gas, and aircraft ordnance shattered the ship. Hundreds of crewmen already were dead, immolated, or blown to bits, when the motion picture from which this frame is taken was filmed. Few photographs convey the real power of the devastating explosions on board the carrier.
U.S. Navy photograph

An aerial view of *Franklin* on fire with the cruiser *Santa Fe* close aboard
U.S. Navy photograph

Franklin afire and listing. What appears to be white smoke around the carrier's island on the left is a wall of flame. The view is from USS *Santa Fe* (CL 60), which was alongside assisting with firefighting and rescue work.
U.S. Navy photograph

Franklin's aft 5-inch, .38-caliber turret burns furiously. Note the flames spilling from the muzzles of the turret's guns. The ready magazine in this turret, filled with shells weighing more than fifty pounds each, exploded, rocking the entire ship and forcing light cruiser *Santa Fe* to withdraw from its position close aboard. Father O'Callahan directed the removal of shells from a forward turret to prevent a similar explosion there.
U.S. Navy photograph

Franklin's flight deck, from *Santa Fe,* seconds after the aft turret ready magazine exploded. Fire crews are running away from the blast. Miraculously, no one was killed by the cloud of debris raining down on both ships after the explosion.
U.S. Navy photograph

Franklin struggling to contain fires off the coast of Japan, photographed from cruiser *Santa Fe*

U.S. Naval Institute Photo Archive

A close-up of the aft flight deck's starboard side, showing flaming fuel spilling from *Franklin*'s hangar deck

U.S. Navy photograph

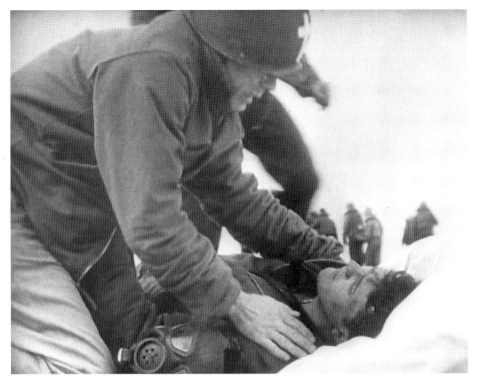

Father O'Callahan comforting crewman Bob Blanchard on the *Franklin*'s flight deck. Blanchard suffered from smoke inhalation but recovered. The white cross on Father Joe's helmet made the padre visible from the carrier's bridge.
U.S. Navy photograph

A photograph from the heavy cruiser *Pittsburgh* as she made ready to take *Franklin* under tow. The carrier's thirteen-degree list is clear in this view.
Photograph courtesy of Robert M. Cieri, via NavSource.com

Reverend Grimes Gatlin, *Franklin*'s Protestant chaplain, conducted a memorial service on the carrier's decimated hangar deck, Sunday, March 25, 1945. Father O'Callahan celebrated Catholic Mass the same day on the flight deck.
U.S. Navy photograph

CV 13 on the way home. Damage on the aft flight deck, where twenty-two aircraft preparing to take off exploded and burned, was especially heavy. Damage on the hangar deck is not visible here, although the force of the blast lifted the forward elevator off of its track, leaving the shaft open.
U.S. Navy photograph

Another view of *Franklin*'s aft flight deck while moored in New York Harbor.
U.S. Navy photograph

Members of *Franklin*'s 704 Club stand at attention in new dress blue uniforms, "manning the rails" as CV 13 makes way up the East River to the New York Navy Yard in Brooklyn. The war ended before the ship completed repairs, and she joined the "mothball fleet" across the Hudson River in Bayonne, New Jersey.
U.S. Navy photograph

CV 13 undergoing repairs in the New York Naval Shipyard in Brooklyn, 1945
Photograph courtesy of Steve Whitby, via NavSource.com

Lieutenant Commander O'Callahan smiles for press photographers during the *Franklin* news conference in New York. The navy emphasized that the chaplain had been recommended for the Medal of Honor. On the right, typical front-page coverage on the day after the news conference.
Photographs courtesy of the College of the Holy Cross

In Washington, D.C., during the summer of 1945, Commander O'Callahan calls on Admiral R. Kent Hewitt, commander of naval forces in the North Africa invasion in 1942 when O'Callahan was chaplain on *Ranger*.

U.S. Navy photograph

President Harry S. Truman, center, presented Medals of Honor to army sergeant John R. McKinney, army first lieutenant Daniel W. Lee Jr., navy lieutenant Donald A. Gary, and navy commander Joseph T. O'Callahan in an Oval Office ceremony on January 23, 1946.

National Park Service, Abbie Rowe, Courtesy of Harry S. Truman Library

A month after receiving the Medal of Honor, Father O'Callahan was chaplain on the aircraft carrier *Franklin D. Roosevelt* for the ship's shakedown cruise to Rio de Janeiro, Brazil, where he celebrated a military Mass in a city cathedral.
U.S. Navy photograph

After his first stroke in December 1949, Father Joe spent much of his time in his Fenwick Hall room at Holy Cross. His poor health exacted a heavy toll on O'Callahan. Less than a decade after the war, he appeared older than most men in their late forties.
Photograph courtesy of the College of the Holy Cross

The O'Callahan family in the early 1960s. Father Joe and his mother Alice are seated left and center, respectively, surrounded by the priest's nieces and nephews.
Photograph courtesy of the College of the Holy Cross

Father Joe, near the end. Years of suffering register on his face.
Photograph courtesy of the College of the Holy Cross

The Jesuits, Holy Cross, and the U.S. Navy shared responsibility for Father O'Callahan's funeral and interment on March 21, 1964. Navy and Marine Corps enlisted men serve as pallbearers in the procession from the college chapel to the small cemetery nearby. O'Callahan's mother Alice is in the wheelchair behind and to the right of her son's flag-draped casket.
Photograph courtesy of the College of the Holy Cross

Franklin in the Portsmouth Salvage Company's scrap yard in Mill Dam Creek, Virginia, after the navy sold the old ship for scrap in 1966. Steel from CV 13 was sold to Japanese mills.
Photograph courtesy of Steve Whitby, via NavSource.com

USS *O'Callahan* (DE 1051) launched at the Defoe Shipbuilding Company's yard in Bay City, Michigan, on October 20, 1965. The ship was reclassified as a frigate in 1975 and remained in U.S. service until 1988.
Photograph courtesy of the College of the Holy Cross

USS *O'Callahan*, "haze gray and underway"
U.S. Navy photograph

Father Joe's headstone in the cemetery by the Chapel at the College of the Holy Cross

Photograph courtesy of the College of the Holy Cross

With more than eight hundred carrier sailors crowding *Santa Fe's* weather decks and her sick bay, the cruiser's men began throwing to *Franklin* any equipment that seemed remotely useful to those still there, including medical supplies, blankets, oxygen-breathing apparatuses, food, and water bottles. Firefighters from the cruiser brought more fully functional hoses into play against the flames still blazing in the hangar deck amidships and broiling the flight deck aft of the island. At one point, a fire hose burst between the two ships. Fireman First Class Gerald S. Smith, a *Franklin* firefighter, crawled over the side, dangled on ropes, and spliced an undamaged section of hose in place to restore water flow. Throughout his task, he apparently ignored the real possibility that the two huge hulls, just feet apart, could collide any minute and flatten him like a pancake.

For more than two hours the two ships rode locked in their mechanical embrace, their crews working together to save the carrier. Destroyers *Hickox* and *Miller* and heavy cruiser *Pittsburgh* also pulled close aboard at CV 13's stern, taking off many other sailors trapped by fires and unable to contact anyone else.

Gehres requested Fitz to take *Franklin* in tow, but the cruiser was not large enough to handle this task. *Pittsburgh,* a bigger ship at 13,000 tons, one-third more in displacement than *Santa Fe,* took the assignment.

Just before 12:30 p.m., *Franklin* requested *Santa Fe* to haul away so *Pittsburgh* could maneuver closely enough to rig a towline. Fitz complied with the request, having earned the undying gratitude of every soul on the carrier. For his actions on March 19 that helped to save the lives of at least eight hundred sailors, Capt. Harold Carlton Fitz merited and later received the Navy Cross, his service's highest military decoration.[14]

Below decks, Lt. (jg) Don Gary had strapped on an oxygen-breathing apparatus (OBA) with about ten minutes of air left in its canister and began the search for a passage to safety. He descended in smoke and near-total darkness through a hatch from the third deck to the fourth, then crawled through another hatchway to an engine uptake shaft. He crawled through the space on his hands and knees, climbed a ladder in the shaft all the way to an opening in the island, then stepped out to the flight deck. After breathing some fresh air deeply and replacing the OBA canister, he headed back to the enlisted mess. This time he took just ten men with him, in case they walked into an explosion or got lost. All of them tried to filter their breathing through handkerchiefs or cloths soaked with any available liquid, including urine. The little group, gripping each other's hands like a line of children in kindergarten, traveled more than six hundred feet, much of it in blackness, through the ship until they emerged six decks above by a 40-mm gun sponson. As the sailors gasped in the chill air, Gary headed back for more. He made two more trips, first with fifty, than with more than two hundred, until every man trapped in the mess was safe.

Gary was not, however, content to rest after his feat. He joined firefighting teams to extinguish blazes on the hangar deck and later went below decks again into the dangerous smoke and oppressive heat, this time to help relight no. 5 boiler in Fireroom 3 and restore power in his ship. For his actions on March 19 that, at repeated risk to his own life, directly saved the lives of three hundred of his shipmates and helped to save his ship, Lt. Donald Arthur Gary merited and later received the Medal of Honor, the nation's highest award for valor above and beyond the call of duty.[15]

Many other heroes emerged that day, including the *Franklin*'s Catholic chaplain. Less than two-and-a-half hours after the bombing, the fire crews on the flight deck had pushed the wall of flame back to the island. Father O'Callahan did what he could topside, helping Commander Hale, the senior officer with the firefighters. Lt. (jg) Stanley S. "Steamboat" Graham, CV 13's fire marshal, with collateral duty as a bomb-disposal officer, rallied sailors around the carrier's bow and soon had about a dozen fire hoses turned on the blaze. Bombs rolled about the deck, their steel casings heated to dangerous levels in the fire. Several sailors burned their hands catching the loose ordnance and rolling it off the deck into the sea.

Lt. (jg) Lindsay E. "Red" Morgan, an assistant aviation maintenance officer, attempted to handle a hose by himself. Father O'Callahan tried to help him but quickly realized the job required several men. As he searched for sailors who could pitch in, the white cross on his helmet drew people like a magnet with "the power of recognition and inspiration." He later wrote:

> As I trudged along a lad spotted the cross on my helmet. He ran over to me, and asked in a not too steady voice, "Father, give me absolution." To the lad, whose name I did not even know, I explained that when the first bomb exploded I had given general absolution, then added, "Say an act of contrition and I'll give you absolution now."
>
> He knelt on the listing flight deck. In the background flames shot high in the air, smoke billowed into the sky. Even during the short time it takes to say an act of contrition, there were explosions. The boy finished his prayer of sorrow for having offended God, and I concluded absolution. As he rose to his feet I recalled Red Morgan and his need of help.
>
> "Look, lad, will you go down now to the fire lines and help Lieutenant Red Morgan with the hose?"

The boy looked me in the eyes, and with complete simplicity and sincerity said, "Sure, Father, I'll go anywhere now."[16]

Other sailors quickly followed suit, and O'Callahan joined them, caught up in the same power of the cross. As *Santa Fe* evacuated the carrier's wounded, Captain Gehres saw flaming gasoline spill from a hangar deck vent into the ocean. The CO also saw liquid pouring from another catwalk vent between two improvised gangways rigged to remove wounded crewmen. If the fluid were gasoline, an explosion could immolate men as they evacuated the ship. Gehres asked O'Callahan to find out what was spouting from the vent. The priest could not see the leak from flight deck, so the captain used hand signals to guide him over it. Father Joe dipped his hands in the stream, tasted salt water then turned, smiled, and flashed thumbs-up to Gehres.

A *Santa Fe* photographer's mate stood with a movie camera on the cruiser's weather deck, filming the rescue efforts from close range. One image he captured was Father O'Callahan offering extreme unction to a dark-haired young man lying on the deck, a billowing parachute splayed under him like a loose sheet. The sailor was Yeoman Third Class Robert C. Blanchard, twenty-one, who normally worked in the gunnery office on the third deck. Blanchard, the son of a naval officer, had enlisted in 1943 after working a couple of years for General Motors in New York. He was one of the three hundred men trapped in the enlisted mess with Lieutenant (jg) Gary, and smoke had seared his lungs during the escape from below decks. The film, later used more than once in war movies, shows the priest, the helmet with the white chaplain's cross obscuring his features, on his knees, his hands holding the young man's shoulders, then clasped in prayer. In fact Blanchard survived, and after several days in *Santa Fe*'s sick bay he returned to *Franklin* when the carrier arrived in Ulithi. He served as one of the crewmen that would bring the carrier home, where the sailor would meet his six-month-old daughter, Violetta, whom he had never seen.

"I just got a lot of smoke," Blanchard, a Catholic, said. "Father O'Callahan gave me a blessing and started last rites. I tried to get up, but he pushed me back." Later, Blanchard spoke to Father Joe several times on the voyage home and thanked him for his care. "He was a real nice guy, as regular as you can get. There was a closeness to him. He could talk to you plain and simple, and he was good in confession. You could be comfortable with a guy like that. Everybody liked him." After *Franklin*'s return to the States, Father O'Callahan traveled across the country visiting the parents of many sailors who had not come home. "I didn't know it then, but he went to Bremerton, Washington, where my father was stationed at the time, and he talked to my father to let him know I was okay."[17]

With the prominent white cross standing out on his helmet, O'Callahan became something of a messenger for directives from the bridge. On the captain's order, he helped to gather engineers so these men could return to their spaces below, restore ship's power, and get the drifting *Franklin* well away from the Japanese coast, now merely forty-five miles distant.

As he searched for men, Father Joe and others came across a live thousand-pound bomb. While the priest stood by, Steamboat Graham and Lt. Cdr. George Stone, an aviation division officer, coolly tried to disarm the fuse, which would not detonate as long as the bomb remained horizontal. Everyone, including the five enlisted men trying to hold the casing steady, understood that it could erupt at any second. The officers were unsure if they had succeeded with the fuse. Before rolling the weapon over the side, they sent O'Callahan below to the forecastle to evacuate men trying to rig a towline. If the bomb rotated as it fell, it could destroy the ship's prow and everything on it. The bomb dropped harmlessly into the water.

Lieutenant Commander McKinney, *Franklin's* gunnery officer, approached next with an urgent task. Flames had swept around a forward twin 5-inch, .38-caliber gun turret. The firefighters had pushed the blaze away from the turret, but it was filled with shells that could cook off in the heat. The aft turret explosion earlier had nearly rocked CV 13 apart, and McKinney was certain the ship could not withstand another blast. He needed a chain of sailors to pass hot 5-inch shells from the ready magazine in the barbette, one level under the turret, to the adjacent catwalk and heave them over the side. More than enough men quickly volunteered, and O'Callahan himself went into the turret, despite the claustrophobia that had nagged him all his life. He later wrote an understated explanation: "For me to enter a small closed space such as that turret demands effort of the will, and it is accomplished only at the cost of cold sweat. I did not so much mind the thought of being blown up. I did very much mind being hemmed in. A silly phobia, I realized, but I confess it took an effort to overcome it."[18]

Inside the dark turret, O'Callahan struggled to breathe in the heat and smoke, but also because fear gripped him so completely. One of the sailors who followed Father Joe inside called out, "Praise the Lord and *dump* the ammunition," as they blistered hands picking up the big shells, each of which weighed about fifty-five pounds, and tossing them into the waiting arms of the next man. The priest had no recollection of the ammunition's weight as he picked up the shells. Several days later he tried lift one again and had far greater difficulty. "I wouldn't want to earn my living at it," he said.[19] After the crew emptied the ready magazine, O'Callahan emerged from the turret, caught Captain Gehres' eye above him on the bridge, smiled again and raised his thumb. Gehres turned to his orderly, marine private Wallace Klimkiewicz, and others on the bridge and said, matter-of-factly, "That's the bravest man I ever saw."

The priest followed Steamboat Graham once again, this time to the hangar deck, where the inferno had consumed almost every combustible object. After inspecting the almost indescribable damage, the men returned to the flight deck, where Graham directed volunteers below with a fire hose. On the way back, several men tripped over a body and recoiled. Their padre helped them move the corpse, and they pressed on, spraying water on the blistering surfaces. When he returned again to the flight deck, he found the firefighters making progress. They had pushed the fires even farther aft and in the process had uncovered at least six more 1,000-pound bombs that had roasted in the flames. The men moved within eight feet of the bombs, playing high-pressure water on the casings to cool them off. O'Callahan told the men not to let the stream hit the sensitive bomb fuses and risk detonation, to which one retorted, "That's right, Father; let's not take any unnecessary chances!"[20]

From the bridge, Pvt. Wally Klimkiewicz had remained by his captain on the bridge through the worst of the carnage. He finally left, with the captain's permission, to join others manning one of the few 40-mm gun tubs still serviceable.

Suddenly, another Japanese attacker appeared, flying over the flight deck on a strafing run as O'Callahan's fire crew continued wetting down bombs. The priest recalled:

> All hands sprawled, crouching beneath their helmets. Placito Abellon, a Filipino boy, Chief Cook, flopped down beside me.
>
> To him, this strafing was the last straw. I've never seen, nor expect to see, a person more completely frightened. With bullets splattering around us, I said the Act of Contrition into his ear. He tried to repeat the familiar prayer, but his jaw muscles wouldn't function. He was inarticulate. I gave him absolution. Quicker than it takes to tell, the strafing was over, and we were still alive. But there was no time to rejoice. Seconds were valuable; we couldn't afford to let the flames reach those bombs again.
>
> "Come on. We have to get back to the hoses."
>
> Physically and psychologically unnerved, green with fright, Abellon came back. And because it was so obvious that he had great fear to conquer, and had conquered it, his example led thirty other boys back

within a matter of seconds. A good share of the credit for preventing the explosion of those six bombs must go to Abellon.[21]

Exec Taylor had witnessed much of the action. "Throughout all this, Father O'Callahan, our Catholic priest, was a soul-stirring sight . . . doing everything he could to help save our ship. He was so conspicuous not only because of the Cross dabbed with paint across his helmet but because of his seemingly detached air as he went from place to place with head slightly bowed as if in meditation or prayer." Navigator Jurika added that O'Callahan was "doing ten men's work." The assistant aviation officer, Lt. Cdr. David Berger, echoed the praise:

> The Catholic chaplain, Father O'Callahan, was very inspiring as he proceeded up and down the flight deck in his tin hat with a large white cross painted on it. He was one of the outstanding leaders in fighting the fires and he could be observed by everybody topside as he would give the Last Rites of the Church to the dying men and then very shortly afterwards would lead parties into the smoke and flames. On more than one occasion I saw him carrying bombs and five-inch ammunition, all of which had been heated to the exploding point, over to a ramp where it could be jettisoned from the ship. His actions throughout were such that we were all inspired by him.[22]

O'Callahan and others believed the removal of the six bombs on the flight deck, all safely rolled into the ocean, marked the turning point for *Franklin*. No more major explosions rocked the ship, although machine-gun rounds continued to pop off.

Cruiser *Pittsburgh,* under the command of Capt. John Gingrich, a native of Dodge City, Kansas, and an Annapolis classmate of Hal Fitz, steamed ahead of *Franklin* and prepared to rig a towline aft. In the carrier's forecastle, Commander Taylor gathered several dozen men, including many of the ship's cooks and stewards, to cut the starboard anchor chain with torches, saws, and chisels, so as to release the anchor itself—Taylor intended to pay out the chain, 540 feet long, as part of the towline. *Pittsburgh* had slowed almost to a full stop, backing down toward the carrier, and worked a messenger line, a manila rope eight inches in circumference, the size and stiffness of a water pipe, to *Franklin.* Men in the forecastle would haul in the messenger, itself attached to a steel tow cable, through the port bulls-eye. The line weighed tons, and the anchor capstan, a huge winch ordinarily capable of hauling it on board CV 13, was useless without power. Taylor's crew would have to muscle enough of the cable, literally inch by inch, into the forecastle to attach it to the anchor chain.

Crews of both ships were uneasy about the situation. With *Franklin* adrift and *Pittsburgh* unable to accelerate quickly once the tow was made up, carrier and cruiser would be especially vulnerable to another air attack. If a Japanese aircraft broke through the overcast, another strike on CV 13 could undo all the progress damage control parties had made through the morning, or create similar carnage on *Pittsburgh*.

Franklin's stewards, nearly thirty in number, chanted a gandy dancer's refrain, setting up a rhythm that helped the forecastle crew get the tow cable on board. The chant "seemed to give us new heart, with colored sailors pulling their hearts out side by side with white sailors and officers," Taylor wrote. "The messenger seemed endless and finally an officer on the *Santa Fe* hollered across and said he could pull it in for us with one of his forecastle winches. This was a tremendous and successful idea. We soon had the thimble of the *Pittsburgh*'s $1^7/_8$-inch wire on deck. We shackled it to a deck stopper from the starboard chain."

The heavy cruiser sent word she required a hundred fathoms of chain in addition to the wire. Taylor's men went back to work, manhandling the anchor chain from its locker. "After much wig-wagging, walkie-talkie conversation, etc., we finally got the *Pittsburgh* to go ahead slow and the old chain just eased out slick as a whistle. We stopped about every five fathoms with the hand brake so it wouldn't go out too fast. When I had 90 fathoms on deck, we put on two deck stoppers and reported to the commanding officer that we were ready to go ahead."[23]

Despite the continuing presence of Japanese aircraft, one of which the combat air patrol splashed just after 1:00 p.m. a few miles from *Franklin,* Commander Jurika's action summary noted CV 13's improved prospects. "At 1404, *Pittsburgh* started towing us, but instead of positioning herself and getting way on us, she towed at right angles, trying to swing *Franklin* towards the South. We called steering aft from the conn and asked that hand gear and tackle be used to shift the rudder from amidships to three degrees right." The five men trapped in that space, despite nearly seven hours in oppressive heat, complied in about fifteen minutes. "The tow then proceeded smoothly, *Pittsburgh* reporting us headed south at five knots." Within an hour, the carrier was making six knots on a course due south, fifty-five nautical miles from Japan, moving away from danger.[24]

Several destroyers and cruisers hovered around the carrier, pulling close aboard to assist with firefighting, passing supplies and equipment, and providing essential protection for both CV 13 and *Pittsburgh,* itself unable to maneuver in case Japanese airplanes showed up. Nearly all of these ships had picked up *Franklin* crewmen from the water. Destroyer *Marshall* had rescued 212, including marine pilot Budd Faught. Destroyers *Miller* and *Hunt* had each fished about 50 sailors from the sea. *Santa Fe*'s roster listed 832 *Franklin* men on board, including about 100 wounded, many of them severely. More than 800 men throughout the carrier had died in the conflagration, and nearly 300 had been wounded. This left 706 on *Franklin,* according to Gehres' count, 103 officers and 603 men, many of them not in condition even to make muster or report for duty until March 21, to handle the carrier.[25]

Jurika reported, "About 1700 [5:00 p.m.], fires on the flight deck were under control as far back as #3 elevator. The deck was a shambles of burned, warped and broken wood and steel, with bodies, debris and wreckage littering the area. Holes were cut in the flight deck with axes, and hoses were poked through in an attempt to quell flames still raging on the gallery deck." Officers sent to inspect the ship returned to the bridge, and on the basis of their reports Jurika wrote, "Our situation seems quite hopeful." Tommy Greene and his engineers went below to get to work in the engines and firerooms. A couple of hours later, officers on the bridge had their first meal of the day, canned pork sausage and orange juice—"a gourmet's delight," Jurika remembered.

As dusk settled in, extinguishing fires became even more critical, since *Franklin* afire would serve as a beacon for Japanese night aerial attacks. Destroyers *Bullard* and *Kidd* joined the ships covering CV 13's retreat, riding shotgun.

Another important chore remained. Lt. (jg) E. Robert Wassman, twenty-four, an assistant navigation officer, volunteered to go below with several other sailors and bring the five men out of Steering Aft, where they had remained in insufferable conditions for more than twelve hours. Wassman had narrowly missed death early on March 19 when he left his office and headed for the wardroom mess for pancakes. The lieutenant had made his way to the forecastle, the flight deck, and ultimately the bridge, where he handled several tasks for Captain Gehres, including damage inspections.

"The captain and others on the bridge phoned Holbrook Davis and told him we were coming down to get him and the others out," Wassman remembered. Using rescue breathers, he worked his way aft and brought a wounded man from the gun sponsons on the fantail up to the flight deck. Deck by deck, the rescuers then descended into the hull, crawling over obstacles of all sorts and through many flooded spaces, flashlights their only source of illumination. "We finally reached a space directly over Steering Aft," Wassman said, "but it was half flooded. If we opened a hatch in the deck to reach Davis, we could have drowned the men inside." Wassman and his helpers headed topside to retrieve hand pumps, then returned and set to work. After eliminating all but about a foot of the water in the compartment, one of the men tapped out a Morse code message to the five hostages, then opened the hatch. Out came the five sailors, soaked but alive, and eager to leave the duty station that had become a de facto prison cell. Lt. Edward H. R. Wassman, Machinist's Mate First Class James H. Gudbrandsen, Machinist's Mate Third Class Laurentino E. Costa, Quartermaster Third Class Holbrook R. Davis, Engineman Third Class William H. Hamel, and Seaman First Class Norman C. Mayer all received the Silver Star for conspicuous gallantry on March 19, 1945.[26]

By 9:00 p.m., engineers including Lieutenant (jg) Gary were working in earnest in Fireroom 3, despite the 150-degree air temperatures. After midnight, steam was up to 1,200 pounds per square inch, enough to turn the engine turbines, and Lieutenant Commander Greene ordered engines warmed up. The engineers cut in more boilers on the after engines at dawn and began turning the ship's screws at fifty-six revolutions per minute, though the tow was not cast off.

While the engineers labored, Captain Gehres ordered counter-flooding in port compartments to reduce and ultimately eliminate the list, which impeded *Franklin*'s safe movement under tow. Men went below to complete the task manually, since all remote controls were out of commission. With no way to control the counter-flooding from the bridge, the men below went too far and induced a list to port of about nine degrees. The ship remained on this uneven keel until it arrived in Ulithi six days later, but it was making way on its own.

March 19, 1945, the date seared into the minds of every sailor still breathing on *Franklin,* drew to a close. Big Ben's tragic hours had forever changed the lives of everyone on board and of many of those who witnessed the horrible event from other ships. The experiences of more than two thousand souls would unite around the conflagration that had nearly destroyed one of the U.S. Navy's most advanced warships. Throughout the ordeal, the sailors involved answered the challenges they faced with actions derived from the training they had received. They responded as a navy crew, part of a great mechanism designed to produce results with efficiency and ruthless precision. After all, from the national point of view, the mechanism and the institution of which it was a part were what really mattered, since global war required massive institutional commitment, far beyond the means of a few men.

Task Force 58 continued its attacks against Japan without significant interruption. Operation Iceberg followed on schedule. Thousands of American marines and soldiers died or suffered grievous wounds on Okinawa as they captured the island and in the process killed tens of thousands of Japanese defenders. Meanwhile, the U.S. Navy, and the entire nation, prepared to invade

Japan with the same efficiency and precision to induce the Empire's unconditional surrender, the outcome engendered fewer than five months later by an exponentially more ruthless and productive secret weapon.

Franklin's awful day also demonstrated beyond doubt that even as institutional capabilities and perspectives apparently triumphed, regardless of the adversity and the cost in lives imposed, individuals still mattered.

The ship's crewmen retained their humanity. Nearly all of those on board acted almost unerringly with decency and generosity, risking their lives—too often giving up their lives—not to meet the navy's mechanistic objectives but to save other individuals about whom they cared. They were sailors—all parts of the great machine—but at the core also human beings, with human frailties, limitations, and imperfections who nevertheless frequently placed other human needs ahead of their own.

The evidence is compelling, moreover, that Father O'Callahan, one of the few on board whose principal mission was to focus on human values, demonstrated enough faith and strength of character to inspire his shipmates and ensure they never lost sight of the attributes they shared, not as war fighters but as men.

11

Operating Independently

"A ship that won't be sunk can't be sunk."[1]

By 10:00 a.m. on March 20, Captain Gehres notified the task unit commander that *Franklin* was ready to cast off *Pittsburgh's* tow and to make fifteen knots. At noon, CV 13's speed of advance was fourteen knots, and half an hour later she cast off the cruiser's tow. *Pittsburgh* hauled off, and *Franklin* steamed under her own power for the Carolines anchorage she had left less than a week earlier.[2]

The carrier's crewmen ate bread, the only food readily available. They found almost no drinkable water. Despite thirst, many of them fell asleep, exhausted, in undamaged officers' bunk rooms around the forecastle. If they reflected on the day's events at all, the sailors on board *Franklin* may have realized that the dead on their ship outnumbered the living. Corpses, broken and charred, already had begun to fester. Small fires still burned, scorching parts of the ship and worsening the pervasive wreckage that made every passageway a terrifying obstacle course. Virtually every system and service on board was out of commission, even as the crew worked ceaselessly to restore functions, and death still lurked behind every hatch.

Death also lurked in the air. Fire blazed on the ship enough to light up the sky, and Japan's air defenses mobilized to destroy the crippled carrier. In the darkness, attackers swarmed around *Franklin's* position while still adrift. Night fighters took on the intruders and claimed as many as forty kills before dawn. Fireballs and streams of light dropping into the sea were visible to many of CV 13's watch standers. O'Callahan showed little respect for his adversaries:

Why didn't the Japs veer from their course and direct their attack against the *Franklin?* Perhaps because they were Japanese.

American pilots would immediately have recognized that their careful calculations had become useless, and would have brought a little individual initiative into play. . . . When they had last observed the *Franklin,* she had been dead in the water, drifting at a definite rate in a definite direction. They refused to heed even the possibility that the situation might have changed, despite the evidence of their senses and our flaming ship. Perhaps, though, the Japs were giving a direct tribute to the work done by Joe Taylor; they probably thought a blazing hulk the size of the *Franklin* could not possibly get a towline rigged.[3]

Even a decade after the war, when O'Callahan wrote his memoir, his language reflected surprisingly little charity toward his former enemy, despite the fact that one of his sisters-in-law, for whom he expressed great affection, was of Japanese heritage.

By midday on Tuesday, March 20, the carrier was well away from the Japanese mainland but still within range of Japanese aircraft that continued searching for CV 13. Two hours later, Captain Gehres reported that

an unintercepted enemy "Judy" made a fast-glide bombing run from out of the sun on the starboard bow of the *Franklin.* This plane was not taken under fire by the screen on its approach. At about 1500 yards, *Franklin's* forward island forty-millimeter quad mount, in manual operation and local control by a volunteer crew, took the plane under a fast and accurate fire which caused it to pull up and swerve at the dropping point, with the result that its heavy bomb (apparently about 500 pounds) crossed the flight deck barely missing the port deck edge and exploded in the water about two hundred feet off the port quarter.

One of the members of the volunteer gun crew was Captain Gehres' marine orderly, Pvt. Wally Klimkiewicz.

By this time Father Joe was on the flight deck with a burial detail. He later marveled at his lack of reaction during the attack. "I should have crouched to the deck to make myself as small a target as possible. I didn't crouch, but not from bravado or fearlessness. The effort involved in having to climb to my feet again seemed just then to be a greater evil than any number of bullets that might be splashing around. Perhaps one can become sated with danger. I was too tired even to be angry, and yet, subconsciously, I did resent any enemy plane strafing us while we were burying the dead."[4]

Radars on screening ships continued to plot bogeys around *Franklin,* so gunner McKinney and his ordnance specialists slaved to bring other batteries on line, including the forward port 5-inch, .38-caliber turret and a 40-mm quad mount on the bow. McKinney and his men also rigged sound-powered telephones to all these guns.[5]

A task more terrifying than any Japanese bomb would begin on Tuesday. Removing the bodies of *Franklin*'s dead was so difficult and unpleasant that nearly every crewman would gladly have faced explosions and fire instead. Everyone on board the carrier shared the grisly responsibility, and several men helped, but Captain Gehres assigned much of the job to the ship's doctors, medical personnel, and chaplains, as well as to the cooks and stewards, all black or Filipino. The enlisted men did most of the work, and many of them broke under the strain. O'Callahan never shied away:

> Some bodies were easily accessible; most were not. It was like wandering through thick underbrush. Ten feet ahead you could see an object; but ten feet of entanglement lay between, and it would take fifteen minutes to break through. The decks and beams of the *Franklin* were a jungle of steel. . . . It was not unusual to work for a full hour, lifting, pushing, breaking though this wreckage in order to go fifteen feet to reach the body of a dead comrade. These boys had not been crushed to death; they had died in the first great flash of gasoline flame. But after death they had been enmeshed in the debris of the explosions. Our burial services were brief but they were reverent. . . . A body would be extricated from the steel debris, gently lifted onto a stretcher, and carried to the quarterdeck. There Chaplain Gatlin or myself would say a brief prayer; and another of our former shipmates would be buried. . . . As the body is consigned to the immensity of the water, so the soul is consigned to the immensity of a merciful God.[6]

Many of the dead were below decks in confined spaces. Sailors had to carry these bodies in their arms up ladders and through blocked or narrow passageways. Men who had faced violence without blinking shrank in deep disgust from dealing with human remains. Father Joe did not. "Boys don't like to carry burned corpses pickaback up steep ladders. I think that I carried most of the corpses. It has been a source of several nightmares since, perhaps because on one trip I was so exhausted that I fell asleep a moment on the step of the ladder. It is disconcerting to awake and find oneself clasping and facing a burned corpse."[7] Indeed!

Dr. Sherman echoed the horror. "The ship's medical officers put the burial functions on my shoulders. I had to declare them dead, take off their identification, remove, along with the chaplains' help, whatever possessions that hadn't been destroyed on them, and then slide them overboard because we had no way of keeping them. A lot of them were my own Air Group people, pilots and aircrew, and I recognized them even though the bodies were busted up and charred."[8]

Sherman remembered later that removal of *Franklin*'s dead continued for a week. He counted 832 bodies. "That was terrible, really terrible to bury that many people."[9]

By the end of the ordeal, everyone involved was "at the end of his rope," as Chaplain Gatlin said. There would be little rest, however. Captain Gehres believed that idle time would damage the men more than the trauma they had faced and overcome. Salvage crews not assigned to remove the dead with care got rid of wreckage by the ton, dumping trash over the side with no ceremony or reverence at all. Somehow, four jeeps emerged from the carnage unscathed, and sailors put them to use pushing and pulling wreckage off the ship. Technicians continued repairs around the clock to restore the ship's systems. The one suspension of regulations everyone remembered and enjoyed was the distribution of beer, after work details scavenging for useful material found several cases of brew. That night O'Callahan also asked Dr. Fuelling, who readily complied with the request, to dispense his inventory of medicinal whiskey to officers who were not part of the burial party. As the men passed a bottle, Red Morgan refused to take it and turned to Father Joe, "Padre, take the bottle. Hand it to me personally. I want to be able to tell my grandchildren that aboard ship, where Navy Regs forbid it, the Padre passed me a quart of whiskey and offered me a drink." O'Callahan's apparent generosity masked an ulterior motive. He asked the officers to give the enlisted men a break and help him remove a dozen bodies from the galley, then clean it up so the cooks could begin preparing food. Not a single officer refused. They worked throughout the night to put the galley in working order.[10]

Steamboat Graham worked his way below into the magazines, discovering to his horror that they were dry. When he reported his findings to the bridge, Captain Gehres turned "an interesting shade of green and purple," and everyone realized how lucky they and *Franklin* truly had been.

As the ship's communication system came back on line, Captain Gehres received messages from his commanders and colleagues. Vice Admiral Mitscher signaled, "You and your historic crew cannot be too highly applauded for your historic and successful battle to save your gallant ship, in spite of the difficulty, the enormity of which is appreciated. Deep regrets for your losses which we feel as our own."

Rear Admiral Davison added, "Congratulations. I may be on a stranger's doorstep now but I claim you again with pride. Battered though you may be you are still my child. Great work."

Gehres replied to all, "My ship's company and I thank you for your message and for the protection received in our worst hours."[11]

To help restore some semblance of good order and discipline on the carrier, Exec Taylor began issuing plans of the day, using a still functional mimeograph machine in a ship's office. The title of his first issue, dated March 22, read:

Big Ben Bombed, Battered, Bruised and Bent, but Not Broken.

1. All hands wear clean dungarees, blue-dyed hats, black shoes to quarters. Chins up, chests out, tails over the dashboard.

2. Gun crews will wear helmets. All usable gun batteries will be manned.

That same day, as the carrier steamed toward the fleet rendezvous point in Fueling Area Bedbug, *Franklin* sighted Task Force 58 and by afternoon had joined carriers *Wasp* and *Enterprise,* cruiser *Santa Fe,* and several destroyers. On orders from Rear Admiral Davison, still Commander, Task Group 58.2, CV 13 steamed in company with destroyers *Miller, Marshall,* and *Hunt* toward Ulithi at twenty knots.

On March 23 Taylor sent out another plan of the day dealing with minutia and morale:

"A Ship That Won't Be Sunk Can't Be Sunk":

1. Due to our after gasoline system being damaged, smoking regulations must be strictly enforced. You may smoke on the forecastle during the daylight hours. You may smoke in the forward messing compartment between reveille and taps. Officers may smoke in the wardroom. Never throw a lighted butt over the side.

2. Keep busy doing something all the time. If you aren't on a scheduled working party, work anyway. We've got the world by the tail, hang on.

3. Do not throw any usable article over the side. If you think it can be salvaged, stack it neatly on the hangar deck just forward of No. 3 elevator on the starboard side.

4. Anyone knowing the whereabouts of any musical instruments report to the chaplain.

5. Any personal effects such as wallets, watches, etc., shall be turned in to the Executive Officer's cabin.[12]

Captain Gehres later wrote, "The voyage to Ulithi was without incident, this ship operating independently, five miles in advance of the task group."

Franklin's crew boasted several musicians who had brought instruments on board and played in a swing band, belting out popular hits of the day. Father O'Callahan recommended reconstituting the band, under the direction of Musician Horace K. "Saxie" Dowell, a well-known performer in civilian life and composer of several popular tunes, including "Three Little Fishes."[13] The instrument inventory consisted initially of a couple of trumpets, a guitar, a clarinet, and an ocarina. Bandsmen scrounged instruments later from other ships, but they also improvised, using a penny whistle as a flute, a jug as a bass fiddle, and making drums out of galley tubs, cymbals out of pie pans, and drumsticks out of wooden spoons. The ensemble rehearsed to the amusement of some and the consternation of others, playing a variety of familiar tunes, most with new lyrics describing Big Ben's ordeal.[14]

Now far from any threat of Japanese attack, *Franklin* released its destroyer screen just outside the Ulithi anchorage and took her place in column astern of *Wasp* and *Enterprise,* entering the lagoon in formation with no assistance. As the carrier neared her assigned berth, Lt. Cdr. D. L. Johnson, commanding officer of *Miller,* signaled CV 13, "Please permit me to express the unbounded admiration of all hands on board *Miller* for you and your gallant ship. We are proud to have been associated with her." Another destroyer, *Stephen Potter,* part of the carrier's screen on March 19, added, "Our hats are off to you. The Japs can't beat the spirit you have displayed." Captain Gehres answered, reflecting the bond among navy men, "Thank you both for your messages, which have been read to the crew. We think you are stout fellows. Thanks for your protection."

As early as March 23, Father Joe realized that notification of the relatives of *Franklin*'s dead and missing would be an enormous and delicate task. He pre-pared a letter of condolence for the families of all those lost, assuring everyone that the crew shared in their sorrow and that everyone would receive per-sonal letters from him and from Captain Gehres. O'Callahan also listed several sources of consolation:

> Your loved one did not suffer. The attack was so sudden and the result-ing explosions so rapid and intense that there was time only for a short prayer and then death came. There were a very few who were injured and lingered in suffering. In almost every case death came as instantaneously as I have described. . . . There is a further source of consolation—the reverence which enshrouds a military burial at sea, however abbreviated the ceremony might be. In times of great catastrophy [sic], the human soul penetrates directly to the important spiritual essences of things; in times of great catastrophy [sic], reverence does not need the usual orna-ments of ceremony. Had you been here you would have been indelibly impressed with the reverence of those who committed the body of your loved one to the depths of the sea.
>
> . . . Those shipmates of your husband and of your son who did survive the combat, showed heroism beyond belief. Completely aware of the dangers that beset them on every side, dangers from bombs and from fires, dangers of suffocation and capsizing, they set about to accomplish what seemed at the time an impossible task—to save the ship. And they

saved it. Your husbands and your sons were the shipmates of these boys and cast in the same mould. Therefore they shared their common characteristics, therefore they were cast in the same heroic mould.

But for your loved ones there is this further tribute; their heroism was complete, their heroism led them to the supreme sacrifice. They laid down their lives in service of their country. May God reward them and may their souls rest in peace.

In the name of all officers and men I express my heartfelt sympathy.[15]

In light rain on Saturday, March 24, the carrier's crew manned the rails, standing at attention in ranks on the flight deck and singing a parody of "The Old Gray Mare," to the accompaniment of Saxie Dowell's troubadours, as the ship slowed to anchor.[16]

Despite continued drizzle, Chaplain Gatlin led a Sunday Protestant service in an open corner of the hangar deck, still awash with water from the fire hoses. Father O'Callahan celebrated Mass on the forward flight deck.

Reverend Gatlin prayed for the living and the dead: "And since it is of Thy mercy, O gracious Father, that another week is added to our lives, we here dedicate again our souls and our bodies to Thee and Thy service, in a sober, righteous and Godly life; during the week we made new resolutions and in these, do Thou, O merciful God confirm and strengthen us; that as we grow in age we may grow in grace, and in the knowledge of our Lord and Savior Jesus Christ who taught us to pray."

After both services, the entire crew gathered on the flight deck for a military memorial service. Father Joe officiated. "In a beautiful heart-touching talk, the priest recalled to the men that their comrades had died on Saint Joseph's Day—Saint Joseph, the patron saint of a merciful death—that their death, though tragic, had been in merciful circumstances, with every man having a brief moment for a last prayer."[17] A marine honor guard fired three volleys, and the men returned to their cleanup. Pumps from other ships were brought on board and emptied several flooded and inaccessible compartments, including sick bay, where the bodies of Dr. Bill Fox, his seven pharmacist's mates, and eleven patients still lay.

The next evening, an entertainment troupe from the hospital ship *Bountiful* came on board, providing a bit of respite from the unrelenting work, which resumed soon after. Several able-bodied crewmen rescued by other ships on March 19 returned to *Franklin* and began assisting in the salvage operations. Removal of a Tiny Tim rocket from the second deck with help from Ulithi service workers provided significant relief. Since Ulithi had no dry docks or heavy repair equipment, *Franklin* was soon preparing for a voyage to Pearl

Harbor, in company with *Santa Fe* and three destroyers. The ships were under way at sunset on Tuesday, March 27. *Santa Fe*'s log noted, "*Santa Fe* steamed toward Mugai Channel with 'Homeward Bound' pennant streaming aft, dipping in the ship's wake a hundred yards astern. This was the moment all men and officers had been waiting for the last six months. This is to be *Santa Fe*'s first period and her crew's first leave period since commissioning on November 24, 1942. At 1836 passed through Point Able headed eastward."[18]

Big Ben's cruise book summed up the week-long trip back to Pearl. "There was little of laughter or gaiety on the shattered decks as men found surcease from tension and memories in the exhaustion of toil." There was little time for rest, since the tasks of cleanup, salvage, and repair seemed insuperable to the relatively small group of men on board. The skeleton crew that ultimately arrived home included 125 officers and 837 enlisted men out of the carrier's full complement of 144 officers and 2,461 men, not including about 800 in the carrier's air group. Although their number had swelled after arriving in Ulithi, those on board who had kept the ship in operation quickly dubbed themselves the 704 Club, based on an apparent miscount on the first complete muster Captain Gehres had ordered on March 21. *Franklin* crewmen in the club would enjoy special cachet, since they could legitimately claim to have saved their ship and brought it home.

During the voyage to Pearl, Saxie Dowell's kazoo band serenaded the ship's company one afternoon, and other crew members performed magic tricks and other entertainments. Captain Gehres watched the show and addressed the crew, "We are going to take this ship back out and get even with the little yellow scoundrels. I for one am going to be the first volunteer to take her back."[19]

Franklin steamed in company with the ever-faithful *Santa Fe* into Pearl Harbor on April 3, 1945, one month to the day after she had departed. The ship passed through the Fort Kamehameha Channel, past the hospital and administration building, then turned toward a pier. As some, but not all, of the 704 Club stood on the forward flight deck at quarters for entering port, CV 13 moved slowly to its mooring. A glee club of fifty WAVES in khaki uniforms stood on the pier, part of an official welcoming committee, singing the traditional tune of hail and farewell, "Aloha 'Oe." On board *Franklin*, several men, standing at attention in grubby dungarees, wept openly, as did sailors on the pier, including Vice Adm. George Murray, representing the Pacific Fleet commander, Chester Nimitz. As the ship slowly glided nearer, the women in the choir realized CV 13 was torn to shreds and that the few men on deck were the remnant of a full crew, many of whom had died horribly, despite Father O'Callahan's repeated reassurances to the contrary. Their voices faltered then, as Father Joe remembered, "melted away" into awkward silence. Saxie Dowell and his bandsmen knew what to do. They broke into a rendition of their "Old Gray Mare" parody, and the ship's company began to sing, "Oh, the Old Big Ben, she ain't what she used to be, ain't what she used to be, ain't what she used to be. Old Big Ben, she ain't what she used to be, just a few days ago."

On arrival at Pearl Harbor, a message from Admiral Nimitz awaited CV 13. He wrote, "It is evident that the return of the *Franklin* to port required skill and courage of the highest degree on the part of those who participated. The officers and men who returned on the *Franklin* and also the officers and men of the *Santa Fe* who rendered invaluable assistance have set a high standard of seamanship, courage and devotion to duty which will always be an inspiration to the fleet. Well done to all hands."[20]

Another message came directly to Father Joe, who later recalled,

The week before I left to board the *Franklin,* I had sent a letter to my sister Alice in the Philippines. It is a queer sensation writing to one who may be long since dead; but on the chance that she was alive I had written to her through the Red Cross units with the Sixth Army, which had just landed in Luzon. The prisoners of Santo Tomas had been liberated, but La was not there.

Then the Japanese devastation of the old walled City of Manila began. As the daily newspapers headlined the atrocity stories, hope for La's safety waned. . . .

Amidst the bustle of activity which accompanies the mooring of a large ship, I head a voice from the dock hailing, "Father O'Callahan."

It was Father Sheehy, district chaplain at Pearl Harbor. . . . His greeting to me was the climax of a drama: "Hi Joe! I can't wait until the gangway is across. . . . I came down to tell you that yesterday we received definite word that your sister is alive in Manila."[21]

O'Callahan's sister later sent her mother a dramatic account of her rescue on February 23, 1945, the same day marines raised the American flag on Iwo Jima's Mount Suribachi. More than a month before, the Japanese guardians of her camp had apparently reconciled themselves to an eventual American victory in the Philippines. On January 7 the camp commandant announced that his forces would withdraw and leave the American captives in charge of their own camp. After months of privation, Rose Marie and everyone else enjoyed three relatively complete and nourishing meals a day. This luxury lasted a week. The Japanese returned and imposed strict discipline once again. The guards seemed intent on starving the prisoners, depriving them of rations. Several prisoners escaped, but the Japanese caught and executed two men.

American planes overflew the camp nearly every day, bombing and strafing nearby areas. At night, Sister Rose Marie and others could see fires in Manila glowing in the sky. Although help was near, few prisoners expected to survive, and several died waiting for American troops to arrive. Finally, on February 23, during the camp's morning roll call, prisoners watched American paratroopers jump from transport aircraft just a few miles away. Sister Rose Marie went as scheduled to chapel with bullets flying around her. "Soon we could hear American voices outside the walls—'How do you get in here? Where are the Japs?' etc., etc. And, then, through the chapel, followed by a band of guerilllas, came our first American G.I. You will never know how good he looked to us. It was no time for demonstration, but we hailed him with hearts full of gratitude as he passed through and across the road apparently oblivious of flying bullets."[22]

The paratroopers arrived none too soon. The Japanese had apparently planned to line up their prisoners and machine-gun them all. Instead, GIs attacked the guards, who had entrenched on a hilltop near the prisoners' barracks. The Americans acted quickly and efficiently. "Not a single Jap escaped," Sister Rose Marie wrote. "After the battle, heads were counted, and every last guard was dead. It's too bad it had to be so—but they asked for it."[23] Once the prisoners were liberated, army amphibious tractors loaded everyone in camp on board and carried them to safety near Laguna Bay, although Japanese troops sniped at the convoy as it left the camp. For both brother and sister O'Callahan, survival clearly was a close-run thing.

Damage to *Franklin* was so extensive that Pearl Harbor's facilities could not hope to complete repairs. The Navy Department ordered CV 13 to return to the Brooklyn Navy Yard in New York, where shipwrights would promise to rebuild the ship and return her to service in eight months, by the first of 1946. For five days at Pearl, members of the 704 Club went ashore for at-best subdued celebrations. Many of the men remained in shock, still traumatized after the near destruction of their ship, and parties were not in order for them. At dawn on April 9, the carrier cast off her lines and shaped a course east, Diamond Head receding astern. As the ship departed, many workers were skeptical of the ship's chances to make it stateside.

O'Callahan noted, "The voyage from Pearl Harbor to New York by way of the Panama Canal was routine, but not restful. The days were filled with work, the same hard laborious work which cleared the ship of wreckage and the mind of psychosis. The evening hours were spent in pleasant conversation. The days passed in work and talk." Quartermaster John O'Donovan also remembered "a leisurely . . . cruise from Hawaii to the Canal Zone, beautiful weather all the way, sunbathing on the flight deck every day, a completely enjoyable ocean voyage. I feel that this repaired our nerves."

En route to Panama, *Franklin* received word that President Franklin D. Roosevelt had died. With the ship's flag at half-staff, Captain Gehres presided at a memorial service on April 15. Assistant aviation officer Berger reported:

> In a dignified and solemn fashion, Captain Gehres spoke, very briefly, bringing out the point that President Roosevelt was a great friend of the Navy and that we had really lost somebody who had the best interest of the Navy at heart. The manner in which Captain Gehres spoke, the setting of the services which were held up forward in the hangar deck in full view of the number one elevator which had been turned to a very absurd angle as a result of the first explosion on March 19, the solemn and dignified fashion the entire ceremony was carried out, made it most memorable. As a matter of fact to a crew which had only too frequently attended memorial services, this one was particularly memorable.[24]

Franklin entered the canal on April 17. Half the crew took liberty in Panama City, and after a two-day transit the other half went ashore in Colon. Once in the Caribbean and headed for the Windward Passage, the carrier picked up air cover, which was welcome since German submarines still threatened American ships. In fact, a U-boat sank a merchant vessel less than one hundred miles from Big Ben as the carrier closed on Cuba. The ship's cruise book noted, "Men who knew what one torpedo would do to the battered carrier breathed more quickly for several days."

Finally, on the afternoon of April 26, 1945, *Franklin* arrived off Gravesend Bay, Long Island, New York, and dropped anchor. Two days later, the crew wore crisp new dress-blue uniforms as the ship steamed into New York Harbor. The 704 Club stood once again at quarters on the flight deck, saluting the Statue of Liberty as *Franklin* sailed without fanfare past Governor's Island, up the East River, and under the Brooklyn and Manhattan Bridges into the Brooklyn Navy Yard, where CV 13 warped alongside Pier 12. After a 10,525-nautical-mile voyage from the coast of Japan, Big Ben had made it home.[25]

Throughout her wartime service, *Franklin* lost 916 men in combat operations, including pilots and air crewmen who did not return from missions and those killed in other mishaps. Fifty-one men in Air Group 13—pilots, aircrew, and mechanics—on board the ship until it sustained damage in October 1944, died, and fifty-nine members of the ship's company were killed in 1944. Wounded that year totaled about seventy-five. On its second campaign, before March 19, 1945, *Franklin* had lost two enlisted men to noncombat causes and two pilots killed in combat missions. Despite reports of about 725 killed that day, the roster shows 802 men killed or dead of wounds, including members of admirals' staffs of Carrier Divisions 2 and 4, the carrier's marine detachment, Air Group 5, the two marine squadrons, and the ship's company on March 19. Wounded numbered 272. Rosters are the only means to determine who died on *Franklin,* and these also may be inaccurate, since crew changes occurred at sea up to the disaster and administrators may not always have recorded these actions in timely ways. Crewman who disposed of the dead believed they removed as many as 834 bodies, but fire had completely incinerated several, leaving behind nothing but ashes. Explosions had dismembered others, and several more who jumped or fell overboard drowned and were not recovered. During news briefings on May 17, the navy reported 832 dead and 270 wounded, for a total of 1,102 casualties on March 19. In any case, CV 13's losses were among the highest any U.S. Navy ship sustained in World War II.[26]

Those who died, and those who survived, clearly had earned national recognition. Recognition would come quickly.

12

Accolades

"Chaplain Courageous"[1]

As *Franklin* made her long voyage home, no one in the United States was remotely aware of the crew's ordeal. Although local papers across the nation published reports on area killed and wounded, U.S. policy prohibited national publication of casualties during military campaigns. The government wanted to avoid giving any advantage to the enemy from information on the damage inflicted on American forces. The national release of the loss of the five Sullivan brothers and all but ten other members of the crew of the light cruiser *Juneau* during the battle of Guadalcanal shocked the entire country in January 1943. The first news photo of dead GIs, lying in the sand on New Guinea's Buna beach, appeared in *Life* magazine in February 1943. D-day, the Bulge, and Iwo Jima killed thousands of American soldiers, sailors, and marines, but the home front remained insulated from most of the horror. Civilians had little real understanding of the misery war entailed for casualties and survivors alike.

The damage on *Franklin* was hard to miss, but the navy did not publicize the carrier's arrival in New York. Few people would have noticed as CV 13 glided into the navy yard or understood what had happened even if they had seen the ship. Once in port, the men moved into barracks, far more comfortable quarters than anything available on board. Since most crew members were more than ready to enjoy long-overdue liberties in New York and leaves home, Captain Gehres was concerned about security breaches. He distributed a lengthy and sobering memorandum to all hands:

> All officers and men are reminded that there has been no release of any
> information concerning the *Franklin,* so you must not discuss, either

orally or in your correspondence, the manner or extent of the ship's damage or your own experiences on board, and you must not reveal the location of the ship. . . . Until such time as higher authority sees fit to announce publicly the facts concerning the *Franklin* it is incumbent on every one of us to guard our tongues and our pens. And when and if any information concerning the ship is officially released you must not in anyway [*sic*] elaborate on the information thus given, except that you are allowed then to tell your family about your own strictly personal experiences. This however, does not extend to telling any details of the ship's damage or about the number of ships involved, or just where we went or when, or the number of casualties. . . .

In the ports where we have stopped enroute [*sic*] there has been a tendency to lionize the ship and her people. You and I know that we did not have a ship load of great heroes. Probably all of us were pretty well scared at times. In saving the ship we really only did our job and we were saving ourselves as well. Never forget that we did not bring out the *Franklin* by ourselves and other ships and crews deserve as much credit as we do. Had it not been for the really heroic work of the *Santa Fe*, the *Pittsburgh*, and all those destroyers, who helped us, towed us, and guarded us we would never have gotten away. And if it had not been for the other task groups whose guns and planes fought off large groups of enemy aircraft reportedly after us we would never have gotten away. Never forget that we did not go out there to save a damaged ship. We went to damage the enemy and when we became a casualty we upset plans and operations by that much.

Wars are not won by saving damaged ships but by those which are still out there fighting day and night. So when you are allowed to talk about all this, be modest and be humble. That we are alive where so many of our shipmates are not. That we are in the states with a chance to see our families is a great privilege and it behooves every one of us to realize and remember that the rest of the fleet is still out there pitching, winning a hard tough battle without any help from us. . . I remind you about your conduct and appearance ashore. Wear your uniforms properly, salute all officers you meet, and behave yourselves. You represent the Navy and the ship—see that you do both credit. I was proud of your perfect record in Pearl Harbor and Panama and gratified by the compliments I received from authorities in those places on your conduct and appearance. I am sure you will do equally well here and on leave.[2]

As navy yard workers began round-the-clock work on CV 13, cutting entire sections away to enable repairs, Captain Gehres and his officers completed comprehensive reports on the March 19 attack, their recollections of events that followed immediately, careful accountings of casualties, and the performance of the surviving crew members. Fighting continued on Okinawa until early July, and before the atomic bombs fell on Hiroshima and Nagasaki in August, the armed forces were planning to invade the Japanese mainland. Complete documentation and understanding of what happened on *Franklin* was important because the navy could use it to eliminate similar structural and system vulnerabilities and capitalize on, and improve, strengths in the *Essex*-class design, as well as other ships. Counting both the October 1944 and March 1945 attacks, CV 13 may have survived more damage than any other U.S. Navy ship during the war. Engineering experts pored over the ship, while technicians repaired it and issued their own reports. Naval authorities probably subjected *Franklin* to the most minute and exhaustive damage evaluation in modern history up to that time. The review led to several significant design changes for carriers already on the ways and completed after the war.

The navy also planned an awards ceremony on *Franklin* to recognize the crew's remarkable heroism and achievements, despite Captain Gehres' deprecatory memo. In fact, the captain had traveled to Washington and recommended nearly five hundred crewmen, officers and enlisted, for decorations and requested rehabilitation leave for everyone on board. The Navy Department reviewed Gehres' recommendations and approved recognition for 391 of Big Ben's heroes. *Franklin* could claim the most decorated crew in the U.S. Navy's 170-year history. Among the awards presented were 233 letters of commendation with ribbons, 115 Bronze Stars (or gold stars in lieu of second awards), 22 Silver Stars, 19 Navy Crosses, and 2 Medals of Honor.

Navy public relations knew it had a good story on its hands and scheduled the award ceremony for many of the sailors on Thursday, May 17—"one bright spring morning," according to Father O'Callahan. Political and military officials, other dignitaries, and family members attended the event, which garnered national news coverage. The crew that had brought the carrier home assembled on the forward flight deck and listened as officers read each citation for bravery, an extraordinary litany of remarkable individual and collective courage. Because the Medals of Honor still required congressional approval, awards for Lieutenant (junior grade) Gary and Lieutenant Commander O'Callahan, would wait for a later presentation.[3]

Father Joe later wrote:

> The Ceremony of Awards on the *Franklin* was so impressive that I became somewhat saddened, not for myself, but for my mother. I knew how she felt. However greatly her son might be honored at a later date in the White House, the cold fact was that when all the ship was honored, her son's name was not mentioned.

Here Captain Gehres reached his noble best. Unknown to me, he talked a long time to my mother. He told her his version of what I had done for the men of the *Franklin* and for *Franklin*.

Captain Gehres is not a sentimental man; and of this I approve. Nor is he a religious man; and of this I disapprove. But Captain Gehres made my mother very happy when, after recounting my exploits, he concluded: "I am not a religious man, but during the height of combat, while I watched your son, I said aloud then, and I say to you now, 'If Faith can do that for a man, there must be something to it.'"[4]

For those who had risked their lives and survived, now standing in depleted ranks at attention to quarters as each sailor stepped forward to receive his decoration, the ceremony must have triggered profound reflection and deep emotion. Father O'Callahan noted its impact. "The sun must have been very strong in my eyes. I had to blink against it quite often." He added:

I didn't mind being blown up with the ship. For those who believe in God, death is a transition between earth and heaven. Frightened? I don't think I was. But I don't think I was particularly brave. . . .

God knows I am not, as a man, more courageous than others, nor did I in fact perform more deeds of courage than many others. There is no measuring rod for heroism, anyway. But what I did do was done from Faith. I was conscious of my office as a priest and conscious of the tremendous graces that continually sustained me in fulfilling that office. Whatever I did was given to me to do. It was done from Faith, which is a gift.[5]

The priest did not add that for more than a week before the event, from May 6 to May 14, he had been a patient at the Navy Convalescent Hospital in Harriman, New York, suffering from "catarrhal fever." Catarrhal fever strikes cattle and sheep, not humans; Father Joe in fact suffered from catarrh, severe congestion, almost certainly brought on by exhaustion.[6]

After the ceremony at the navy yard, Captain Gehres and about thirty *Franklin* officers and sailors, including Father Joe, visited the navy's New York district public affairs office at 90 Church Street for a press briefing. Nearly every major paper in the country made *Franklin*'s story front-page news the next day. Among the typical headlines, that of the *New York Times* read, "Marines Win Foothold in Naha; Infantry Gains in East Okinawa; Loss of 832 on U.S. Ship Revealed: American Aircraft Carrier Ablaze In the Pacific: Carrier Wrecked by Bombs, Gets Home Despite Big Loss." Tabloid newspapers featured photographs of *Franklin* on fire and, more often than not, a close-up of Father O'Callahan, kneeling in prayer over Bob Blanchard on *Franklin*'s flight deck.

Alvin McCoy's long and detailed first-person account of *Franklin*'s trial ran in many papers. McCoy's story was a comprehensive accounting of events, but the New York press focused more on the personalities involved. When Captain Gehres listed the officers and men who had earned special recognition, reporters quickly latched onto the bespectacled priest from Boston. *Franklin*'s story suddenly became equally Father Joe's story, if not more. The *New York Journal American*'s headline read, "Saga of Stricken Carrier *Franklin*: Chaplain No. 1 Hero: Hail Hero Chaplain." The *New York World-Telegram*'s headline noted, "Dauntless Carrier *Franklin* Being Readied to Fight Again: 'The Bravest Man I Ever Knew:' Tribute by His Skipper Disclaimed by Chaplain Who Couldn't Feel Fear." Captain Gehres' recommendation of O'Callahan for the Medal of Honor, a recommendation nearly every senior officer on *Franklin* instantly endorsed, riveted the entire nation on this unlikely warrior and set off a firestorm of public and media attention.[7]

Congratulatory messages poured in. A letter to O'Callahan's mother from the Father Provincial was typical: "Every Jesuit in the country is walking in the clouds these days because of the heroism of your Jesuit son under fire and because of the great honor it brings on us all. I am sure that in such a happy moment every Jesuit would want me as their Provincial to write you a note of great felicitations to yourself, the mother of such a Jesuit son. Yours is really the honor and the reward." So, too, was a letter from the provincial to O'Callahan himself: "No words of mine will afford the slightest indication of the joy and pride of your fellow Jesuits in the heroic action aboard the *Franklin* at the gates of Japan. No children will read the story in their history books later with more thrill and inspiration than we are reading it fresh from the newspaper dispatches. Your fellow Jesuits salute you with profound affection and esteem. *Ad Majorem Dei Gloriam* [to the greater glory of God]."[8]

Once the extent of *Franklin*'s losses became public, Captain Gehres also sent condolence letters to the families of those missing in action.

> It is with deep sorrow that I write you concerning your son . . . who was reported missing in action on 19 March 1945. I regret to say that a careful review of the known facts has failed to disclose any further information. That part of the ship where he had his battle station, and from which he might have made his way into the sea was thoroughly searched. A number of ships, planes and small boats patrolled the area of the disaster rescuing survivors from the sea, but he was not among the men who were found. . . .

> I fully realize the inadequacy of my words to lighten the burden of grief and anxiety that must be yours at this sad time, but the lack of definite

information requires listing him as missing. I wish I could offer you some encouragement, but unfortunately I feel that there is slight hope for his survival.

Your son's devotion to duty and his splendid service to his country were in keeping with the highest traditions of the Navy. His shipmates will always remember him as a real sailor.[9]

On Memorial Day, May 31, *Franklin's* crew gathered once again, this time in Rockefeller Plaza by a display model of an *Essex*-class aircraft carrier, for another ceremony. Father Joe presided over the event, broadcast over national radio.

The war continued to engorge human fodder, and tired but able-bodied sailors were in demand. Several lucky *Franklin* crewmen began a thirty-day leave in June as new recruits reported on CV 13 to take their places and help with the ship's overhaul. One of these boys was Henry Syrek, whose older brother Frank had died in *Franklin* on March 19. The navy began reassigning many other members of *Franklin's* crew to advanced firefighting and damage-control training.

A final award ceremony took place on June 20 for those not previously honored. By month's end, Captain Gehres had detached from *Franklin* and assumed command of Naval Air Station San Diego. Gehres later retired as a rear admiral and ran unsuccessfully for Congress in 1950. He became a businessman, working into his seventies as the head of a San Diego commercial fishing fleet.

Other officers also transferred and won promotions. Exec Joe Taylor became the commanding officer of Naval Air Station Brunswick, Maine. The air officer, Henry Hale, assumed command of *Franklin* during her stay in the navy yard.

Not surprisingly, shipwrights discovered the remains of one more victim of the March 19 attack as they stripped wrecked components from the ship. Despite the yard's diligence, the repair work, the largest task of its kind in the navy's history, continued until mid-1946, well beyond the original schedule.[10]

Father Joe, too, left the ship to which he had given so much. On June 14, 1945, he detached from CV 13 and reported in Washington, D.C., as chaplain for the navy's Office of Public Information. In this assignment, Commander O'Callahan—promoted to that rank in July—would travel across the country meeting with the families of crew members, promoting the navy's interests, and incidentally raising money for the Jesuits.

The public focus on Father Joe inevitably led to interest from Hollywood and the country's growing media machine. Quentin Reynolds, a well-known writer and editor at *Collier's,* a popular weekly magazine, contacted O'Callahan about an article. The priest referred the writer to his brother Neil, then a businessman in Philadelphia. Reynolds' letter to Neil in early May 1945 reflected efforts to capitalize on Father Joe's new celebrity.

> I was no sooner home last night when Paramount called and said they might be interested in making a picture about the Commander. The Navy has tied this story up until mine is written. Now, when my story is done there is a possibility that Paramount would want to make a film about the Commander. As soon as this gets around other companies will be after the story.
>
> If I may be so bold as to make a suggestion. I would suggest that you appoint yourself the Commander's business agent and manager and when any negotiations arise they must go by you. The Commander doesn't know the ramifications of picture deals perhaps and if there is a chance of making some dough for the family, especially for the sister in Manila, we might as well make these people (assuming that this turns out to be a project financially profitable) pay as much as a tropical bear. If any of them call you why not call me and we will talk it over because that's one business I know like I know the back of my hand.[11]

The first installment of Reynolds' article, entitled "Chaplain Courageous," appeared in *Collier's* on June 23, 1945. *Reader's Digest* and other publications soon reprinted it. Within days, more honors materialized. Springfield, Massachusetts, designated June 24–30 as "Father O'Callahan Week," and the Massachusetts General Assembly invited him to address a joint session.[12]

For the remainder of the summer and fall, O'Callahan was almost constantly on the go. A travel schedule for August and September 1945 directed him to San Diego, Los Angeles, San Francisco, Portland, Oregon, Seattle, Salt Lake City, Denver, Oklahoma City, Tulsa, New Orleans, and Atlanta. He said later the travel and public obligations he undertook—meeting with as many as 100,000 people at dinners, luncheons, receptions, and other social functions, conducting press conference and interviews in nearly every city he visited—were more grueling than combat.[13]

Nevertheless, O'Callahan worked diligently to meet expectations. "I believe you realize that I'm almost shot, and that I realize same. Thus far the publicity has all been favorable—very complimentary," he wrote the Father Provincial on August 7. "But there is the constant dread of misquoting or misinterpretation, as well as the dread awareness of how easy it is to make a major mistake. This mental strain is the hardest to endure. The point of this note is that I want you to keep me informed of adverse press reports, but try to shield me from the unfair ones if you can. I feel like the camel upon whose back someone is about to lay the last straw."[14]

While on his national tour, O'Callahan received disturbing news. The navy had evaluated Captain Gehres' recommendation and planned to downgrade his award from the Medal of Honor to the Navy Cross, the navy's second most prestigious decoration. In fact, the Medal of Honor apparently had never really been in the cards for O'Callahan, although *Franklin's* senior officers had not hesitated to raise the issue in public at every opportunity during the press meetings after the ship's return to New York. These discussions cemented the idea, at least in the minds of the press, that Father Joe would receive the medal, so news to the contrary immediately raised questions. Reporters knew a story when they had one. The circumstances surrounding O'Callahan's recognition were complex, involving navy tradition, the judgment of the navy's senior leadership, politics, religion, and publicity.

In a letter to Massachusetts senator David Walsh, chairman of the Senate Committee on Naval Affairs, Secretary of the Navy James Forrestal explained the award process, noting that Rear Adm. Ralph E. Davison, Captain Gehres' immediate superior as commander of Task Group 58.2, which had included *Franklin* on March 19, had decided almost immediately after receiving Gehres' recommendation to turn down Medals of Honor for both Father Joe and Lieutenant (jg) Gary, and to propose Navy Crosses instead to recognize their heroism. Forrestal added that the task force commander, Vice Adm. Marc Mitscher, had concurred with Davison and had forwarded the amended recommendation to the Pacific Fleet commander in chief, Fleet Adm. Chester Nimitz. Nimitz had established a review board, "consisting of two Rear Admirals, two Navy Captains and a Colonel in the U.S. Marine Corps."

> This Board carefully evaluated the recommendation submitted on behalf of Father O'Callahan and, after a comparison with similar reports of acts of personal heroism, recommended to the Commander in Chief, U.S. Pacific Fleet, that the Navy Cross be awarded in lieu of the Medal of Honor. Admiral Nimitz concurred in the recommendation of this Board and made the award. It is most regrettable that, contrary to the instructions which I have issued relative to publicity concerning recommendations for awards which have not been made, the officers of the *Franklin* were overzealous in recounting the heroic exploit.[15]

The navy clearly believed the system had adequately reviewed O'Callahan's situation and wanted the case closed. Newly promoted Lieutenant Gary had already received a Navy Cross. Forrestal received a brief memorandum on Monday, July 9, 1945, from his naval aide, Capt. E. B. Taylor, noting that Father Joe would be in Washington the following Thursday, when Admiral Nimitz would award him the Navy Cross. Taylor asked Forrestal if he wished to present the medal.

The ceremony never took place. The Massachusetts congressional delegation and the Society of Jesus both understood the potential for favorable publicity the Medal of Honor could bring to the state and the Jesuits, respectively. These interests wanted O'Callahan to receive the medal and apparently suggested that he not accept the Navy Cross. There is no record of O'Callahan taking this action, and it would have been out of character for him to buck the system. It is possible, however, that the navy decided not to push forward, knowing the issue remained unresolved in the public press and among powerful political interests.

In the meantime, politicians and priests alike lobbied heavily for a change in policy. Father Joseph Maxwell, president of Holy Cross, and J. J. McEleney, provincial of the Society of Jesus, were among the prelates who wrote to Senator Walsh and other representatives throughout the autumn urging intervention. A letter dated October 8, 1944, from James Dolan, O'Callahan's Father Provincial since 1944, to Walsh was typical:

> It has come to my attention that the Navy is planning to award the Navy Cross to our Chaplain, Fr. Joseph T. O'Callahan. I wish to call your attention to the fact that such an award will be a public disappointment. No one individual episode of the War, I am inclined to think, called forth such universal admiration for valor and heroism. The Congressional Medal itself was recommended. And the U.S. Navy authorities released all the publicity upon this matter, even upon the recommendation of the Congressional Medal. To do less now, and to merely award the Navy Cross, will be a source of no little disappointment to the American Public and will make them anxious to know why the Navy Department is failing to carry out the recommendation.
>
> I know that it is personally distasteful to Father O'Callahan to have anyone intervene in a matter of this nature. But there is a larger issue involved. I am sure I can count on yourself to investigate the matter, and to make a recommendation that the Congressional Medal be awarded to Father O'Callahan.[16]

Walsh, who clearly mattered to Forrestal and the navy's uniformed leadership, relayed these concerns to the secretary in several notes and letters.

On October 31, entertainment writer, fellow Irish Catholic, and future television variety-show impresario Ed Sullivan mentioned the O'Callahan issue in his "Little Old New York" column in the *New York Daily News,* one of the nation's most widely circulated tabloid newspapers. "No word from the Navy on the Congressional Medal of Honor for Chaplain O'Callahan by former USS *Franklin* skipper Gehres. (Rumor has it that they turned it down.)"[17] Among the column's readers was Secretary Forrestal. The secretary was an astute political operative who had worked briefly as a journalist early in his career. He understood the public portent of even brief mention in Sullivan's column and in a typed memo asked his personal assistant, Eugene S. Duffield, another former newspaperman, to check into the matter: "I notice Ed Sullivan has a paragraph on Father O'Callahan. I wonder if it wouldn't be well to clarify this with him. The reason O'Callahan didn't get the C.M. of H. as I understand it is that such awards are only for persons engaged in actual combat, and obviously a Chaplain is not in that category. You might talk with Admiral Hayler [then senior member of the Navy's Board of Decorations and Medals] about it. I am sure there is no disposition to withhold it from him for any small reason."[18]

Duffield quickly replied in handwriting on Forrestal's note: "There is no explanation except that Adm. Ralph Davison, task group commander, did not think, for reasons unstated, that O'Callahan deserved the Medal of Honor. CinCPac [Commander in Chief, Pacific Fleet, i.e., Admiral Nimitz] agreed and gave him the Navy Cross."[19]

Based on Duffield's assessment, Forrestal realized that the navy's official justification for downgrading O'Callahan's medal, which he would send that same day to Senator Walsh, might not be adequate. He closed his letter to the senator with a promise to investigate the matter.

> In much of the information contained in the published accounts and in the radio reports of this action, there appears to be quite a variance with the official reports submitted by the Commanding Officer of the U.S.S. *Franklin.* I have, therefore, directed that the Commanding Officer institute an investigation relative to the cases of Father O'Callahan and Lieutenant Gary and the publicity which has been released in sending these recommendations. He has been directed to submit to me any additional information of a reliable nature which may have any bearing on the award of the Medal of Honor to these two officers. If sufficient additional substantiating information is received, the case will be reconsidered by the Navy Department Board of Decorations and Medals.

> I am most confident that Fleet Admiral Chester W. Nimitz, in making the awards of the Navy Cross to these officers in accordance with his authority which I have delegated, was most equitable and just in his deliberations and made an award which was appropriate for the official information which he had available.[20]

A week later, House Majority Leader John McCormick, who represented O'Callahan's home in Cambridge, called Forrestal. A transcript of the conversation shows that Forrestal was unwilling to make a final decision on the matter. McCormick asked for any news on the award, and Forrestal replied his only intervention would be to request additional investigation on the circumstances. McCormick emphasized his own unwillingness to lobby directly on the issue, but the message was clear nevertheless.[21]

Forrestal followed up quickly. On November 21 his naval aide, Captain Taylor, requested additional review of the O'Callahan case, as well as a reconsideration of the award for Lieutenant Gary. The navy then called Captain Gehres to Washington to discuss both matters with the navy's Board of Decorations and Medals at month's end.[22]

In Washington, Leslie Gehres, forceful as ever, made a cogent case for O'Callahan and Gary. He argued that all the criteria for the Medal of Honor applied completely to both Father Joe and Lieutenant Gary. Both were actively serving members of the armed forces and had distinguished themselves "conspicuously by gallantry and intrepidity at the risk of their lives life above and beyond the call of duty while engaged in an action against any enemy of the United States." No one was in a better position to assess the deeds of these officers than Gehres, he insisted. He had witnessed them, adding that their actions reflected personal bravery and self-sacrifice that conspicuously distinguished both men, even in the company of the heroes *Franklin*'s crew became on March 19.

The logic of Gehres' advocacy was incontrovertible, his eyewitness testimony unimpeachable. The board took the case under advisement and spent several days considering a final decision. During the review, newspaperman Drew Pearson, in his "Washington Merry-Go-Round" column, added more weight on the side of a favorable decision. Sources involved with the board had obviously discussed the matter with Pearson, who wrote in his column that one reason for downgrading the award was that approval of the medal for Father Joe would obligate the navy also to present it to Captain Gehres. Gehres was a career naval officer, Pearson added, but he was not an Annapolis graduate, and that did not sit well with many admirals. General officers in other services had varied backgrounds, but Naval Academy graduates predominated in the navy's flag ranks. Awarding the Medal of Honor to enlisted men or reserve officers, such as Commander O'Callahan, was one thing, but the navy's leaders apparently recoiled at recognizing a "mustang" like Gehres.[23]

Pearson also claimed another likely reason for this decision was O'Callahan's noncombatant status. No member of the Chaplain Corps in any uniformed service had ever received the Medal of Honor. Although requirements for the medal had changed over the years, by World War II nearly every recipient had conclusively demonstrated extraordinary valor in direct combat, above and beyond the call of duty and at risk to his life, in the face of the enemy.

In the reviewers' judgment, O'Callahan's achievements apparently had not completely fulfilled all these conditions, although Captain Gehres and other *Franklin* officers were adamant about his heroism. Father Joe, in a typically modest comment, later agreed that his actions were "overrated." Captain Gehres had expressed a similar view about his own performance on *Franklin*. He argued that he should not receive the medal, having merely fulfilled the duties of a commanding officer at sea.

Father Joe, wrote Pearson, "has become the only man in history to turn down the Navy Cross. This lesser decoration has been offered to him by the Navy but he has politely declined. The Navy itself gave out the information that he was to receive the Medal of Honor, and he is waiting for them to carry out that public statement."[24]

In the meantime, Father Joe drew a short assignment at the naval training station in Newport, Rhode Island, close enough to Boston to enable frequent visits home. He then reported to the New York Navy Yard in Brooklyn as a "plank owner," a member of the commissioning crew, of the new 45,000-ton *Midway*-class carrier *Franklin D. Roosevelt* (CVB 42). With twice the displacement of the *Essex* carriers, "FDR" earned its designation "CVB," which stood for "aircraft carrier, large." *Roosevelt,* built in the navy yard, entered commissioned service on Navy Day, October 27, 1945, which became Commander O'Callahan's first official day as the ship's chief chaplain. The ship continued to fit out after commissioning and would not put to sea for several months, so Father Joe's duties were routine.

Just before Christmas, the decorations board reported its findings after consulting the officers involved in the original recommendation. Captain Taylor prepared a brief memorandum for Secretary Forrestal:

> As a result of a full investigation and discussions with members of his staff who remained aboard the *Franklin,* Rear Admiral Ralph Davison has now recommended the award of the Medal of Honor to Commander Joseph T. O'Callahan and Lt. Donald A. Gary.
>
> Admiral Nimitz concurs and our Board of Decorations and Medals after due deliberation and consideration recommends the withdrawal of the Navy Cross to these officers and the award of the Medal of Honor in lieu thereof.[25]

Senator Walsh, other members of the Massachusetts congressional delegation, and the Jesuits were elated at the decision. The Jesuits, not known for their acumen in military or government procedures, even proposed holding the presentation ceremony at a Jesuit institution in Washington or Boston. Secretary Forrestal explained that President Truman would be delighted to present the medals at the White House. Clark Clifford, then President Truman's assistant naval aide, confirmed the president's willingness to preside over the ceremony and set the date for late January.[26]

Drew Pearson, always interested in demonstrating his Washington insider status, took a final swipe at the navy in his January 22 column, claiming that another reason for the navy's initial reluctance to honor O'Callahan was that its leaders were not happy with Captain Gehres, who had attempted to court-martial six of *Franklin's* junior officers. Several officers had allowed enlisted men, some shivering in their underwear, to don their own coats in the earliest moments of the carrier's distress on March 19. Some of these men had jumped from *Franklin* because they had no other avenue of escape, and several other sailors, observing officer insignia on the clothing, had followed them into the sea. The navy's chain of command ignored Gehres' hard-line request, apparently chalking up his actions to his "mustang" pedigree, which as we have seen was suspect among the Annapolis-trained flag-officer fraternity.[27]

January 23, 1946, finally brought the long-awaited award presentation in Washington, D.C. Harry S. Truman, president of the United States, officiated at a White House ceremony for four Medal of Honor recipients. Army sergeant John R. McKinney and 1st Lt. Daniel W. Lee Jr., both of Georgia, won their medals for heroism in the Philippines and France, respectively. Navy lieutenant Donald A. Gary and Cdr. Joseph T. O'Callahan, the two *Franklin* heroes, received their awards together. President Truman hung the bright blue ribbons around their necks and greeted their proud families, including O'Callahan's mother, Alice. "One of the pleasantest tasks of a President is to bestow this medal on the men who have earned it at the risk of their lives," Truman said, "with never a thought of selfish interest." Truman had remarked more than once, "I'd rather win the Medal of Honor than be President."[28]

Father O'Callahan's citation read:

> For conspicuous gallantry and intrepidity at the risk of his life above and beyond the call of duty while serving as chaplain on board the U.S.S. *Franklin* when that vessel was fiercely attacked by enemy Japanese aircraft during official operations near Kobe, Japan, on March 19, 1945.
>
> A valiant and forceful leader, calmly braving the perilous barriers of flame and twisted metal to aid his men and his ship, Commander O'Callahan groped his way through smoke-filled corridors to the open flight deck and into the midst of violently exploding bombs, shells, rockets and other armament.
>
> With the ship rocked by incessant explosions, with debris and fragments raining down and fires raging in ever-increasing fury, he ministered to

the wounded and dying, comforting and encouraging men of all faiths; he organized and led fire-fighting crews into the blazing inferno on the flight deck; he directed jettisoning of live ammunition and the flooding of the magazine; he manned a hose to cool hot, armed bombs rolling dangerously on the listing deck, continuing his efforts despite searing, suffocating smoke, which forced men to fall back gasping and imperiled others who replaced them.

Serving with courage, fortitude and deep spiritual strength, Commander O'Callahan inspired the gallant officers and men of the *Franklin* to fight heroically and with profound faith in the face of almost certain death and to return their stricken ship to port.[29]

After the ceremony, Father Joe and his family enjoyed a luncheon that featured cream of tomato soup and roast stuffed turkey with trimming. The entire Jesuit community and his college home celebrated. *The Tomahawk,* the Holy Cross student newspaper, noted, "Probably no single act of fearlessness ever thrilled us here at Holy Cross as much as that of Lt. Comdr. Joseph T. O'Callahan. . . . The Congressional Medal of Honor now rests on the chest of 'that Irishman from Boston.' A country that is quick to recognize, but slow to reward has finally honored the first Jesuit to enter the armed services of the U.S. in this war. In honoring Fr. O'Callahan, Congress is also honoring Holy Cross for it was the same priest who headed the mathematics department here. . . . And it is to this college that we hope he returns."[30]

In February 1946, despite the fact that his award had earned him an accelerated discharge, O'Callahan put to sea once again, as FDR made a shakedown cruise to Brazil. On arrival for a port call in Rio de Janeiro, the priest celebrated Mass at the high altar of Candaleria Cathedral. Father Joe wrote Father Dolan, "While there I organized a big Church Party from the ship and took over one of the principal churches of the city for Mass. From reports it was one of the most impressive events of our officers' call in Brazil. Some 1,200 men marched through the streets & crowded the church for a military Mass."[31] Father Joe left the ship in mid-April just before she joined Eighth Fleet maneuvers off the East Coast, the first large navy training exercise after the war.

The commander accepted another brief assignment, with the Navy Department's Office of Public Relations in Washington, in preparation for his expected discharge, even as he continued to receive invitations to attend ceremonies and events around the country. He expected to work on the Navy Education Program. "There is much work to be done there & it will be much less pleasant than the ship cruise to Cuba [on FDR]. . . . Will stay at Georgetown & still hope to get out in June."[32] O'Callahan was ready to leave the navy, although he mentioned in another letter that he was under "much pressure" to remain in the service.[33] His discharge was delayed, however, for yet another mission at sea. He explained in a brief, handwritten letter dated June 14, 1946, to the Father Provincial: "I had expected to be demobilized tomorrow—June 15, but at last minute was assigned as special chaplain escort [for] the body of the late Pres. Quezon back to the Philippines. I leave Norfolk tomorrow morning, & I don't know finish date. Apart from being a special mission, it is an undreamed of opportunity of seeing my sister."[34]

Manuel Quezon had been the first president of the Commonwealth of the Philippines, elected in 1935. When Japan invaded the islands, he had fled to the United States, escaping just before Gen. Douglas MacArthur. Quezon had suffered from tuberculosis and died in Saranac Lake, New York, in 1944. He had been buried in Arlington National Cemetery, but his family and nation wanted him returned home. The new *Ticonderoga*-class aircraft carrier *Princeton* (CV 37), named for a light carrier lost at Leyte Gulf, drew the assignment to carry Quezon's body to the Philippines.

Just before departing on his new assignment, O'Callahan accepted an invitation to be commencement speaker at Georgetown University in Washington, where he received a doctor of science degree, *honoris causa*. His remarks to the graduating class were direct and reflected his war experience: "Take life seriously," he advised, "which means for your happiness, that you live your life as God would have you lead it."[35]

Father Joe, having completed his military and personal missions, left the ship in Manila in early August, flying home to Boston through Cairo and Rome, with an expected return by the first of September.[36]

At long last, the return to civilian life was at hand. The commander completed his separation paperwork at the Bureau of Personnel and then reported to the Officer Personnel Separation Center in Boston. The navy released him from active duty on November 12, 1946. Although continued service was out of the question, he remained in the inactive Naval Reserve, and the navy administratively promoted him to the grade of captain just before transferring him to the retired list in October 1953.[37]

Joseph O'Callahan had served on active duty in the U.S. Navy's Chaplain Corps for more than six years, advancing from lieutenant (jg) to commander, and ultimately to captain. He had fulfilled a variety of assignments, with sea duty on four aircraft carriers and participation in four combat campaigns. He was awarded the Purple Heart, American Area Medal, World War II Victory Medal, American Defense Medal, Asiatic Pacific Area Medal with one campaign star, the European African Middle Eastern Area Medal with three campaign stars, and the Congressional Medal of Honor—one of 464 awarded in all services, and just fifty-seven in the navy, during World War II.[38]

As for the ship on which he earned most of these military decorations, *Franklin* never returned to active service. Naval budget reductions in 1946 kept CV 13 from joining the Fourth Fleet as planned. She transferred instead to the inactive Sixteenth Fleet. As part of Operation Zipper, the carrier completed extensive preservation at the Navy Yard Annex in Bayonne, New Jersey, once the superintendent of the Brooklyn Navy Yard, Lt. Cdr. J. M. McMullen, declared her repaired and ready for duty. In November 1946 a skeleton crew of seventy men and six officers buttoned up Big Ben and left her moored with the "mothball fleet" in Bayonne. The navy decommissioned *Franklin* in February 1947, and the carrier remained at rest for years in the Hudson River, its empty hull a quiet haven for the ghosts of glory and violence.[39]

13

The Room in Fenwick Hall

"The Hidden Hermit of Pain"[1]

Father Joe did not intend at first to return to Holy Cross and teaching. He wanted instead to follow another Jesuit tradition, mission work. "Father O'Callahan planned to spend the remainder of his life working for the Japanese missions, and the missions of the Caroline Islands. His religious superiors readily cooperated with his wishes. But his yearnings far surpassed his strength."[2]

"I first saw Joe after the war at a Jesuit retreat," his colleague Father Nelligan would recall. "He was an emotional wreck, completely nervous and exhausted."[3] Father Dowling wrote, "What effect Father O'Callahan's traumatic experience aboard the *Franklin* had on his physical and mental well-being must now remain a medical mystery. Suffice it to say that never again in life would he enjoy adequate health to carry out professional duties."[4]

In fact, there was little if any mystery about O'Callahan's condition. He and many of his *Franklin* shipmates suffered from post-traumatic stress disorder, known in World War II as "combat fatigue" and in World War I as "shell shock." His ailment was neither trivial nor transitory, and available medical treatment was rudimentary. Father Harkins understood that O'Callahan's force of character had enabled him to cope with the stress of navy responsibilities and the exponentially more difficult stresses of combat. "He was a man who was dedicated to God and to his vocation. That caused him to be heroic, not natural instinct. There may be some who are naturally heroic, but he wasn't." Father Harrington added, "The Navy used him, and he got worn out."[5]

Father Joe was much like any other frontline veteran. He had difficulty adjusting to civilian life. With no pressing travel schedule or other duties, the priest truly could relax for the first time in years, but he also had no further need to put up a front in response to his sense of the navy's expectations. Just as importantly, O'Callahan had time to reflect on what had happened to him and others. The continuous activity his wartime celebrity had generated disappeared, and the priest began to deal with his experiences. Repression no longer was a haven. Compounding Father Joe's condition was his untreated hypertension, the same illness that had killed his father in 1920. Heavy smoking also did not help. O'Callahan smoked unfiltered Camels, and his doctors actually encouraged him, believing the habit helped control hypertension.[6]

O'Callahan's situation may have dashed his hopes for a future overseas, but Holy Cross was happy to have him back. He soon returned to teaching, despite the psychological difficulties that plagued him. Father Harrington remembered, "It was really amazing to me that after the war when he got the Congressional Medal of Honor that he took up teaching without trouble, one hundred percent, teaching the branches of philosophy—logic, epistemology and cosmology—even though I'm sure he had read none of it in the Navy."[7]

He asked the college administration to put his Medal of Honor in a safe, and he did nothing to promote his past. "He was not at all vociferous about politics and current events," Harkins added, "He joked about the Navy, but he also had a great pride in the Navy."[8]

"His room was always open," Father Harrington said. "He still loved to argue, and a group would barge in and talk and debate with him. We had a lot of fun. He never brought up any incidents of the war. I never heard anything mentioned about the *Franklin* or the war at all."[9]

In addition to his teaching, Father Joe reserved enthusiasm for sports and for his family. "Joe was a big fan of the Boston Red Sox, as was Father Crosby, another faculty member. Crosby loved shortstop Johnny Pesky, a native of his home town, Lynn, Massachusetts, and the priests attended several games," said Father Harrington.[10]

"He was fun, he liked to talk to you," said Maureen Madell. "He was precise and careful, and he expected the same from his nieces and nephews. After the war, people stopped to talk to him a good deal. In 1948, when I was twelve, he took us to New York City. He went to see Joe Louis fight—he loved sports— and I argued that boxing was a terrible sport. We also had a carriage ride in Central Park."[11]

Unfortunately, this peaceful routine did not last long. As Father Dowling noted, "his anguished body refused to cooperate. In December 1949, he suffered his first stroke. . . . [T]he acclaim of the Medal of Honor would yield to the silent suffering of Gethsemane."[12]

"It was a terrible stroke," Maureen Madell remembered. "He valued the mind the most—that was the most important thing. He had a very disciplined mind, and the stroke was horrible for him."[13] "Yet the same unflagging spirit which merited him the Medal of Honor aboard the *Franklin* now flared anew—and even stronger," Father Dowling wrote. "His first stroke had left his right arm paralyzed. Hour after hour, day after day, he exercised that weak member, to restore it to efficient usefulness."[14]

O'Callahan, however, never fully recovered. The stroke left him debilitated and in great pain. He also had difficulty speaking clearly. Father Joe's physicians suggested corrective surgery. Another priest at Holy Cross had tried the procedure, known as a sympathectomy, with some success. The surgery destroys nerves in the sympathetic nervous system, cutting or destroying ganglia along the thoracic or lumbar spinal cord, and can increase blood flow and reduce pain from certain diseases that cause narrowed blood vessels, including hypertension and strokes.[15]

Unfortunately for O'Callahan, the sympathectomy, performed in 1950, failed. It did not help control his blood pressure and may have caused even more pain. Moving around, even for short distances, was a trial. He used the elevator to get from his room on Fenwick Hall's third floor, and he walked very slowly. After shuffling along for a hundred yards or so, he had to sit and rest. While he recuperated from surgery at the family home in Cambridge, Father Joe received a personal note from President Truman in May. Secretary of Labor Maurice J. Tobin had asked the president to write, having received a request from Henry Smith, business manager of the Boston School Committee. Nearly a year later, while visiting friends at the Naval Air Station in Miami, O'Callahan dutifully responded to Truman and asked to visit him at the Little White House in Key West. The president's secretary, William D. Hassett, replied immediately, politely but firmly turning down Father Joe's request.[16]

Father Joe found it impossible to continue in the classroom; teaching strained him both physically and intellectually. The stress was evident. He had left the navy at age forty-one with dark, wavy hair and a youthful, ready smile. After his stroke, his hair turned gray, and he cropped it closely around a face creased and furrowed with pain. "I knew how deeply his whole being was affected. He repeatedly asked his doctor to let him get back to his students, but it was too much for him," said Father Harkins. "One thing he did, he started the 'Dante Academy.' Five or six students and faculty members would come to his room in Fenwick Hall and read and study *The Divine Comedy*. That made him very happy."[17]

He also enjoyed coffee, serving it black. Father Harkins preferred his coffee light, but O'Callahan remonstrated. "He said, 'Why don't you take it straight like the Navy? That way you get the real flavor of coffee,'" Harkins recalled, adding, "It took me three years to get used to it."[18]

All of O'Callahan's colleagues at the time agree that he faced his difficulties with admirable courage and patience. He did not complain, and he seemed outwardly to be the same friendly man he had been before his illness. "He stayed for the most part in his room," Father Harrington recalled. "He had no radio or television in his room. There was a TV in the Hall's common room, but he spent no time there. Instead, he passed the time reading newspapers and other things."[19]

Maureen Madell also knew how important reading was to her uncle. "My husband was working on his thesis in nuclear physics, and Father Joe asked to read it," she said. "He said, 'I don't read easy stuff. If I let myself go and read *Time, Life* or novels, I'll lose my grip.'"[20]

Father Joe was not, however, completely disciplined. He drank immoderately to help deal with his constant pain and enjoyed it, although his friends and relatives agreed that they never saw him out of control. The combination of slurred speech and his staggering walk, however, often gave people who did not know him well the impression that he was drunk. He also tried to visit his family. "I drove him to his sister's house in Cambridge," Father Harrington said. "He was able to get out in the beginning, but was confined more and more as time passed. His brother Neil also visited him from Philadelphia."[21]

There were other small diversions. In the spring of 1950 he received a brief letter from his former commander in chief:

> I am distressed to learn of your continued illness and wish it were in my power to say a word of comfort to you. I can only hope that you will find great satisfaction in the consciousness of the selfless and patriotic service as a chaplain which you rendered in the War—a service which brought you the highest honor within the gift of a grateful nation. And may God bless you.
>
> Very Sincerely Yours,
> Harry Truman.[22]

Other letters involved much less worldly but equally significant events, as far as O'Callahan was concerned. An example is this note to his nephew, Kevin O'Brien:

> Dear Kevin:
>
> As your mother can tell you, her father (and mine) was most severe about studying. The men I had in class thought I was severe, but compared to

my father, I was gentle. However, I am sure that even he would be satisfied with your report card for the first term at Boston College High.

Congratulations,

Uncle Joe.[23]

Father Joe also enjoyed card games. He played cribbage and acey-deucey
with his friends. Father Harkins recalled, "Once I was sitting with him, and
he became very agitated and said, 'Fire! There's fire!' I calmed him down and
walked down the hall. There was a clothes hamper on fire. Someone had
thrown a cigarette in it, so I put the fire out. He sensed that, I guess, from his
experience on the *Franklin*."[24]

Fire haunted O'Callahan. One of his caregivers recalled:

The one and only time that I ever saw Father betray emotion was on the
occasion of having a small tumor removed from his forehead. A local
anesthetic was injected and the surgeon began to cauterize. Instantly,
Father's pulse changed, a great pallor came over his face, beads of cold
perspiration stood out, tears trickled down his cheeks. With a husky
voice he asked the surgeon to please stop, adding, 'The stench of burning
flesh is more than I can bear; it brings back such horrible memories. Can
you not use a knife?' A moment of reverent silence and inactivity passed.
Then a "considerate" surgeon picked up his scalpel. Meanwhile, Father's
composure returned.[25]

In September 1954 several navy visitors came to Worcester and the Holy
Cross campus to visit Father Joe and present him a copy of a thirty-minute film
about *Franklin*'s ordeal, using images navy cameramen had shot on the scene.
O'Callahan sat during the ceremony, a cane by his side, and reminisced about
his own experiences to the audience, typically focusing on the actions of others
rather than his own. The ceremony brought a special pleasure. Captains Steven
Jurika and Kirk Smith, O'Callahan's *Franklin* shipmates, attended and renewed
their friendship with the carrier's chaplain.[26]

Another navy honor came several weeks later, during a college football
game. Father Joe made his way down the hill to the stadium. Hundreds of
Reserve Officers' Training Corps students, all in uniform, were there waiting
for him. An admiral, a guest of the ROTC program, also had attended the
game to see the Holy Cross Medal of Honor recipient. "Uncle Joe started up
the stairs," Jay O'Callahan recalled. "The admiral stood up, and all the ROTC
students rose silently. It was a most moving moment. Father Joe was completely unaware of what was happening. The admiral and everyone else were
saluting, and Father Joe was unaware of it."[27]

In the mid-1950s, sufficient time had passed for Father O'Callahan to consider telling his own story. Early interest from Hollywood had waned, but several publishers were enthusiastic about a book. With help from his younger brother Edward and Father Frank Shea—"Father Joe's ghost writer," according to Father Nelligan—the priest completed the prosaically titled *I Was Chaplain on the Franklin*. Edward submitted the manuscript to the Jesuits and the navy for review and censorship, and Macmillan published the memoir in 1956, to moderate and brief success. The book, highly selective and constrained, nevertheless provided several important insights into O'Callahan's character.

Written after his stroke, the narrative focused only on Father Joe's military service, as if the wartime episodes in his life constituted a chapter he considered complete and closed. There was no mention of his life after the war or any other personal issues, including his family, except when they were material to the story he wanted to share.[28]

As part of its publicity campaign, Macmillan provided comments from one of O'Callahan's friends:

> His room is a favorite spot for anyone on the faculty with a class period free and a yen for good conversation. For the room is almost always filled with talk—challenging, allusive, humorous, informed, sometimes profound. Anyone with the stamina to abide by his convictions and the grace to laugh at himself would find it a delight. Should he command the luxury of any ability to make phrases he would find himself a prized visitor, in fact his genius will probably be noted, dated and bylined in a book for that purpose.[29]

Also in 1956, Columbia Pictures issued a low-budget motion picture entitled *Battle Stations*, loosely based on O'Callahan's story. Actor John Lund played Father Joe McIntyre, chaplain of an *Essex*-class aircraft carrier, in conflict with the carrier's strict and tough captain, played by Richard Boone. Other notable actors in the film were William Bendix and Keefe Brasselle. The film, however, was anything but notable, just one more release from the Hollywood movie factory.[30]

As the years rolled on, Father Joe was less and less able to leave the confines of his room in Fenwick Hall, but he continued to visit his family despite the great effort that required. Maureen Madell remembered a visit to Boston in 1958: "We met him in the Ritz-Carlton Hotel, and we all went to dinner. Father Joe wasn't drinking, but it was very hard for him to walk because he was in such pain," she said. "He suddenly had a change in blood pressure, and his color changed. He got sick and stood up to go to the men's room. He staggered in the dining room, and a woman sitting nearby said, 'Look at that drunken priest! Do you know who that is?' I know he was greatly upset by that comment."[31]

Father Dowling later summed up Father Joe's suffering:

> Truly, the glamour hero of acclaim was now the hidden hermit of pain. Patient, he was, but his was the perceptive patience of Job, "the Lord hath given, the Lord hath taken away." Come glory, come torture, all was God's will. Yet never was he bitter. Few humans could realize more vividly, "man's humanity to man" in the awful Armageddon that is modern warfare. Still, each summer he prepared meticulously for fall classes, trusting and hoping that by September he would be strong enough to return to the classroom. . . . Perhaps his deepest source of strength was his daily Mass. He had received ecclesiastical permission to offer his Mass sitting down. Some days, he literally dragged himself to the altar to share with Christ the infinite sacrifice of love.[32]

The final chapters of Father Joe's life had been written. Soon the book would close.

14

Requiem Aeternam Dona Ei

Misere mei, Deus, secundum magnum misericordiam tuam.[1]

For more than a decade, Father Joseph O'Callahan had endured unspeakable pain. His body, already weak, was wearing out. "My sense is that he would have been glad to go, by listening to my father and his other brothers," Jay O'Callahan said. "I think he knew toward the end. His mind was slipping, even though he only was in his mid-fifties."[2]

Several friends and relatives noted that Father Joe stopped drinking altogether in the early 1960s, perhaps to try to minimize his diminishing intellectual acuity. Father Dowling noted, "Then came a deceptive plateau of peace. During the last year of his life, his health and spirits seemed to improve. His ready grin was often in evidence."[3]

Father Harrington recalled, "He was always tense because of the pain, and wearing down over the years, but he never showed any awareness of nearing death. He remained just the same. Joe never made demands on you as a sick person might. He took things with a smile and never whined. He was a regular guy, who held on to his enthusiasm for work. He was always interested in others. It was always you, not him. Joe made a great impression on everyone who came in contact with him. He knew what he had done, and what he was doing, and never boasted about it. It was a gradual thing, wearing down."[4]

"As he declined, Father Joe often went to Saint Vincent's Hospital for treatment," Father Nelligan said. "While there, Sister Elizabeth Mary, a member of the nursing order, the Sisters of Providence, took Joe under her care. He called her Sister Liz, and she became part of his family. I think it is fair to say that they truly loved and respected each other and were mutually dependent. She considered herself his muse. She was one of his main care givers right up until the end. I am sure everyone at Holy Cross and in Joe's family recognized and appreciated what she did for him."[5]

O'Callahan inscribed a copy of his book, its original sale price $2.75, for Sister Liz, the single sentence conveying both the oddly entwined formal constraint and open humor of his character: "To Sr. Elizabeth Mary, S.P., With much gratitude for bearing up under the peskiness of an author-patient. In Xto [*Christo*], Father Joe. God bless you."[6]

Tuesday, March 17, 1964, was Saint Patrick's Day. Father Joe offered his morning Mass with a colleague, Father Frank Hart. O'Callahan was looking forward to the day, the nineteenth anniversary of the general absolution he had offered on *Franklin* before the ship entered combat. At breakfast after Mass, however, he suffered another stroke. His friends had the priest taken to Saint Vincent's Hospital as quickly as possible, and the college summoned his family. "His mind remained very clear; his wit was never sharper. He was in God's hands," Father Dowling wrote. "Even if this were to be his last battle, let God's holy will be done. As ever in his life, he was prepared."[7]

Father Joe passed a restless night but seemed better in the morning. Suddenly, however, on the afternoon of March 18, a massive stroke spelled his end.

"When he was dying, the doctors came to my Dad and asked about another operation," Maureen Madell remembered. "But Dad said no—we don't want to leave him more debilitated, so don't do any more surgery. Then Father Joe died. It was very hard on my Dad."[8]

O'Callahan's family gathered and remained with him until 10:30 that night. "He was conscious to the last moment. He raised his hand, blessed his family and all present. He thanked everyone, then joyously asked, 'Why is everyone so solemn? This is a great day for me.'"[9] Within five minutes he had suffered a convulsion. Several priests, Sister Liz, and another nurse and his doctor stood at Father Joe's bedside when he died moments later. The diagnosed cause of death was a ruptured aortic abdominal aneurysm.[10]

"Joe wore the medal of the Sacred Heart around his neck until his death," Father Nelligan said. "Sister Liz took his medal and wore it until she died in 1985, when it was returned to Holy Cross."

Massachusetts, the state's Irish community, Holy Cross, and the Jesuits, not to mention the U.S. Navy, all regarded Father Joe as a national hero, and each claimed him as its own. Dozens of condolence messages arrived at Holy Cross from naval officers, colleagues (including Richard Cardinal Cushing of Boston), and friends.

His funeral on Saturday, March 21, 1964, combined the rituals of the institutions O'Callahan had served. The bishop of Worcester presided at the Solemn High Mass in the Holy Cross Chapel. The bishop of Springfield, Massachusetts, represented the Military Ordinate, and the archbishop of Boston attended, as did several monsignors and more than a hundred priests, as well as Rear Adm. David F. White, CHC, USN (Ret.), the former Chief of Chaplains. Six sailors and marines in full dress uniform served as pallbearers. Hundreds of navy and government representatives were there, as were many *Franklin* shipmates, to pay last respects. Father Raymond Swords, president of Holy Cross, spoke at the service:

> It is not traditional to deliver a eulogy at the funeral of a Jesuit—and Father O'Callahan would be the last to wish the tradition broken. However, he belongs not to the Jesuits alone, but to the entire nation. . . . In the hour of our country's deepest crisis he gave to her the full measure of his own devotion and won her signal gratitude in the highest award which a grateful nation could bestow. . . . We honor him today as a loyal man of God, a truly humble and pious man, of deep simplicity and faith, whose habit of courage was the serving out of an inner strength which flowed from his allegiance to his Supreme Commander-in-Chief. . . . May his noble soul rest in peace."[11]

Father Joe had asked Holy Cross not to display his Medal of Honor until he was gone. The college complied, placing the decoration on his casket beside the crucifix he had received when he took his vows as a Jesuit.

When the Mass ended, the naval honor guard led a short procession from the chapel to the small burial ground reserved for Jesuit luminaries. After a brief graveside service, marines fired three volleys in salute and a bugler sounded "Taps." The service concluded with the presentation of the American flag that had covered Father Joe's casket to his mother, sitting by the grave in a wheelchair. Alice O'Callahan, ninety years old and living in a nearby nursing home, broke down, weeping quietly. She had outlived one of her children, the last fate any parent could wish.[12]

The great adventure had ended. Over Father Joe's grave the Jesuits placed a simple white headstone, slightly larger than the rest. Its Latin inscription lists the essential details of his life—his name, date of birth, entry into the Jesuits, and his death. There is more, however, to reflect the immense human pride of his nation and his Jesuits in a man so brave and so frail:

Hero, USS *Franklin*
19 Mar. 1945
First Naval Chaplain Awarded
Medal of Honor.[13]
Requiescat in pacem![14]

15

Postscript

"He was a leader."[1]

Big Ben and Father Joe had faded from public memory even before the priest's death in 1964. The advent of pervasive media, riveting short-term attention and exaggerated focus on successive global catastrophes, blinded most people to the significance of past events. World War II had brought such enormous change that people found it impossible to keep even the most profound and touching occurrences in proper perspective. *Franklin's* story was just another minor chapter in the century's greatest tragedy.

There were small exceptions to the neglect. On July 13, 1968, Father Joe's beloved sister "La," Sister Rose Marie, became the first nun ever to sponsor a warship. The navy commissioned its tenth and last *Garcia*-class destroyer escort, USS *O'Callahan* (DE 1051), at the Boston Naval Shipyard. Sister Rose Marie also had christened the ship at its launching in the Defoe Shipbuilding Company's yards at Bay City, Michigan, in 1965. *O'Callahan* was based in San Diego and cruised on eight deployments in the western Pacific and Indian Ocean in the U.S. Seventh Fleet, including combat missions during the Vietnam War. Redesignated a frigate in 1975, the ship displaced 3,500 tons with a crew of 16 officers and 231 enlisted men.[2]

In April 1969 NBC aired an hour-long documentary on *Franklin* and her crew entitled "The Ship That Wouldn't Die." Actor and dancer Gene Kelly, who had served as a navy public information officer in World War II, was the show's host and narrator. The navy had sold CV 13, originally costing $57 million in 1944, for scrap to Portsmouth Salvage Company in Chesapeake, Virginia, for $228,000 in July 1966. A towing company moved the old carrier from its berth in Bayonne, New Jersey, to the company's yard in Mill Dam Creek, Virginia, where camera crews filmed the demolition work that stripped *Franklin*'s structures to provide material for Japanese steel mills.

Early in the process, the show's producer invited about a dozen members of *Franklin*'s crew to visit their ship one last time. Retired rear admiral Leslie Gehres was there, as were Don Gary, Bob Blanchard, Bob Wassman, James Turner, Gilbert Abbott, Steve Nowak, John Kennedy, Fred Masters, and others. Each crewman recounted his own experience on the ship in vignettes that conveyed genuinely deep feelings that resonated with everyone watching the program.

Gene Kelly read from an intelligent script that accurately reflected the crew's achievement. As the camera swept the ship's weathered flight deck, Kelly said, "Here men fought and freely offered their lives, not to destroy an enemy, but to save their shipmates." As the show ended, Kelly concluded, "The ship is dead, but the heritage of the *Franklin* lives on. Dean Kincaide, one of the ship's company, remembers, 'In that terrible time, we were transformed into a living whole, utterly without bias, color consciousness, creed. In my lifetime, nothing will compare to those hours when everybody was his brother's keeper.'"[3]

A few small pieces of *Franklin*—the ship's bell, photographs, and other mementoes—may still be found in museums, tiny fractions of the navy's World War II legacy, itself a fading remnant of a seemingly endless battle fleet that once stretched across the oceans and ensured the safety of continents.

The men of *Franklin* returned home, raised families, pursued careers in the navy and many other fields—and in time they began to grow old and die, an infinitesimal segment of the more than 16 million World War II veterans now passing away at the rate of more than a thousand each day. Leslie Gehres died in 1975. Don Gary passed in 1977. The active roster of *Franklin* crewmen who still proudly maintain an active alumni organization that sponsors reunions and supports museum exhibits shrinks every year.[4]

The navy, Holy Cross, and Worcester, Massachusetts, have regularly commemorated Father O'Callahan's achievements over the years, especially on anniversaries of the *Franklin* disaster. Articles in newspapers and magazines rarely evoke lasting interest, however.[5]

Father Joe's Medal of Honor eventually went on display in the Dinand Library, and then joined other O'Callahan materials in the library's special-collections archive. There it remained in the 1990s, in a plain blue box with a typed label, "Commander Joseph T. O'Callahan, Chaplain Corps, U.S.N.R." The medal, still attached to a wrinkled blue ribbon, is inscribed "Lt. Comdr. Joseph Timothy O'Callahan (CHC) U.S. Naval Reserve."

Father Joe's immediate family also passed into history. His mother Alice, who attended her son's funeral, died in 1967, aged ninety-three. His oldest brother John passed away in 1972, followed over the next several years by Neil, Rose, and Edward, who died in 1988. After John's death, Ann returned to Canada, living with her younger sister Rosemary in British Columbia until her death in 1987. Sister Rose Marie, the Maryknoll nun who endured years of captivity in a Japanese internment camp and spent decades as a Catholic missionary, died in 2004 at the order's New York retirement facility. She was ninety-seven years old.[6]

The mystic chords of memory are fragile indeed but somehow remain miraculously unbroken. Father Joe's example still serves those who struggle to balance institutional and individual expectations and values. His nephew, Jay O'Callahan, summed up his life and character: "He was a leader. He taught us that you just deal with things, deal with them at the moment, and strive for the best, even when you have to take great risks. He was a fine man and wonderful example for all of us."[7]

So he was—and is—for everyone who knows in his deepest fiber that our real purpose on this earth, the true meaning all of us may derive from our unique human lives, is to strive for decency, tolerance, and kindness.

On Big Ben and throughout his life, Father Joe showed us that our true role is to fill our lifetimes with those hours when everybody *is* his brother's keeper.

Notes

Introduction

1. Translation: "As it was in the beginning, is now, and ever shall be, world without end. Amen." "Latin Mass: Ordinary of the Mass, 1962 edition of the Tridentine Ordo, Mass of the Catechumens," *Internet Sacred Text Archive,* http://www.sacred-texts.com/chr/lmass/ord.html (accessed December 18, 2005).

2. Harrison E. Salisbury, *Black Night, White Snow: Russia's Revolutions 1905–1917* (Garden City, N.Y.: Doubleday, 1978), pp. 116–28.

3. Robert K. Massie, *Castles of Steel: Britain, Germany and the Winning of the Great War at Sea* (New York: Random House, 2003), p. 122.

4. Fred Howard, *Wilbur and Orville: A Biography of the Wright Brothers* (New York: Alfred A. Knopf, 1987), pp. 133–40.

5. Massie, *passim*; "Conference on the Limitation of Armament, Washington, November 12, 1921–February 6, 1922," Treaty Series no. 671, *Papers Relating to the Foreign Relations of the United States: 1922*, vol. 1, pp. 247–66.

6. "The 20th Century: 1905–1907," *Timelines of History,* http://timelines.ws/20thcent/1905_1907.html (accessed December 18, 2005).

7. *Boston Family History.com: The Place to Meet Your Past,* http://www.bostonfamilyhistory.com/ir_main.html (accessed August 2, 2003).

8. Ibid.

9. Walter Muir Whitehill and Lawrence W. Kennedy, *Boston: A Topographical History,* 3rd. ed., enlarged (Cambridge, Mass.: Belknap Press of Harvard University Press, 2000), pp. 1–141.

10. Oscar Handlin, *Boston's Immigrants 1790–1880: A Study in Acculturation* (Cambridge, Mass.: Belknap Press of Harvard University Press, 1991), p. 25.

11. Thomas H. O'Connor, *The Boston Irish: A Political History* (Boston: Northeastern University Press, 1995), p. 59.

12. *Boston Family History.com;* Betty G. Farrell, *Elite Families: Class and Power in Nineteenth-Century Boston* (Albany: State University of New York Press, 1993), p. 71.

13. "Boston," *Ask.com,* http://www.spartacus.schoolnet.co.uk/USAboston.htm (accessed August 2, 2003).

14. Handlin, *Boston's Immigrants 1790–1880,* p. 37.

15. Farrell, *Elite Families,* p. 21.

16. O'Connor, *Boston Irish,* p. 69.

17. Peter K. Eisinger, *The Politics of Displacement: Racial and Ethnic Transition in Three American Cities* (New York: Academic, 1980, p. 41; reprinted *Political Science Quarterly* 93 [Summer 1978]), pp. 217–39.

18. *Boston Family History.com* (accessed August 3, 2003).

Chapter 1. Prologue

1. The characters depicted here, Shin and Fu, also translate from Japanese as *kami* and *kaze,* "divine wind." The phrase derives from the late thirteenth century, when a typhoon destroyed much of a 3,500-ship Sino-Mongol fleet, carrying more than 100,000 warriors, bent on invading Japan, then wracked by civil war and unable to resist. The storm stopped the assault, and China never again attempted an invasion of the home islands. From Bernard Millot, *Divine Thunder: The Life and Death of the Kamikazes* (New York: Bair McCall, 1970), p. 42.

2. Ikuhiko Hata and Yasuho Izawa, *Japanese Naval Aces and Fighter Units in World War II* (Annapolis, Md.: Naval Institute Press, 1989), pp. 74–75; Rikihei Inoguchi and Tadashi Nakajima, *The Divine Wind* (Annapolis, Md.: Naval Institute Press, 1958), pp. 137–39; Rene J. Francillon, *Japanese Aircraft of the Pacific War* (Annapolis, Md.: Naval Institute Press, 1990), pp. 454–61; "Yokosuka D4Y Suisei 'Judy,'" *D4Y Suisei Multimedia,* http://214th.com/ ww2/japan/d4y/index.htm (accessed December 19, 2004).

3. Kazuhiko Oshio, ed., *Kamikaze: Imperial Japanese Naval Air Force Suicide Attack Units, No. 458* (Tokyo: Model Art, 1995), *passim.*

4. Ian Gow, *Okinawa 1945: Gateway to Japan* (Garden City, N.Y.: Doubleday, 1985), pp. 2–22.

5. A. A. Hoehling, *The* Franklin *Comes Home* (New York: Hawthorne Books, 1974), p. xi; Roger Chesneau, *Aircraft Carriers of the World, 1914 to the Present: An Illustrated Encyclopedia* (Annapolis, Md.: Naval Institute Press, 1995), pp. 198–253. Hoehling incorrectly claims that 113 new U.S. carriers were commissioned before the war's end. He confuses production starts (i.e.,

keels laid down) with commissionings (ships' official commencement of naval service).

6. Ronald H. Spector, *Eagle against the Sun: The American War with Japan* (New York: Free Press, 1985), *passim*.

7. Gow, *Okinawa 1945*, pp. 30–42.

8. Edwin P. Hoyt, *The Last Kamikaze: The Story of Admiral Matome Ugaki* (Westport, Conn.: Praeger, 1993), pp. 171–72.

9. Ibid., p. 173.

10. Millot, *Divine Thunder*, pp. 34–35.

11. Ibid., p. 36.

12. Ibid., pp. 37, 44–45; Inoguchi and Nakajima, *Divine Wind*, pp. 3–13, 57–60.

13. James Bradley, *Flags of Our Fathers* (New York: Bantam Books, 2000), p. 137. Despite exhortations from the their commander, Lt. Gen. Tadamachi Kuribayashi, the Japanese on Iwo Jima killed about one American for every four of their own, but this tally, more than 6,800, was horrible enough.

14. Inoguchi and Nakajima, *Divine Wind*, p. 114; Samuel Eliot Morison, *The Two-Ocean War: A Short History of the United States Navy in the Second World War* (Boston: Little, Brown, 1963), pp. 436–63; Chesneau, *Aircraft Carriers of the World, 1914 to the Present*, pp. 214–17, 238–41.

15. Inoguchi and Nakajima, *Divine Wind*, pp. 121–31; Morison, *Two-Ocean War*, pp. , 486, 513–20; Hata and Izawa, *Japanese Naval Aces and Fighter Units in World War II*, p. 74.

16. Inoguchi and Nakajima, *Divine Wind*, pp. 131–33; Francillon, *Japanese Aircraft of the Pacific War*, pp. 462–67; John W. Lambert, *Bombs, Torpedoes and Kamikazes* (North Branch, Minn.: Specialty, 1997), pp. 70–71; Richard O'Neill, *Suicide Squads: Axis and Allied Special Attack Weapons of World War II: Their Development and Their Mission* (London: Salamander Books, 1981), pp. 166–67. Lambert, O'Neill, and Inoguchi and Nakajima disagree on the number of aircraft that made it to Ulithi Atoll. Lambert and O'Neill write that only two *Gingas* (Frances) penetrated the atoll, while Inoguchi and Nakajima assert that eleven made it. Since none returned, and given the lack of damage, the lower number of attackers seems more likely.

17. Clark G. Reynolds, *The Fast Carriers: The Forging of an Air Navy* (Annapolis, Md.: Naval Institute Press, 1968), p. 337.

18. Masataka Chihaya, trans., *Fading Victory: The Diary of Admiral Matome Ugaki, 1941–45* (Pittsburgh: University of Pittsburgh Press, 1991), pp. 549–52; Hoyt, *Last Kamikaze*, pp. 174–76.

19. Hoyt, *Last Kamikaze*, pp. 175–77.

20. Ibid.; Inoguchi and Nakajima, *Divine Wind*, p. 224.

21. "Yokosuka D4Y Suisei 'Judy,'" in Francillon, *Japanese Aircraft of the Pacific War,* pp. 527, 531.

22. Ibid.; Hata and Izawa, *Japanese Naval Aces and Fighter Units in World War II,* pp. 405–408.

23. Hata and Izawa, *Japanese Naval Aces and Fighter Units in World War II,* pp. 409–16; Oshio, *Kamikaze; U.S.S.* Franklin *(CV13) War Damage Report No. 56* (Washington, D.C.: U.S. Navy Department Bureau of Ships, 15 September 1946), p. 9. Japanese flight training and unit operational records are rarely available in English. I am indebted to James Sawruk, who specializes in World War II Japanese naval aviation history, not only for the translations of names and records from this text but also for guidance in evaluating its implications. While I am confident that my identification of Lieutenant Kawaguchi as the pilot who bombed *Franklin* is correct, it remains conjecture. My reasoning derives from Kawaguchi's well-documented experience and ability, especially in comparison to the other aviators in his flight. Furthermore, the location and timing of aircraft takeoffs and distance to target are persuasive. Only Ensign Kawabata and Lieutenant Kawaguchi were in position to strike at 7:08 a.m., the time *Franklin* was hit. A single bomb struck and badly damaged *Wasp* (CV 18) at 7:10 a.m., as well, so it is clear that both Kawabata and Kawaguchi scored. *Wasp,* in Carrier Task Group 58.1, was several miles from *Franklin,* assigned to Carrier Task Group 58.2, but close enough to make it impossible to determine which pilot hit which ship. Nevertheless, the extraordinary performance of the Judy that bombed *Franklin* reflects more than simple luck, and Ensign Kawabata would have needed considerably more than luck to do as well as Kawaguchi almost certainly could do, and did. Furthermore, it is likely that Kawabata, the less experienced pilot, carried one bomb mounted under his fuselage. Kawaguchi would have been better able to handle an asymmetric load if he could drop only one bomb at a time. In any case, the conjecture, although slight, is mine alone, and I welcome rebuttal. The bomb load carried on Kawaguchi's aircraft is derived from *Franklin's* battle damage report.

24. Oshio, *Kamikaze.*

25. Hoyt, *Last Kamikaze,* pp. 178–79.

26. Translation: "One! Two!"

27. Alvin S. McCoy, "Eyewitness on U.S.S. *Franklin:* Holocaust on Big Flat Top as Own Bombs Exploded," *Boston Daily Globe,* May 18, 1945, p. 13; Hoehling, Franklin *Comes Home,* p. 31; John Pomeroy Condon, *Corsairs and Flat Tops: Marine Carrier Air Warfare, 1944–45* (Annapolis, Md.: Naval Institute Press, 1998), pp. 67–68. My account reflects contemporary testimony and more recent scholarship. Of interest is a major discrepancy in descriptions attributed to 1st Lt. Kenneth E. Linder, a Marine pilot assigned to VMF-214, the "Black Sheep Squadron," then on CV 13, who was flying combat air patrol during *Franklin's* bombing. The newspaper

article cited quotes Linder as a witness to the Judy's destruction. Linder credits *Franklin*'s air group commander, Cdr. Edwin Parker Jr., with the kill. The U.S. Navy's record of air-to-air claims shows eighty Japanese planes shot down on March 19, with twenty-six probables and sixteen damaged. That morning near Task Force 58, Lt. (jg) Locke H. Trigg of VF-47, from *Bataan* (CVL 29), claimed a Myrt, a Nakajima C6N *Saiun* (Painted Cloud) single-engine reconnaissance aircraft with a three-seat-in-tandem cockpit, at 0700. Commander Parker claimed a Judy, Kawaguchi's plane, at 0708. Ens. Robert E. Wolfard of VF-86, from *Wasp* (CV 18), claimed another "radial Judy," almost surely the plane with Kawabata and Kashi on board, which had bombed his ship. The remaining *Suiseis*, well away from the task force and flying toward it after sunrise with their inexperienced pilots, all fell to American fighters before they posed a threat to *Franklin*.

However, Major General Condon's account, published in 1998 after his death, awards partial credit for Parker's Judy kill to Linder. He quotes Linder in some detail, describing a delayed takeoff that led to his encounter with the Judy, its "red meat balls on the wings," his tracers hitting the plane and the gunner "slumped over and not firing." Linder reported here that he, not Parker, followed the D4Y3 into its loop and that he rolled out when he realized he had insufficient altitude to complete the maneuver. Condon concludes that Parker, who had fired earlier on the same Judy, and Linder shared credit for the kill, and Linder "also laid claim to the sad distinction of being the last Black Sheep to shoot down an enemy aircraft in World War II." Clearly, the record does not support Condon. There is no shared claim i n the record. Furthermore, Linder's account at the time contradicts his later version, even though the Judy's actions and fate are consistent throughout.

28. Inoguchi and Nakajima, *Divine Wind,* pp. 207–208, 233–34; Lambert, *Bombs, Torpedoes and Kamikazes,* p. 6; Millot, *Divine Thunder,* pp. 158–69; Andrieu D'Albas, *Death of a Navy: Japanese Naval Action in World War II* (New York: Devin Adair, 1957), p. 341.

Chapter 2. Introit

1. Translation: "I will go to the altar of God. To God, who giveth joy to my youth." Ordinary of the Mass.

2. U.S. Census 1880, Boston, Suffolk, Massachusetts, roll T9-566, Family History Film 1254566, p. 250D, Enumeration District 670, image 0163.

3. *Stimpson's Boston City Directory, 1887, 1889, 1890* (Boston: C. Stimpson, 1887, 1889, 1890), available at http://www.ancestry.com (accessed December 21, 2005).

4. U.S. Census Reports for 1880 and 1900, www.ancestry.com (accessed December 23, 2005).

5. U.S. Census Reports for 1900 and 1910, www.ancestry.com (accessed December 23, 2005); Cambridge Historical Commission, Materials on

origin and ownership of 9 Leonard Avenue, Cambridge, Massachusetts, July 10, 2000.

6. Obituary for Cornelius J. O'Callahan, *Boston Globe,* December 28, 1920, p. 4; and Funeral notice for Cornelius J. O'Callahan, *Cambridge Chronicle,* January 1, 1921, p. 3.

7. "A Brief History of Boston College High School," *Boston College High School: The Jesuit High School of Boston,* http://www.bchigh.edu/home/content. asp?id=1 (accessed December 28, 2005).

8. Statement by Father Ben Fiekers, S.J., College of the Holy Cross, Worcester, Massachusetts, April 10, 1964, Joseph T. O'Callahan papers, Special Collections, Dinand Library, College of the Holy Cross, Worcester, Massachusetts.

9. Madell telephone conversation, June 15, 2003; "The Sponsor: Sister Rose Marie, M.M.," *United States Ship O'Callahan (DE 1051) Commissioning Brochure,* July 13, 1968.

10. Jay O'Callahan, Marshfield, Massachusetts, nephew of Joseph O'Callahan, telephone conversation with author, September 5, 2000; Madell telephone conversation.

11. "Wilson and Harding Administrations, Postwar Recession, 1920–1921," http://www.u-s-history.com/pages/h1362.html (accessed December 28, 2005); "The Economy of the Twenties: The Recession of 1920–21," http:// www.wou.edu/las/socsci/kimjensen/ economy%20of%20the%20twenties.htm (accessed December 28, 2005).

12. Jay O'Callahan telephone conversation.

13. Joseph P. Roel, MPH, MHA, and Richard H. Grimm, Jr., MD, PhD, "Management of Hypertension: Contributions of Clinical Trials," *Medscape: WEBMD,* http://www.medscape.com/viewarticle/407692_print (accessed December 28, 2005).

14. Cornelius O'Callahan obituary.

15. Jay O'Callahan telephone conversation.

Chapter 3. *Iudicium*

1. Translation: chapter title, "Judgment." Epigraph, "Judge me, O God, and distinguish my cause from the nation that is not holy." *Internet Sacred Text Archive.*

2. Fiekers statement.

3. Jay O'Callahan and Maureen Madell telephone conversations.

4. "The Society of Jesus (Company of Jesus, Jesuits)," *The Catholic Encyclopedia,* http:// newadvent.org/cathen14081a.htm (accessed June 27, 2000).

5. "St Andrew-on-Hudson," http://www.geocities.com/Heartland/Acres/2843/ StAndrewOnHudson.html (accessed December 29, 2005). In 1970, as the numbers of Jesuit novices declined, the order sold St. Andrew to the Culinary Institute of America, which operates its East Coast campus there today.

6. Gary Wills, *Bare Ruined Choirs: Doubt, Prophecy and Radical Religion* (Garden City, N.Y.: Doubleday, 1972), p. 25.

7. Harold D. Donohue, "Requiem for a Hero: Rev. Joseph T. O'Callahan, S.J., Medal of Honor Recipient," *Congressional Record*—Appendix, Volume 110, no. 139, Tuesday, July 21, 1964. Extension of Remarks of Hon. Harold D. Donohue of Massachusetts, in the House of Representatives, Containing Requiem by Rev. Richard J. Dowling, S.J.," pp. A3795–A3797; Jack O'Connell, "Editor's Note," *Holy Cross Magazine,* April/May 1998, http://www.holycross. edu/departments/publicaffairs/hcm/hcmam98/ letters/letterfromeditor.html (accessed December 29, 2005); "Captain Joseph T. O'Callahan, Chaplain Corps, Unites States Naval Reserve," USS *O'Callahan* commissioning brochure; Biographical form, Joseph T. O'Callahan, August 28, 1963, O'Callahan Papers; "Joseph Timothy O'Callahan," *Dictionary of American Biography, Supplement 7: 1961–1965,* American Council of Learned Societies, 1983; document number BT2310006515, reproduced in Biography Resource Center, Farmington Hills, Mich.: Gale Group, 2003, http://www.galenet. com/ Servelet/BioRC (accessed July 10, 2003); Father Frederick Harkins, S.J., professor emeritus, College of the Holy Cross, personal interview with author, Worcester, Massachusetts, December 29, 1993; C. A. Phillips, "Wings over Pensacola: News of 'The Annapolis of the Air,'" *Pensacola News-Journal,* December 1, 1940.

Chapter 4. *In Hoc Signo Vinces*

1. Translation: "In this sign wilt thou conquer," the motto of the College of Holy Cross, http://www.holycross.edu/about/history/website/seal.html (accessed December 29, 2005), Translation: "Send forth Thy light and Thy truth: they have led me and brought me unto Thy holy hill, and into Thy tabernacles." *Internet Sacred Text Archive.*

2. Walter J. Meagher, S.J., and William J. Grattan, *The Spires of Fenwick: The History of the College of the Holy Cross, 1843–1963* (New York: Vantage, 1966), pp. 17, 58, 156, 216.

3. Harkins interview.

4. Translation: "Let us proclaim the mystery of faith," Internet Sacred Text Archive.

5. Father Eugene Harrington, S.J., professor emeritus, College of the Holy Cross, personal interview with author, Worcester, Massachusetts, December 29, 1993; Phillips, "Wings over Pensacola."

6. Ernest J. Passaro, "For God and Country: A Priestly Profile of the First Navy Chaplain to Receive the Medal of Honor: Chaplain Joseph T. O'Callahan, 1904–1964" (unpublished manuscript, New England Jesuit Archives, Holy Cross College Archives, June 1984), p. 5.

7. Joseph T. O'Callahan, S.J., to Rev. James H. Dolan, S.J., Father Provincial, New England Province, Society of Jesus, June 23, 1940, Joseph T, O'Callahan Papers, College Archives and Jesuit Province Archives, Special Collections, Dinand Library, College of the Holy Cross, Worcester, Massachusetts.

8. James H. Dolan, S.J., to Joseph T. O'Callahan, S.J., June 25, 1940, O'Callahan Papers.

9. O'Callahan to Dolan, June 26, 1940, O'Callahan Papers.

10. Harkins interview; Father Paul Nelligan, S.J., College Archivist, College of the Holy Cross, personal interview with author, Worcester, Massachusetts, December 29, 1993.

11. Donohue, "Requiem for a Hero," p. A3796.

12. Ibid.

13. Jay O'Callahan telephone conversation.

14. Record of Service, Form H-5 (1940), Joseph T. O'Callahan, National Personnel Records Center, St. Louis, Missouri, March 16, 1994.

Chapter 5. Pensacola

1. O'Callahan to Dolan, November 23, 1940, O'Callahan Papers.

2. Dolan to O'Callahan, November 27, 1940, O'Callahan Papers.

3. "NAS Pensacola: The Cradle of Naval Aviation," http://www.pensacola chamber.com/armed services/nas_pensacola.htm (accessed January 3, 2006); "Naval Air Station Pensacola," *Pensacola Area Flight Watch,* http://www.pafw. com/nasp.htm (accessed January 3, 2006).

4. "Naval Air Station Pensacola."

5. O'Callahan to Dolan, November 29, 1940; O'Callahan to Dolan, March 26, 1942, O'Callahan Papers.

6. Letters from O'Callahan to Dolan, December 2 and 5, 1940, O'Callahan Papers.

7. Letter and Report from O'Callahan to Dolan, n.d., O'Callahan Papers.

8. O'Callahan to Dolan, January 28, 1941, O'Callahan Papers.

9. O'Callahan to Dolan, May 15, 1941, O'Callahan Papers. A gosport was a primitive communication device, similar to a stethoscope, used in early flight training. A student aviator, ensconced in the front seat of a trainer,

wore a cloth flight helmet with earphones connected to rubber tubes, themselves connected to a long tube leading to a speaker in the flight instructor's rear cockpit. Although sitting in tandem, instructors had the ability to give students instant feedback on every move they made by yelling into the unamplified speaker, a surprisingly effective method, despite constant engine noise and wind over the wings.

10. O'Callahan to Dolan, n.d., O'Callahan Papers.

11. O'Callahan to Dolan, September 10, 1941, O'Callahan Papers.

12. O'Callahan to Dolan, n.d., February 1942, O'Callahan Papers.

13. Ibid.

14. Ibid.

15. Ibid.

16. Joseph T. O'Callahan, *I Was Chaplain on the* Franklin (New York: Macmillan, 1956), p. 3.

17. Father Maurice Sheehy to Father Joseph O'Callahan, February 2, 1942; O'Callahan to Dolan, February 9, 1942, O'Callahan Papers.

18. O'Callahan, *I Was Chaplain on the* Franklin, p. 4.

19. Letters from O'Callahan to Dolan, March 26 and March 27, 1942, O'Callahan Papers.

20. Navy Department, Bureau of Navigation, Washington, D.C. 30380, memorandum, Nav-318-FCM, 87280, April 10, 1942, with first endorsement dated April 13, 1942, O'Callahan Papers.

Chapter 6. *Ranger*

1. Naval History Center, Office of the Chief of Naval Operations, Navy Department, *Dictionary of American Naval Fighting Ships* (Washington, D.C.: U.S. Government Printing Office), vols. 1–9, http://www.history.navy.mil/danfs/r-list.htm (accessed January 5, 2005); Norman Friedman, *U.S. Aircraft Carriers: An Illustrated Design History* (Annapolis, Md.: Naval Institute Press, 1983), pp. 57–77, 390–91; Chesneau, *Aircraft Carriers of the World, 1914 to the Present,* pp. 205–206.

2. *Ranger* CV-4 World War II Aviation History Diary File, Action Reports, April and May 1942; United States Government microfile E108, September 1, 2001, Joseph T. O'Callahan, 87280, Ships and Stations, Form H-5 (1940), National Personnel Records Center, St. Louis, Missouri, March 16, 1994. O'Callahan's report date for *Ranger* is not clear on the Ships and Stations Form, and his report date is not noted in *Ranger*'s war diary. The carrier's daily log, which contains this report, is not available.

3. "Argentia Timeline," *U.S. Military Honors: Milgen.htm*, http://www.sid-hill.com/honors/hon-04c.htm (accessed January 7, 2006).

4. O'Callahan to Dolan, July 30, 1942, O'Callahan Papers.

5. "Narrative Report of Torch Operations," Commanding Officer, U.S.S. *Ranger*, Carrier Division Three, Aircraft, Atlantic Fleet, United States Atlantic Fleet, CV4/A8, November 28, 1043, p. 70.

6. Harkins interview.

7. "Organic Army Aviation in World War II—Combat: Mediterranean Theater of Operations," *United States Army Aviation Museum*, http://www.army avnmuseum.org/history/war/ww2/overview4.html (accessed January 14, 2006).

8. "Casablanca to Tokyo: The *Ranger* Air Group over Casablanca," Air Group 4, http://www.airgroup4.com/torch.htm (accessed January 4, 2006).

9. "Narrative Report of Torch Operations," pp. 65, 70.

10. Ibid., p. 71.

11. "Operation "Leader": Report of," memorandum CV4/A16-3, Commanding Officer, U.S.S. *Ranger*, October 9, 1943, pp. 1–3; "Casablanca to Tokyo," Air Group 4.

12. "Casablanca to Tokyo," Air Group 4.

13. Ibid.; *Ranger* CV-4 World War II Aviation History Diary File; O'Callahan Ships and Stations. *Ranger* completed the war as a training carrier on the West Coast, based in San Diego. She returned to the East Coast after war's end, completing an overhaul. The Navy decommissioned her, clearly obsolete, in Norfolk on October 18, 1946, and sold her for scrap to Sun Shipbuilding & Drydock Co., Chester, Pa., on January 28, 1947.

14. O'Callahan, *I Was Chaplain on the* Franklin, pp. 2–5.

Chapter 7. Interlude

1. Yves Buffetaut, *D-Day Ships: The Allied Invasion Fleet June 1944* (Annapolis, Md.: Naval Institute Press, 1994), pp. 8, 16–17.

2. "Historic California Posts: Naval Air Station, Alameda (Benton Field)," California State Military Department, California State Military Museum, http://www.militarymuseum.org/NASAlameda.html (accessed January 16, 2006).

3. O'Callahan to Dolan, June 20, 1944, O'Callahan Papers.

4. *The Ford Islander*, Ford Island Naval Air Station Newspaper, January 6, 1945, p. 3.

5. Morison, *Two-Ocean War*, pp. 56–69.

6. O'Callahan, *I Was Chaplain on the* Franklin, p. 1.

7. *O'Callahan* commissioning brochure.

8. Phone conversation with Rose Sperry, Father O'Callahan's niece, in Cambridge, Massachusetts, 2008.

9. E-mail correspondence with Richard Yoshida, nephew of Ann Yoshida, Toronto, Ontario, Canada, August 18, 2008.

10. "The Internment of Japanese Canadians in Canada during World War II," *Moments in Time,* http://timeinmoments.wordpress.com/2007/11/06/the-internment-camps-of-japanese-canadians-in-canada-during-world-war-ii/ (accessed January 4, 2009).

11. Richard Yoshida correspondence.

12. E-mail correspondence with Jay O'Callahan, nephew of Joseph O'Callahan, Marshfield, Massachusetts, September 24, 2007, and Maureen Madell, niece of Joseph O'Callahan, Chicago, Illinois, November 23, 2007.

13. E-mail correspondence with Rose Sperry, niece of Joseph O'Callahan, Cambridge, Massachusetts, 2008; Richard Yoshida correspondence.

14. Sperry, pp. 1–2.

15. Ibid., p. 2.

16. Ibid., pp. 5–7.

Chapter 8. *Franklin*

1. *Dictionary of American Naval Fighting Ships,* vol. 2, pp. 442–44.

2. Friedman, *U.S. Aircraft Carriers,* pp. 79–101, 133–57; Chesneau, *Aircraft Carriers of the World, 1914 to the Present,* pp. 205–206.

3. Alan Raven, *Essex-Class Carriers* (Annapolis, Md.: Naval Institute Press, 1988), pp. 3–16.

4. Friedman, *U.S. Aircraft Carriers,* pp. 133–57

5. O'Callahan, *I Was Chaplain on the* Franklin, p. 25.

6. *Dictionary of American Naval Fighting Ships,* vol. 2, 1963, pp. 442–44.

7. Ibid.; Marvin K. Bowman, *Big Ben the Flattop: The Story of the U.S.S. Franklin CV-13* (Atlanta: Albert Love, 1990), pp. 1–5. The WAVES were "Women Accepted for Volunteer Emergency Service."

8. Ibid., pp. 6–54.

9. Spector, *Eagle against the Sun,* pp. 142–343; Reynolds, *Fast Carriers,* pp. 113–210; Robert St. Peters, ed., *USS* Franklin *(CV-13): Original Documents 1943–1946* (Paducah, Ky.: Turner, 1994), pp. 80–93.

10. Bowman, pp. 33–54.

11. Ibid., pp. 55–66.

12. Ibid.; Spector, *Eagle against the Sun*, pp. 417–44; Reynolds, *Fast Carriers*, pp. 253–300.

13. Bowman, *Big Ben the Flattop*, pp. 67–78; Gow, *Okinawa 1945*, pp. 9–107.

14. E. B. Potter, *Bull Halsey* (Annapolis, Md.: Naval Institute Press, 1985), p. 130.

15. O'Callahan, *I Was Chaplain on the* Franklin, *passim*; Robert Sherrod, *History of Marine Corps Aviation in World War II* (Washington, D.C.: Combat Forces, 1952), pp. 326–32, 359; Hoehling, Franklin *Comes Home*, *passim*; Bowman, *Big Ben the Flattop*, pp. 67–123; St. Peters, *USS* Franklin *(CV-13)*, pp. 168–72.

16. Bowman, *Big Ben the Flattop*, pp. 67–123; St. Peters, *USS* Franklin *(CV-13)*, *passim*.

Chapter 9. Murderers' Row

1. O'Callahan, *I Was Chaplain on the* Franklin, p. 30; Translation: "Who takest away the sins of the world, hear our prayer."

2. Ibid., pp. 26–27.

3. Ibid., pp. 31–35. Translation: "By His authority I absolve you of your sins in the name of the Father, the Son, and the Holy Spirit."

4. Passaro, "For God and Country," p. 7.

5. Ibid., pp. 36–45.

6. Ibid., p. 47.

7. *Franklin* War Diary, CV-13/A16-3, serial 00212, part I, summary, p. 2; Hoehling, Franklin *Comes Home*, pp. 18–23; ibid., pp. 36–50.

Chapter 10. March 19, 1945

1. *Franklin* War Diary, summary, p. 2.

2. O'Callahan, *I Was Chaplain on the* Franklin, pp. 50–51; Hoehling, Franklin *Comes Home*, pp. 22–25; U.S.S. *Franklin* (CV-13), Bomb Damage, Honshu—19 March 1945, in St. Peters, *USS* Franklin *(CV-13)*, pp. 343, 349–50.

3. *Franklin* War Diary, summary, pp. 2–3.

4. St. Peters, *USS* Franklin *(CV-13)*, pp. 343, 350–51; Hoehling, Franklin *Comes Home*, pp. 29–36.

5. *Franklin* War Diary, summary, p. 4.

6. "USS Franklin," video, U.S. Navy Department, Washington, D.C., copied by Holy Cross College, Worcester, Massachusetts.

7. Ibid., pp. 6–7, 45–46, 49–50; Hoehling, Franklin *Comes Home,* pp. 29–30, 43–45; St. Peters, *USS* Franklin *(CV-13),* pp. 350–51.

8. O'Callahan, *I Was Chaplain on the* Franklin, pp. 61–63.

9. Ibid., pp. 64–69; *Franklin* War Diary, summary, p. 7.

10. *Franklin* War Diary, summary, pp. 46–47.

11. O'Callahan, *I Was Chaplain on the* Franklin, pp. 70–71.

12. Ibid., pp. 68–83; Hoehling, Franklin *Comes Home,* pp. 49–76; *Franklin* War Diary, pp. 7–8, 51, 55–56; Bowman, *Big Ben the Flattop,* pp. 67–123.

13. "Recollections of LCDR Samuel Robert Sherman, MC, USNR, Flight Surgeon on USS Franklin (CV 13) When It Was Heavily Damaged by a Japanese Bomber near the Japanese Mainland on 19 March 1945," Oral Histories: Attacks on Japan, 1945, Naval Historical Center, Department of the Navy, http://www.history.navy.mil/faqs/faq87-3i.htm (accessed July 11, 2000), pp. 4, 6.

14. Hoehling, Franklin *Comes Home,* pp. 68–91; *Franklin* War Diary, summary, pp. 7–8, 51–52; O'Callahan, *I Was Chaplain on the* Franklin, pp. 79–97.

15. Hoehling, Franklin *Comes Home,* pp. 69–71.

16. O'Callahan, *I Was Chaplain on the* Franklin, p. 85.

17. Robert C. Blanchard, South Amboy, New Jersey, telephone conversation with author, July 31, 2001. After his discharge in 1946, Blanchard returned to GMC, where he worked for thirty-seven years. He and his wife had nine children, six girls and three boys. At the time of the interview, he had sixteen grandchildren and eight great grandchildren.

18. Ibid., p. 104.

19. Holy Cross *Alumnus,* June 1945, p. 30.

20. Ibid., pp. 97–111.

21. Ibid., pp. 111–112.

22. *Franklin* War Diary, summary, pp. 42, 56, 59.

23. Ibid., pp. 47–48; Hoehling, Franklin *Comes Home,* pp. 62, 82–83, 89–92; O'Callahan, *I Was Chaplain on the* Franklin, pp. 112–13.

24. *Franklin* War Diary, summary, p. 53.

25. Hoehling, Franklin *Comes Home,* pp. 94–95.

26. Mr. Wassman, a professional engineer, retired as a vice president of Rockefeller Center.

Chapter 11. Operating Independently

1. O'Callahan, *I Was Chaplain on the* Franklin, p. 126. *Franklin* (CV-13) Order of the Day, March 23, 1945, in St. Peters, *USS* Franklin *(CV-13).*

2. *Franklin* War Diary, summary, pp. 6–7, 57; Hoehling, Franklin *Comes Home,* pp. 100–104.

3. O'Callahan, *I Was Chaplain on the* Franklin, pp. 117–18.

4. Ibid., p. 128.

5. *Franklin* War Diary, summary, p. 7.

6. O'Callahan, *I Was Chaplain on the* Franklin, pp. 120–21.

7. Ibid., p. 122.

8. Sherman oral history, p. 5.

9. Ibid.

10. O'Callahan, *I Was Chaplain on the* Franklin, pp. 124–25.

11. Hoehling, Franklin *Comes Home,* pp. 104–107.

12. Ibid., pp. 108–109.

13. "Saxie Dowell," http://www.artistdirect.com/artist/bio/saxie-dowell/607490 (accessed December 6, 2010).

14. Ibid.; O'Callahan, *I Was Chaplain on the* Franklin, p. 129; *Franklin* War Diary, summary, p. 8.

15. St. Peters, *USS* Franklin *(CV-13),* pp. 320–21.

16. Hoehling, Franklin *Comes Home,* pp. 104–107; *Franklin* War Diary, summary, pp. 8, 15; Bowman, *Big Ben the Flattop,* pp. 67–123.

17. *Franklin* War Diary, p. 59.

18. Hoehling, Franklin *Comes Home,* pp. 111–12.

19. Ibid.; Bowman, *Big Ben the Flattop,* pp. 67–123.

20. Hoehling, Franklin *Comes Home,* p. 113; Ibid.; O'Callahan, *I Was Chaplain on the* Franklin, pp. 128–29.

21. O'Callahan, *I Was Chaplain on the* Franklin, pp. 129–30.

22. Sister Rose Marie to Alice E. O'Callahan, May 10, 1945, p. 6, O'Callahan Papers.

23. Ibid.

24. O'Callahan, *I Was Chaplain on the* Franklin, p. 130; Hoehling, Franklin *Comes Home,* p. 114; Bowman, *Big Ben the Flattop,* pp. 67–123.

25. O'Callahan, *I Was Chaplain on the* Franklin, p. 130; Hoehling, Franklin *Comes Home,* p. 114; Bowman, *Big Ben the Flattop,* pp. 67–123.

26. St. Peters, *USS* Franklin *(CV-13),* pp. 206–209.

Chapter 12. Accolades

1. Title of an article by war correspondent and author Quentin Reynolds about Father O'Callahan's heroism on *Franklin,* published in *Collier's,* June 23, 1945.

2. St. Peters, *USS* Franklin *(CV-13),* pp. 322–23.

3. Bowman, *Big Ben the Flattop,* pp. 67–123; Hoehling, Franklin *Comes Home,* p. 114; O'Callahan, *I Was Chaplain on the* Franklin, p. 131.

4. O'Callahan, *I Was Chaplain on the* Franklin, p. 135.

5. Ibid.; Holy Cross *Alumnus,* June 1945, p. 30, O'Callahan Papers.

6. O'Callahan, 87280, Ships and Stations.

7. Newspaper articles dated Friday, March 18, 1945 from the *New York Journal American,* pp. 1–2, and March 19, 1945, pp. 1–2; *New York Times,* pp. 1, 18 ; *New York Daily Mirror,* vol. 21, no. 282, pp. 1, 3, 8 ; *New York Post,* pp. 1, 3; *New York Herald Tribune,* pp. 1 ; *New York World-Telegram,* vol. 77, no. 269, pp. 1, 18 ; *New York PM Daily*, vol. V, no. 287, pp. 1, 10–11, 14–15; *Baltimore Sun,* pp. 1, 18; *New York Daily News,* vol. 26, no. 281, pp. 1, 3, 23–24, 40; *Washington Post,* pp. 1 *Washington Public Ledger,* vol. 232, no. 138, pp. 1, 3; *Philadelphia Inquirer,* pp. 3, 16 a, and *Philadelphia Evening Bulletin,* p. 4 ; *Boston Traveler,* May 18, 1945 *Boston American,* May 18, 1945, pp. 1, 4; *Boston Daily Globe,* May 18, 1945, pp. 1, 12; *Boston Evening Globe,* May 18, 1945, pp. 1, 9–10; *Boston Herald,* May 18, 1945, pp. 1, 18, 22–23; *Boston Pilot,* May 19,1945, p; *Boston Herald,* May 22, 1945, ; *The Tomahawk* (Holy Cross College, Worcester, Massachusetts), May 23, 1945; Boston *Guardian*, May 25, 1945, ; all in O'Callahan Papers.

8. Father Provincial, Society of Jesus, to Alice E. O'Callahan and to Lt. Cdr. Joseph T. O'Callahan, May 19, 1945, O'Callahan Papers.

9. St. Peters, *USS* Franklin *(CV-13),* p. 315.

10. Bowman, *Big Ben the Flattop,* pp. 121–23; O'Callahan, 87280, Ships and Stations.

11. Quentin Reynolds to Neil O'Callahan, May 2, 1945, O'Callahan Papers.

12. Quentin Reynolds, "Chaplain Courageous," *Collier's,* June 23, 1945, pp. 11–13, p. 79, and June 30, 1945, pp. 14–15, 27; House Joint Resolution no. 51, June 25, 1945, Massachusetts General Assembly, O'Callahan Papers.

13. Lt. Cdr. Joseph T. O'Callahan, Tour schedule, n.d., O'Callahan Papers; *Southern Cross,* August 3, 1945, p. 1; *Los Angeles Times,* August 4, 1945, pp. 1, 8; *Los Angeles Daily News*, August 4, 1945,; *Los Angeles Times,* August 6, 1945, pp. 1; *San Francisco Examiner,* August 13, 1945, p. 3; Madell and Jay O'Callahan telephone conversations.

14. O'Callahan to Father Provincial, August 7, 1945, O'Callahan Papers.

15. James V. Forrestal to Hon. David I. Walsh, Chairman, Committee on Naval Affairs, United States Senate, October 31, 1945, James V. Forrestal Papers, Seeley G. Mudd Manuscript Library, Princeton University, Princeton, New Jersey.

16. Father James Dolan, S.J., New England Provincial, to Senator David I. Walsh, October 8, 1945, O'Callahan Papers.

17. Ed Sullivan, "Little Old New York," *New York Daily News*, October 31, 1945, p. 60.

18. James V. Forrestal, memorandum to Mr. Duffield, October 31, 1945, Forrestal Papers.

19. Ibid.

20. Forrestal to Walsh.

21. James V. Forrestal, "Excerpts from Telephone Conversation between the Secretary of the Navy and Cong. John W. McCormick of Massachusetts, 8 November 1945," Forrestal Papers.

22. E. B. Taylor, memorandum to Chief of Naval Personnel, 21 November 1945, Forrestal Papers; travel authorization from BUPERS, Washington, D.C., to Commanding Officer, Naval Air Station San Diego, California, November 27, 1945, Miscellaneous Correspondence and Memoranda Pertaining to CDR Joseph T. O'Callahan, Modern Military Records, Textual Archives Services Division, National Archives and Records Administration, College Park, Maryland.

23. Drew Pearson, "Washington Merry-Go-Round," *Baltimore Sun,* December 8, 1945.

24. Ibid.

25. E. B. Taylor, memorandum to the Secretary of the Navy, 12 December 1945, Forrestal Papers.

26. Telephone conversation between Mr. Forrestal and Father McNally, 12/18/1945; Senator David I. Walsh to Honorable James Forrestal, Secretary of the Navy, December 22, 1945; and James Forrestal to Hon. David I. Walsh, December 27, 1945; memorandum for the Naval Aide to the President, January 2, 1946; Matthew J. Connelly to Father McNally, January 3, 1946; John W. McCormick to Matthew J. Connelly, Secretary to the President, January 4, 1946; Clark M. Clifford, memorandum for the Secretary of the Navy, 10 January 1946; Miscellaneous Correspondence and Memoranda Pertaining to CDR Joseph T. O'Callahan, Modern Military Records, Textual Archives Services Division, National Archives and Records Administration, College Park, Maryland.

27. Drew Pearson, "Washington Merry-Go-Round," *Washington Post,* January 22, 1946, p. 8.

28. Congressional Medal of Honor Ceremony Brochure, Cdr. Joseph T. O'Callahan, January 23, 1945, O'Callahan Papers.

29. Ibid.

30. Ibid.; "Fr. O'Callahan Wins Highest Decoration for Valor," *Tomahawk,* January 23, 1945, pp. 1, 3.

31. O'Callahan to Father Provincial, February 15, 1946, O'Callahan Papers.

32. O'Callahan to Father Provincial, April 16, 1946, O'Callahan Papers.

33. O'Callahan to Father Provincial, May 1, 1946, O'Callahan Papers.

34. O'Callahan to Father Provincial, June 14, 1946, O'Callahan Papers.

35. Donohue, "Requiem for a Hero," p. A3796.

36. O'Callahan to Father Provincial, August 7, 1946, O'Callahan Papers.

37. O'Callahan, 87280, Ships and Stations.

38. O'Callahan, 87280, Ships and Stations and BUPERS file; Joseph T. O'Callahan personal information, College of the Holy Cross, August 28, 1963, in O'Callahan Papers.

39. *Dictionary of American Naval Fighting Ships,* vol. 2, pp. 442–44.

Chapter 13. The Room in Fenwick Hall

1. Donohue, "Requiem for a Hero," p. A3797.

2. Ibid.

3. Nelligan interview.

4. Donohue, "Requiem for a Hero," p. A3797.

5. Harkins interview; Harrington interview.

6. Madell telephone conversation.

7. Harrington interview.

8. Harkins interview.

9. Harrington interview.

10. Ibid.

11. Madell telephone conversation.

12. Donohue, "Requiem for a Hero," p. A3797.

13. Madell telephone conversation.

14. Donohue, "Requiem for a Hero," p. A3797.

15. "Sympathectomy," *Health AtoZ: Your Family Health Site,* http://www. healthatoz.com/healthatoz/Atoz/ency/sympathectomy.jsp (accessed December 18, 2005).

16. Correspondence, April 10, 1950 to March 7, 1951, Papers of Harry S. Truman, President's Personal File, Harry S. Truman Library, Independence, Missouri.

17. Harkins interview.

18. Ibid.

19. Harrington interview.

20. Madell telephone conversation.

21. Harrington interview.

22. Harry S. Truman to Father Joseph T. O'Callahan, May 5, 1950, O'Callahan Papers.

23. O'Callahan to Kevin O'Brien, February 4, 1952, O'Callahan Papers.

24. Harkins interview.

25. Comments by Sister Elizabeth Mary, S.P., at launching of USS *O'Callahan*, October 20, 1965, O'Callahan Papers.

26. "Honor Medal Priest Gets Film of Deeds," *Worcester Daily Telegram*, September 22, 1954, pp. 1, 14.

27. Jay O'Callahan telephone conversation.

28. Edward J. O'Callahan to Father Provincial, undated, O'Callahan Papers.

29. Macmillan publicity material for *I Was Chaplain on the Franklin*, undated, O'Callahan Papers.

30. "Battle Stations (1956)," *IMBd*, http://www.imdb.com/search (accessed December 21, 2005).

31. Madell telephone conversation.

32. Donohue, "Requiem for a Hero," p. A3797.

Chapter 14. *Requiem Aeternam Dona Ei*

1. Translations: "Eternal rest grant unto him; have mercy on me, O God, according to Thy great mercy." Ordinary of the Mass.

2. Jay O'Callahan telephone conversation.

3. Donohue, "Requiem for a Hero," p. A3797.

4. Harrington interview.

5. Nelligan interview.

6. Inscribed copy of *I Was Chaplain on the* Franklin, O'Callahan Papers.

7. Donohue, "Requiem for a Hero," p. A3797.

8. Madell telephone conversation.

9. Sister Elizabeth Mary comments.

10. Donohue, "Requiem for a Hero," A3797; Very Reverend Raymond J. Swords, S.J., to Sister Rose Marie O'Callahan, M.M., March 24, 1964, O'Callahan Papers.

11. Eulogy for Father Joseph T. O'Callahan, S.J., by the Very Reverend Raymond J. Swords, S.J., College of the Holy Cross, Worcester, Massachusetts, March 21, 1964, O'Callahan Papers.

12. Swords to O'Callahan; Donohue, "Requiem for a Hero," p. A3797; "Reverend J. T. O'Callahan, Hero-Priest, Is Dead," *Catholic Free Press,* March 27, 1964; M. C. Blackman, "'The Bravest Man I Ever Knew,'" *New York Herald Tribune,* March 20, 1964, O'Callahan Papers.

13. Headstone inscription, Joseph T. O'Callahan, S.J., College of the Holy Cross, Worcester, Massachusetts.

14. Translation: "Rest in peace."

Chapter 15. Postscript

1. Jay O'Callahan telephone conversation.

2. *O'Callahan* commissioning brochure; Sister Maria Del Rey, "Sister Rose Marie Launches the USS *O'Callahan,*" *Catholic Digest,* January 1966, pp. 41–45.

3. "The Ship That Wouldn't Die," video, Bennett Media Corporation, Venice, California, 1990.

4. Thomas W. Leo, Mount Prospect, Illinois, to author, May 3, 1993.

5. Tom Horgan, "Navy Chaplain Recalls Anniversary of USS Franklin Holocaust," *Newport News–Hampton–Warwick (Va.) Daily Press,* March 13, 1955, p. D1; "The Ship That Wouldn't Be Sunk: Story of the USS *Franklin,*" Special Supplement, *All Hands,* November 1964, pp. 54–62; Joseph R. McGinness, "Saga of Fr. O'Callahan on USS *Franklin* Began 20 Years Ago Today," *Worcester Telegram,* March 19, 1965, p. 21; David Davidson, "The Ordeal of the U.S.S. 'Franklin,'" *Catholic Digest,* pp. 90–96; Wesley J. Christensen, "Looking Back Thirty Years," *Crossroads* (March/ April 1975), pp. 1, 5; Douglas S. Crockett, "Fr. O'Callahan Tended Dying as Shells Burst around Him," *Boston Sunday Globe,* March 22, 1984; Bernard Carolan, "Father O'Callahan, Hero," *Brunswick (Me.) Church World,* March 17, 1985, p. 15; Cdr. Frank E. Evans, USN, "Carnage and Heroism aboard the *Franklin,*" *Virginian-Pilot and Ledger-Star,* March 17, 1985, pp. C1–C2; Michael D. Hull, "Chaplain Helped Save Ship That Wouldn't Die," *Worcester (Mass.) Morning Union,* March 18, 1985, n.p.; Bernard Carolan, "Remembering a Hero of the USS Franklin," *Worcester (Mass.) Gazette,* March 18, 1985, O'Callahan Papers.

6. "Social Security Files," *Ancestry Plus,* www.ancestry.com (accessed December 23, 2005).

7. Jay O'Callahan telephone conversation.

Bibliography

Primary Sources

Cambridge Historical Commission. Materials on origin and ownership of 9 Leonard Avenue, Cambridge, Massachusetts, July 10, 2000.

"Conference on the Limitation of Armament, Washington, November 12, 1921–February 6, 1922." Treaty Series No. 671, *Papers Relating to the Foreign Relations of the United States: 1922,* vol. 1.

Funeral notice for Cornelius J. O'Callahan. *Cambridge Chronicle,* January 1, 1921.

Harry S. Truman Papers. President's Personal File, Harry S. Truman Library, Independence, Missouri.

James V. Forrestal Papers, 1941–1949. Seeley G. Mudd Manuscript Library, Princeton University, Princeton, New Jersey.

Joseph T. O'Callahan. 87280. Ships and Stations. Form H-5 (1940). National Personnel Records Center, St. Louis, Missouri, March 16, 1994.

Joseph T. O'Callahan Papers

[*This collection—in the College Archives and Jesuit Province Archives, Special Collections, College of the Holy Cross, Dinand Library, Worcester, Massachusetts—contains personal correspondence, many personal papers, newspaper reports from U.S. Navy press briefing on May 18, 1945, obituary articles, and U.S. Navy documents, all cited in endnotes.*]

"Captain Joseph T. O'Callahan, Chaplain Corps, Unites States Naval Reserve" and "The Sponsor: Sister Rose Marie, M.M." USS *O'Callahan* (DE 1051) Commissioning Brochure, July 13, 1968.

Donohue, Harold D. "Requiem for a Hero: Rev. Joseph T. O'Callahan, S.J., Medal of Honor Recipient." *Congressional Record,* appendix, vol. 110, no. 139. Tuesday, July 21, "Extension of Remarks of Hon. Harold D. Donohue of Massachusetts, in the House of Representatives," containing requiem by Rev. Richard J. Dowling, S.J.

Memorandum, Navy Department. Bureau of Navigation, Washington, D.C., 30380, Nav-318-FCM, 87280. April 10, 1942, with first endorsement, April 13, 1942.

Ford Islander, Naval Air Station Newspaper, January 6, 1945.

"Narrative Report of Torch Operations." Commanding Officer, U.S.S. *Ranger.* Carrier Division Three, Aircraft, Atlantic Fleet, United States Atlantic Fleet. CV4/A8, November 28, 1943.

Miscellaneous Correspondence and Memoranda Pertaining to CDR Joseph T. O'Callahan, Modern Military Records, Textual Archives Services Division, National Archives and Records Administration, College Park, Maryland.

Obituary for Cornelius J. O'Callahan, *Boston Globe,* December 28, 1920.

Ranger CV-4 World War II Aviation History Diary File,. Action Reports, April and May 1942, United States Government Microfile E108, September 1, 2001.

Record of Service, Form H-5 (1940), Joseph T. O'Callahan. National Personnel Records Center, St. Louis, Missouri, March 16, 1994.

U.S. Census 1880, Boston, Suffolk, Massachusetts, roll T9_566, Family History film1254566, p. 250D, Enumeration District 670, image 0163.

U.S. Census Reports for 1880 and 1900, www.ancestry.com (accessed December 23, 2005).

U.S. Census Reports for 1900 and 1910, www.ancestry.com (accessed December 23, 2005).

U.S.S. Franklin *(CV13) War Damage Report No. 56.* Washington, D.C.: U.S. Navy Department Bureau of Ships, 15 September 1946.

Personal and Telephone Interviews and E-Mail Correspondence

Blanchard, Robert C., South Amboy, New Jersey, telephone conversation with author, July 31, 2001.

Cummings, Kathleen, niece of Joseph T. O'Callahan, Oceanside, California, e-mail correspondence, 2008.

Harkins, Father Frederick, S.J., Professor Emeritus, College of the Holy Cross, personal interview with author, Worcester, Massachusetts, December 29, 1993.

Harrington, Father Eugene, S.J., Professor Emeritus, College of the Holy Cross, personal interview with author, Worcester, Massachusetts, December 29, 1993.

Nelligan, Father Paul, S.J., College Archivist, College of the Holy Cross, personal interview with author, Worcester, Massachusetts, December 29, 1993.

Madell, Maureen, Chicago, Illinois, niece of Joseph T. O'Callahan, telephone conversation with author, June 15, 2003, and subsequent e-mail correspondence, 2003–2008.

O'Callahan, Jay, Marshfield, Massachusetts, nephew of Joseph O'Callahan, telephone conversation with author, September 5, 2000, and subsequent e-mail correspondence, 2003–2008.

Sperry, Rose, Cambridge, Massachusetts, niece of Joseph O'Callahan, e-mail correspondence with author, 2008.

Wassman, E. Robert, telephone conversation with author, July 13, 2001.

Books

Bowman, Marvin K. *Big Ben the Flattop: The Story of the U.S.S.* Franklin *CV-13.* Atlanta, Georgia: Albert Love, 1990.

Bradley, James. *Flags of Our Fathers.* New York: Bantam Books, 2000.

Buffetaut, Yves. *D-Day Ships: The Allied Invasion Fleet June 1944.* Annapolis, Md.: Naval Institute Press, 1994.

Chesneau, Roger. *Aircraft Carriers of the World, 1914 to the Present: An Illustrated Encyclopedia.* Annapolis, Md.: Naval Institute Press, 1995.

Chihaya, Masataka, trans. *Fading Victory: The Diary of Admiral Matome Ugaki, 1941–45.* Pittsburgh: University of Pittsburgh Press, 1991.

Condon, John Pomeroy. *Corsairs and Flat Tops: Marine Carrier Air Warfare, 1944–45.* Annapolis, Md.: Naval Institute Press, 1998.

Crosby, Donald S., S.J. *Battlefield Chaplains: Catholic Priests in World War II.* Lawrence: University Press of Kansas, 1996.

D'Albas, Andrieu. *Death of a Navy: Japanese Naval Action in World War II.* New York: Devin Adair, 1957.

Drury, Clifford Merrill, Captain, Chaplain Corps, U.S. Naval Reserve. *The History of the Chaplain Corps, United States Navy,* vol. 2, *1939–1949.* Washington, D.C.: Naval Personnel Command, 1950.

Farrell, Betty G. *Elite Families: Class and Power in Nineteenth-Century Boston.* Albany: State University of New York Press, 1993.

Francillon, Rene J. *Japanese Aircraft of the Pacific War.* Annapolis, Md.: Naval Institute Press, 1990.

Friedman, Norman. *U.S. Aircraft Carriers: An Illustrated Design History.* Annapolis, Md.: Naval Institute Press, 1983.

Gow, Ian. *Okinawa 1945: Gateway to Japan.* Garden City, N.Y.: Doubleday, 1985.

Handlin, Oscar. *Boston's Immigrants 1790–1880: A Study in Acculturation.* Cambridge, Mass.: Belknap Press of Harvard University Press, 1991.

Hata, Ikuhiko, and Yasuho Izawa. *Japanese Naval Aces and Fighter Units in World War II.* Annapolis, Md.: Naval Institute Press, 1989.

Hoehling, A. A. *The Franklin Comes Home.* New York: Hawthorne Books, 1974.

Howard, Fred. *Wilbur and Orville: A Biography of the Wright Brothers.* New York: Alfred A. Knopf, 1987.

Hoyt, Edwin P. *The Last Kamikaze: The Story of Admiral Matome Ugaki.* Westport, Conn.: Praeger, 1993.

Inoguchi, Rikihei, and Tadashi Nakajima. *The Divine Wind.* Annapolis, Md.: Naval Institute Press, 1958.

Lambert, John W. *Bombs, Torpedoes and Kamikazes.* North Branch, Minn.: Specialty, 1997.

Massie, Robert K. *Castles of Steel: Britain, Germany and the Winning of the Great War at Sea.* New York: Random House, 2003.

Meagher, Walter J., S.J., and William J. Grattan. *The Spires of Fenwick: The History of the College of the Holy Cross, 1843–1963.* New York: Vantage, 1966.

Millot, Bernard. *Divine Thunder: The Life and Death of the Kamikazes.* New York: Bair McCall, 1970.

Morison, Samuel Eliot. *The Two-Ocean War: A Short History of the United States Navy in the Second World War.* Boston: Little, Brown, 1989.

Naval Historical Center, Office of the Chief of Naval Operations, Department of the Navy. *Dictionary of American Naval Fighting Ships,* vol. 2. Washington, D.C.: U.S. Government Printing Office, 1963.

O'Callahan, Joseph T. *I Was Chaplain on the* Franklin. New York: Macmillan, 1956.

O'Connor, Thomas H. *The Boston Irish: A Political History.* Boston: Northeastern University Press, 1995.

O'Neill, Richard. *Suicide Squads: Axis and Allied Special Attack Weapons of World WarII: Their Development and Their Mission.* London: Salamander Books, 1981.

Oshio, Kazuhiko, ed. *Kamikaze: Imperial Japanese Naval Air Force Suicide Attack Units, No. 458.* Tokyo: Model Art, 1995.

Potter, E. B. *Bull Halsey.* Annapolis, Md.: Naval Institute Press, 1985.

Raven, Alan. Essex-*Class Carriers.* Annapolis, Md.: Naval Institute Press, 1988.

Reynolds, Clark G. *The Fast Carriers: The Forging of an Air Navy.* Annapolis, Md.: Naval Institute Press, 1968.

Salisbury, Harrison E. *Black Night, White Snow: Russia's Revolutions 1905–1917.* Garden City, N.Y.: Doubleday, 1978.

Sherrod, Robert. *History of Marine Corps Aviation in World War II.* Washington, D.C.: Combat Forces, 1952.

Spector, Ronald H. *Eagle against the Sun: The American War with Japan.* New York: Free Press, 1985.

St. Peters, Robert, ed. USS Franklin *(CV-13): Original Documents 1943–1946.* Paducah, Ky.: Turner, 1994.

Whitehill, Walter Muir, and Lawrence W. Kennedy. *Boston: A Topographical History.* 3rd ed., enlarged. Cambridge, Mass.: Belknap Press of Harvard University Press, 2000.

Wills, Gary. *Bare Ruined Choirs: Doubt, Prophecy and Radical Religion.* Garden City, N.Y.: Doubleday, 1972.

Articles

Davidson, David. "The Ordeal of the U.S.S. 'Franklin.'" *Catholic Digest* (September 1969).

Del Rey, Sister Maria. "Sister Rose Marie Launches the USS *O'Callahan.*" *Catholic Digest* (January 1966).

Eisinger, Peter K. *The Politics of Displacement: Racial and Ethnic Transition in Three American Cities.* New York: Academic, 1980. Reprint, *Political Science Quarterly* 93 (Summer 1978).

"Honor Medal Priest Gets Film of Deeds." *Worcester Daily Telegram,* September 22, 1954.

"Joseph Timothy O'Callahan," *Dictionary of American Biography, Supplement 7: 1961–1965.* American Council of Learned Societies, 1983, document number BT2310006515, reproduced in Biography Resource Center, Farmington Hills, Mich.: Gale Group, 2003, http://www.galenet.com/Servelet/BioRC (accessed July 10, 2003).

McCoy, Alvin S. "Eyewitness on U.S.S. *Franklin:* Holocaust on Big Flat Top as Own Bombs Exploded." *Boston Daily Globe,* May 18, 1945.

O'Connell, Jack. "Editor's Note." *Holy Cross Magazine* 32, no. 3 (April/May 1998),. http://www.holycross.edu/departments/publicaffairs/hcm/hcmam98/letters/letterfromeditor.html (accessed December 29, 2005).

"Organic Army Aviation in World War II—Combat: Mediterranean Theater of Operations." *United States Army Aviation Museum.* http://www.armyavnmuseum.org/history/war/ww2/overview4.html (accessed January 14, 2006).

Passaro, Ernest F. "For God and Country: A Priestly Profile of the First Navy Chaplain to Receive the Medal of Honor: Chaplain Joseph T. O'Callahan, 1904–1964." Unpublished manuscript, New England Jesuit Archives, Holy Cross College Archives, June 1984.

Pearson, Drew. "Washington Merry-Go-Round." *Baltimore Sun,* December 8, 1945.

Phillips, C. A. "Wings over Pensacola: News of "The Annapolis of the Air." *Pensacola News-Journal,* December 1, 1940.

"Reverend J. T. O'Callahan, Hero-Priest, Is Dead." *Catholic Free Press,* March 27, 1964.

Reynolds, Quentin. "Chaplain Courageous, Part I." *Collier's,* June 23, 1945.

———. "Chaplain Courageous, Part II." *Collier's,* June 30, 1945.

Roel, Joseph P. MPH, MHA, and Richard H. Grimm, Jr., MD, PhD. "Management of Hypertension: Contributions of Clinical Trials." Medscape. WEBMD.http://www.medscape.com/viewarticle/407692_print (accessed December 28, 2005).

"The Society of Jesus (Company of Jesus, Jesuits)." *Catholic Encyclopedia.* http://newadvent.org/cathen14081a.htn (accessed June 27, 2000).

Newspapers Reviewed

Baltimore Sun

Boston American

Boston Daily Globe

Boston Evening Globe

Boston Guardian

Boston Herald

Boston Sunday Globe

Boston Traveler

Brunswick (Me.) Church World

Los Angeles Daily News

Los Angeles Times

Newport News (Va.) Daily Press

New York Daily Mirror

New York Daily News

New York Herald Tribune

New York Journal American

New York PM Daily

New York Post

New York Times

New York World-Telegram

Norfolk Virginian-Pilot and Ledger-Star

Philadelphia Evening Bulletin

Philadelphia Inquirer

Philadelphia Public Ledger

Pilot (Archdiocese of Boston, Massachusetts)

San Francisco Examiner

Southern Cross (Archdiocese of San Diego, California)

Springfield (Mass.) Morning Union

Tomahawk (Holy Cross)

Worcester (Mass.) Catholic Free Press

Washington Post

Worcester (Mass.) Telegram

Videos

"The Ship That Wouldn't Die." Video. Bennett Media Corporation, Venice, California, 1990.

"USS *Franklin.*" Video. U.S. Navy Department, Washington, D.C., 1954.

Internet Sites

"A Brief History of Boston College High School." *Boston College High School: The Jesuit High School of Boston,* http://www.bchigh.edu/home/content.asp?id=1 (accessed December 28, 2005).

"Argentia Timeline." *U.S. Military HONORS: Milgen.htm.* http://www.sd-hill.com/honors/hon-04c.htm (accessed January 7, 2006).

"Battle Stations (1956)." *IMBd,* http://www.imdb.com/search (accessed December 21, 2005).

"Boston." http://www.spartacus.schoolnet.co.uk/USAboston.htm (accessed August 2, 2003).

Boston Family History.com: The Place to Meet Your Past, http://www.bostonfamilyhistory.com/ir_main.html (accessed August 2, 2003).

"Casablanca to Tokyo: The *Ranger* Air Group over Casablanca." *Air Group 4,* http://www.airgroup4.com/torch.htm (accessed January 4, 2006).

"Yokosuka D4Y Suisei 'Judy.'" *D4Y Suisei Multimedia,* http://214th.com/ww2/japan/d4y/index/htm (accessed January 14, 2001).

"Historic California Posts: Naval Air Station, Alameda (Benton Field)." *California State Military Department: The California State Military Museum.* http:// www. militarymuseum.org/NASAlameda.html (accessed January 16, 2006).

"Latin Mass: Ordinary of the Mass, 1962 edition of the Tridentine Ordo, Mass of the Catechumens." *Internet Sacred Text Archive,* http://www.sacred-texts.com/chr/lmass/ord.html (accessed December 18, 2005).

NAS Pensacola: The Cradle of Naval Aviation, http://www.pensacolachamber.Com/armed services/nas_pensacola.htm (accessed January 3, 2006).

"Naval Air Station Pensacola." *Pensacola Area Flight Watch, Inc.,* http://www.pafw.com/nasp.htm (accessed January 3, 2006).

Naval History Center, Office of the Chief of Naval Operations. Navy Department. *Dictionary of American Naval Fighting Ships*, vols. 1–9. Washington, D.C.: U.S. Government Printing Office, http://www.history.navy.mil/danfs/r-list.htm (accessed January 5, 2005).

"Saxie Dowell Biography." http://www.artistdirect.com/artist/bio/saxie-dowell/607490 (accessed December 6, 2010).

"St Andrew-on-Hudson." http://www.geocities.com/Heartland/Acres/2843/StAndrewOnHudson.html (accessed December 29, 2005).

Stimpson's Boston City Directory, 1887, 1889, 1890. Boston: C. Stimpson, 1887, 1889, 1890. http://www.ancestry.com (accessed December 21, 2005).

"Sympathectomy." *Health AtoZ, Your Family Health Site,* http://www.healthatoz. com/healthatoz/Atoz/ency/sympathectomy.jsp. (accessed December 18, 2005).

"The Economy of the Twenties: The Recession of 1920–21." http://www.wou. edu/las/socsci/kimjensen/economy%20of%20the%20twenties.htm (accessed December 28, 2005).

"The Internment of Japanese Canadians in Canada During World War II." *Moments in Time,* http://timeinmoments.wordpress.com/2007/11/06/the-internment-camps-of-japanese-canadians-in-canada-during-world-war-ii/ (accessed January 4, 2009).

"The Order of the Mass: Mass of the Catechumens." *Catholic Liturgy,* http://www. CatholicLiturgy.com/the_mass/tridentine1.shtm (accessed June 27, 2000).

"The 20th Century: 1905–1907." *Timelines of History,* http://timelines. ws/20thcent/1905_1907.html (accessed December 18, 2005).

"Wilson and Harding Administrations, Postwar Recession, 1920–1921." http:// www.u-s-history.com/pages/h1362.html (accessed December 28, 2005).

Index

About the Author

Jack Satterfield writes about military history and weapon systems. A retired naval reserve officer, he worked in defense industry public relations and lectures on topics including British and U.S. naval history and World War II. He and his wife live in Delaware near the state's only Revolutionary War battle site.